MW00449669

Praise for *Managing Care*

"A lifetime of wisdom honed through practicing medicine and teaching others how to manage today's challenging healthcare delivery organizations is now available in this profoundly engaging book. A must read for leaders in healthcare—whether in the C-suite or practicing medicine on the front lines of care delivery."
—Amy C. Edmondson, PhD, Professor, Harvard
Business School, and author of *The Fearless Organization*

"Dr. Bohmer, marries his vast experience as a clinician, consultant, teacher, and long-time student of health care delivery to provide a clear guide to effective and efficient medical care."
—David M. Lawrence, MD, MPH, Dean, School of Medicine,
Keck Graduate Institute, and former Chairman and
CEO, Kaiser Foundation Health Plan and Hospitals

"This book is a testament to the need for strong clinical leadership during times of uncertainty and conflict. Bohmer outlines a clear path forward for achieving socially responsible outcomes for those we're dedicated to serve."
—Marc Harrison, MD, President and CEO,
Intermountain Healthcare

"For those who are persuaded that we will never be able to reduce the administrative burdens of healthcare, Bohmer provides a meticulous argument for a way forward. He understands that to improve the effectiveness and efficiencies in healthcare delivery, organizations must include innovation and insight from members of the care team."
—Jeanette Ives Erickson, RN, DNP, Chief Nurse Emerita
and Distinguished Paul M. Erickson Endowed Chair
in Nursing, Massachusetts General Hospital

"I highly recommend this book for all clinician leaders and administrators who see the pressing need for change and are passionate about transforming healthcare systems toward better patient care."

—Ivy Ng, MD, Group CEO, Singapore Health Services

"With pragmatism and wisdom, Bohmer shows how to reliably translate care design into practice—and more importantly, how to continually learn, modify, and improve as we work to transform healthcare to provide better value for patients. The lessons shared are powerful as illustrated by the experience of the Covid-19 pandemic, but they go far beyond the needs of today by providing a systems approach that will endure."

—Gregg S. Meyer, MD, MSc, President of the Community Division and Executive Vice President of Value Based Care, Massachusetts General Hospital, and Professor of Medicine, Harvard Medical School

Managing Care

MANAGING CARE

HOW CLINICIANS CAN LEAD CHANGE
AND TRANSFORM HEALTHCARE

RICHARD M. J. BOHMER

Berrett–Koehler Publishers, Inc.

Copyright © 2021 by Richard Bohmer

All rights reserved. No part of this publication may be reproduced, distributed, or
transmitted in any form or by any means, including photocopying, recording, or other
electronic or mechanical methods, without the prior written permission of the publisher,
except in the case of brief quotations embodied in critical reviews and certain other
noncommercial uses permitted by copyright law. For permission requests, write to the
publisher, addressed "Attention: Permissions Coordinator," at the address below.

Berrett-Koehler Publishers, Inc.
1333 Broadway, Suite 1000
Oakland, CA 94612-1921
Tel: (510) 817-2277   Fax: (510) 817-2278   www.bkconnection.com

ORDERING INFORMATION
Quantity sales. Special discounts are available on quantity purchases by corporations,
associations, and others. For details, contact the "Special Sales Department" at the
Berrett-Koehler address above.
Individual sales. Berrett-Koehler publications are available through most bookstores. They
can also be ordered directly from Berrett-Koehler: Tel: (800) 929-2929; Fax: (802) 864-7626;
www.bkconnection.com.
Orders for college textbook / course adoption use. Please contact Berrett-Koehler:
Tel: (800) 929-2929; Fax: (802) 864-7626.

Distributed to the U.S. trade and internationally by Penguin Random House Publisher Services.

Berrett-Koehler and the BK logo are registered trademarks of Berrett-Koehler Publishers, Inc.

Printed in the United States of America

Berrett-Koehler books are printed on long-lasting acid-free paper. When it is available,
we choose paper that has been manufactured by environmentally responsible processes.
These may include using trees grown in sustainable forests, incorporating recycled paper,
minimizing chlorine in bleaching, or recycling the energy produced at the paper mill.

Library of Congress Cataloging-in-Publication Data
Library of Congress Control Number: 2021930309
ISBN: 978-1-5230-9354-0

First Edition
27 26 25 24 23 22 21   10 9 8 7 6 5 4 3 2 1

Book producer: Westchester Publishing Services
Text designer: Westchester Publishing Services
Cover illustration: Asher Bohmer
Cover design: Dan Tesser, Studio Carnelian

For Lynette,
Asher, and Isobel

Table of Contents

Preface

Early in my career I confronted an uncomfortable reality. I was privileged to be a member of a three-person team recruited to reopen a small surgical hospital in northern Sudan, train local staff, and treat refugees wounded in one of the region's several wars. We operated in a difficult environment: I delivered anesthetics in searing heat, without electricity or pressurized gases. However, over time it became clear that our work was more than performing safe operations under challenging conditions. We had to establish routines—of preoperative preparation, sterile practice, and postoperative surveillance—where there were none previously. It was a sobering realization: our patients' well-being was as much determined by the small-scale systems we built as by our own work as individual professionals. The organization mattered as much, if not more, than I did.

The importance of the way care delivery is organized and managed has only increased during my lifetime. As a junior doctor in a rich country, New Zealand, I had entered a world much less complex than today. Patients had only one or a few diseases and a handful of medications. Primary practitioners had more time to listen and console and to coordinate with hospital specialists and care providers in the community. As clinicians, we gave little consideration to cost, as interventions were less expensive and national budgets less strained.

The current generation of junior nurses, therapists, pharmacists, and doctors is confronting very different circumstances. Multi-comorbid patients with bags full of medicines are common.

As the knowledge base and therapeutic armamentarium have expanded, so too have the number of specialists and institutions. Patients now transition from one professional or specialist to another across multiple organizational boundaries and over long periods of time. It is all too easy to become lost in the system, or invisible to it, as many minorities are. The way we design and manage the systems of care—to ensure the right care, delivered by the right professional, with the right knowledge, in the right place, at the right time, done right—has real impact on our patients' well-being: it determines both their clinical outcome and their experience of care. It also defines our and our colleagues' working lives.

Unfortunately, the systems in which clinicians do their work have changed less during my career. Although innovations such as artificial intelligence and internet-based delivery models threaten to completely upend what we think of as "care," who can be a caregiver, and where and how care can be delivered, our systems have changed little to address this new reality. The legacy of the nineteenth century persists: the visit, the hospital, the individual doctor. In spite of the increasing importance of care delivered in the community, large institutions that centralize human and technical assets still dominate our thinking and consume the lion's share of most developed societies' healthcare resources. The typical response to increased demand and complexity has been to do more of the same, rather than something different. Healthcare has been notoriously slow to adopt innovations. Managers have continued to focus on increasing clinician productivity and training more clinicians so as to maximize the events of care, such as appointments, procedures, and discharges, all within their limited budgets. Patients still come to the system, although modern technology has made it so much easier to take the system to the patient.

One early effect of the Covid-19 pandemic in 2020 was to reveal the cracks in our systems for all to see: the fragility of critical supply chains, the extent of medical uncertainty, the stress of the work of care delivery, the structural racism, and the persisting imbalance between hospital and community care, to name a few. Although patients generally hold their healthcare providers in high esteem, even before Covid-19 they were increasingly dissatisfied with the cost, quality, and accessibility of our systems. Now individuals' risk calculations have changed. It is no longer clear that patients want what our current systems offer in return for a clinical outcome and a care experience: delay, cost, disrespect, inconvenience, and risk.

THE CHALLENGE AHEAD

How can we bring about the changes necessary to respond to a new environment and adapt existing organizations so that they can support new models of care and better serve all patients? Politicians are often drawn to sweeping policy reforms, academics to neat models with broad applicability, and executives to large-scale institutional investments. Their hope is that a national target, a merger, a physician incentive system, or a new electronic health record will change the way patients flow through the delivery system and the way individual professionals behave, and that these changes will result in better patient outcomes and experiences. But such high-level interventions can neglect the important role that local operating systems and individual routines play in the delivery of care. And single solutions imposed uniformly can miss important distinctions between different diseases, patient subpopulations and cultures, and individual preferences that necessitate different approaches to the delivery of care. Moreover, they can fail to account for the nature of the work of delivering care. You have to understand the work before you can redesign it: the difficulty of proning an intubated patient, the diagnostic value in a simple bed bath, the different purposes of an outpatient appointment, the challenge of caring for the homeless, the impact of missing key pieces of information, or the grief, and occasional self-recrimination, staff can feel when they lose a patient.

To improve the quality and efficiency of care delivery often means changing the way care is organized and managed at the local level: how work is divided among members of a multidisciplinary team within an organization, or among organizations in a larger system, how decisions are made, how information flows, how change is led. Professionals must learn new ways of practicing alone and working together in teams on the wards and in the clinics, practices, operating rooms, and community settings if we are to accommodate innovations or novel diseases with the potential to fundamentally change the nature of health care. An inability to change local operating systems both dampens the impact of technology and service innovations and slows the pace of internal cost, quality, and safety improvement activities.

Historically, many working clinicians have held themselves apart from these organizational concerns. They have tended to remain focused on their patients and the care they personally deliver while taking their working environments as a given. But because management decisions have clinical impacts and local operating systems exert a powerful influence on the care our patients receive, unit-level operational design and management matters more than ever. Effective, efficient, and compassionate care systems that are satisfying and safe places to work are not an accident. They are deliberately built. It is no longer enough for clinicians to focus solely on their personal practice: they also have to engage with managers to ensure that clinical insights inform operational design and the systems supporting their work are fit for purpose. Clinicians' understanding of different subpopulations' needs, new technologies' potential, and the work of delivering care ideally positions them to lead local operational change. And taking greater operational control is one way for them to address that sense of isolation and disenfranchisement that so many increasingly feel. Healthcare transformation depends as much on leadership in the middle of delivery organizations as from the top.

Clinical practice and the management of delivery organizations, for generations treated as unrelated disciplines, have now become more and more intertwined as care and systems grow more complex and our focus shifts from the management of hospitals to the management of populations. The rigid distinction between workers and managers began breaking down in many industries during the twentieth century, as it became widely recognized that workers not only have a key role in improving systems but also are essential in managing them. Thankfully, these days I increasingly encounter clinicians who want to be engaged in the design and management of their own delivery organizations, and managers who want to build organizations that better support clinical practice. Clinicians no longer regard the word "management" with as much distaste as they did when I first worked as a hospital administrator in Boston almost thirty years ago.

This book is for clinicians who want to manage the care they participate in delivering and change the systems that support their work. It is for managers who want to create more sophisticated delivery systems that better reflect important differences among diseases and patients. I argue that the way we organize care matters and that the people best positioned to reorganize care are those who deliver it.

The book's primary focus is on how care is managed and change is led. It derives from my years spent working with individuals and teams to help them create organizations that manage care, not transactions. It deliberately draws together insights from healthcare, cognitive psychology, organizational behavior, and operations management to create an intersection between medical and management science. It aims to help leaders in the middle of delivery organizations of all types be simultaneously fluent in the languages of medicine and management. By design it does not endorse a particular model of care, course of action, nor decision for those who want to take control of and reform their local operating systems. Instead, it describes the many tools they can choose: how to use them and how to match each to the corresponding situation. It focuses on the work of leading local operational change, identifies some of the key decisions that must be made and actions to be taken, and discusses factors that may need to be taken into account in making them.

I write at a time when the term *value-based health care* dominates thinking about health system design and management. What is more often meant by this is "value for money" rather than "what does the patient value?" And indeed, many of the management tools this book describes have an engineering flavor: they are the tools of operational design and control. The purpose of putting these tools in the hands of clinicians, of all professions and disciplines, is to ensure that systems reliably deliver what patients value. In healthcare the tools are used in the service of a special human mission: the compassionate care of unique individuals. This book's goal is to put control back into the hands of local clinicians and managers, recognizing that with that control will come responsibility. It is not only possible for working clinicians to acquire the skills to redesign and manage their working environments to provide better care for patients and greater job satisfaction for themselves—at this point it is necessary.

STRUCTURE OF THE BOOK

This book's goal is to address the question of how operational control is exercised at the front line in an industry characterized by uncertainty and changeability, and how the work of operational transformation in healthcare can be systematized and orchestrated. It aims to resolve some of the apparent conflict between the worlds of clinical medicine and organizational management and find a balance between the technology and humanity of healthcare delivery. It takes the perspective that change is local and that what works for one delivery organization may not work for another. How you choose to design and oversee care delivery in your organization will depend on many factors, such as the disease burden of your patients and their communities, the resources you have available, and ultimately, on what you, your colleagues, and the patient communities you serve, value.

To the extent that this book provides a "blueprint" for transformation, its focus is on how to lead change rather than what change to lead. I deliberately concentrate on principles over tactics and process over content. I do not prescribe a single, preferred organizational structure, management philosophy, or reimbursement model. Rather, the focus is on the design principles for patient care operations, the behaviors of leaders far below the top of the delivery organization that can result in organizational transformation, and the internal structures and processes needed to create an environment that encourages and supports those leading from the middle.

Chapter 1 discusses the rationale for transforming healthcare at the front line and the case for greater clinician engagement in the design and day-to-day management of their local delivery organizations. Chapter 2 focuses on the goal of a delivery organization and the purpose of operational redesign. It considers the question of patient value and how this relates to both setting an appropriate goal for operational redesign and creating a unified sense of purpose among a diverse staff.

Chapters 3 through 5 consider the design decisions local clinicians and managers need to make to ensure that their system supports their work in delivering value to patients and the important considerations in making these design choices. These chapters discuss the way control is exercised through the design and management of local unit-level systems, the principles of operations design, and the characteristics of highly functioning operating systems.

Chapters 6 and 7 focus on the problem of bringing about the change needed to implement a new operating system in an existing delivery organization. They discuss the challenge of influencing professionals' behavior and address such issues as motivating behavior, changing unit-level culture, the effective use of incentives, and dealing with unprofessional behavior. Their focus is on the challenges of leading change in a clinical environment, in particular the problems faced by clinicians aiming to lead change among their colleagues.

Few operational changes fully achieve their goals the first time. Hence Chapter 8 looks at strategies for maintaining flexibility through the use of structured approaches to improvement and innovation and considers the adoption of new technology into existing systems.

Together, the first eight chapters focus on the requirements for frontline operational redesign and change management. They try to reconcile the tensions between clinical instincts and the requirements of managerial control. The last two chapters, in contrast, look at transformation from an organizational perspective. Chapter 9 considers the way delivery organizations learned rapidly during the early phases of the Covid-19 pandemic and describes the structure and functioning of learning systems in healthcare and the leader's role in encouraging learning. Finally, Chapter 10 describes an orchestrated approach to enterprise-wide transformation and considers what senior leaders need to do to support the widespread frontline change needed to adopt new technologies, respond to evolving models of care, and implement organizational strategy. It describes the infrastructure needed to support multiple, distributed, and clinician-engaged operational redesigns and an organizational program that comprises multiple frontline changes.

What follows unashamedly takes the point of view of existing delivery organizations. The notions of transformation and innovation are often taken to imply action from the outside, either by policymakers or insurers setting new rules or entrepreneurial companies creating new organizations or implementing innovative services and technologies into existing ones. This book frames transformation as a task internal to the delivery organization, as much an act of maintenance as of innovation. In these organizations, to "transform" means to redesign interorganizational relationships in networks and systems to redistribute and redesign the work of care, and to rebuild intraorganizational frontline operating systems so that patients can more easily move through complex systems that are more capable of meeting their needs.

Transformation will require clinicians to collaborate with managers and take more control of their local practice environments to improve performance and regain some of their professional satisfaction. It will require senior leaders to disseminate the authority and accountability that local staff need to do this in a disciplined, rigorous, and effective way. This book describes the nature of that work: the work of leaders in the middle, close to care and far from the boardroom. It describes the tools they have available and the approaches they need to apply to put them to the most effective use.

Finally, some definitions: in what follows the term "delivery organization" will be used to describe for-profit and not-for-profit organizations that exist to deliver individual patient care: a group that includes entities as diverse as hospitals, community agencies, aged care facilities, and physician group practices. The term "operating system" will mean that subunit of a delivery organization that directly interfaces with an individual patient, sometimes called a "micro-system," although Chapter 3 will define an operating system in a particular way. To "manage care" will mean to design an operating system, to oversee its day-to-day functioning, and to improve its performance over the long term. And finally, by "clinician," I mean anyone who provides some aspect of patient care—including nurses, therapists, pharmacists, paramedics, and social workers—not only doctors.

PART ONE

Why Transform Healthcare?

CHAPTER 1

Leading Healthcare Transformation from the Middle

The Covid-19 pandemic only made what has long been apparent to all even more obvious: modern healthcare is in desperate need of reform. Books, articles, and academic papers typically begin with the same refrain: health care is expensive, hard to access, difficult to navigate, and prone to failure. Despite years of policy and operational changes aimed at improving quality and reducing cost, healthcare systems all over the world are swamped with demand and are short of resources.

In part, the current predicament is the result of past successes creating new problems. Decades of medical innovation have helped grow the aging population and increase the numbers of patients living well with multiple complex conditions. Rapidly advancing science has caused an explosion in medical knowledge. At the same time, increasing subspecialization fragments patients' care across multiple doctors and offices and fractures the clinician-patient relationship, which has been the bedrock of healing practice and a key source of clinicians' job satisfaction for centuries.

Although past successes have increased demand, past failures have worsened supply. Quality remains an issue despite years of academics' and practitioners' work to reduce waste, delay, unwarranted variation, and harm. Uneven spread of resources and quality of care reinforce inequality and are part of a long-standing pattern of structural racism in healthcare delivery.[1] Providers' unrelenting hunt for efficiency has contributed to worsening patient experience. The pooled labor models used in urgent care centers and inpatient hospitalist staffing often mean patients can no longer expect to see the same doctor twice.

Healthcare delivery organizations are under constant pressure to deliver more care at lower overall cost. They have responded by growing, to spread their fixed costs over a larger patient volume, and increasing productivity, to deliver more care with the same resources. Recent decades have seen a wave of mergers, acquisitions, and partnerships of delivery organizations, the substitution of cheaper clinicians and care sites for more expensive ones, and analytic and communication tools that help spread the existing workforce around a larger patient population. On both sides of the Atlantic, healthcare delivery organizations have been driven by performance targets imposed by governments (in the United Kingdom) or insurance contracts (in the United States), typically focused on maximum waiting times or minimum patient volumes and aimed at wringing every ounce of productivity from existing human, technological, and spatial resources.

Unfortunately, many of these responses have only worsened the situation by alienating staff. Clinicians, who have been called upon to do more with less, see their work reduced to a series of isolated transactions and administrative tasks. A deep sense of disenfranchisement and loss of control are contributing to the burnout that is exacerbating workforce shortages. Doctors and nurses are leaving their professions early because they feel they are no longer respected independent professionals but instead are cogs in a machine. Burnout is both a cause and a symptom of health system dysfunction.[2]

But the common narrative of demand and productivity risks missing a deeper secular trend that is pushing delivery organizations to rethink the fundamental models on which they are based and the way they are managed. Healthcare is, at its heart, the organized delivery of science to the patient. Care underpins human compassion with social, psychological, biological, and engineering sciences and brings this all to bear on patients' health problems. As the science changes, so too must the organization of its delivery.

New information, decision support, and diagnostic and communication technologies are changing who can deliver care, and where and how it is delivered. They also enable more precise targeting of care to the unique needs of smaller patient subpopulations. Such new technologies are already allowing a new generation of clinical operating models, such as self-care, virtual consultation, supermarket-based services, health coaching, and disease-specific smartphone applications.

Less obviously, these technological advancements are also forcing delivery organizations to reconsider both how they design new models of care and how they manage change. Although large-scale interventions such as mergers or electronic health record implementations create the essential infrastructure of a modern delivery organization, they are insensitive to subtle differences in the clinical particularities of different patient disease or risk groups. Organizations have to become more operationally diverse as they deploy different models of care to target the needs of different subpopulations, each of which may need a different blend of technology, staff, and site of care to meet its particular needs. If existing organizations are to cope with upcoming technology, they will need to redesign the front line of care at their many locations.

To be successful, redesigning the front line of delivery organizations must occur in ways that are sensitive to needs of patients suffering with specific diseases, respectful of their cultures and values, feasible given current technology, and implementable in the context of existing organizational, regulatory, and financial structures. This requires merging the science of clinical medicine with the disciplines of organizational design and managerial control.

For organizations to transform, clinicians and managers working in thousands of inpatient and outpatient units will need to apply managerial insights to medical, nursing, and therapy practice. In other words, clinicians will need to think like managers and managers like clinicians. Furthermore, organizations will have to develop and support a generation of clinical change leaders.

ALL HEALTH CARE IS LOCAL

It is becoming increasingly clear that simply doing more of the same, only faster and cheaper, will be insufficient to address the issues of demand and productivity, the impact of novel diseases, and evolving technology. A more fundamental transformation is necessary. Thinkers from different disciplines tend to offer solutions framed in terms of their own specialty: economists propose market and payment reforms, such as value-based contracting, and management scholars focus on alternative organizational forms and philosophies, such as focused factories, integrated practice units, and lean manufacturing.

Indeed, many argue that the answer lies in management models drawn from other industries. After all, they reason, healthcare is not the only high-cost, high-risk industry where the cost of failure is measured in human lives. Other dangerous or complex industries have dramatically improved their performance over the years. Landing a jet on an aircraft carrier deck, operating a nuclear power reactor, and flying in a complex air traffic system have become cheaper, safer, and more reliable. Moreover, many of these industries have published their methodologies for all to see, such as High Reliability Theory (nuclear power), Crew Resource Management (airline industry), and the Toyota Production System (manufacturing).

Yet uptake of workable solutions and validated approaches has been uneven. These managerial approaches are still not routine in healthcare, and in some quarters they are still viewed with suspicion. Individual examples of successful system and institutional improvements abound, but there are fewer examples of systemic, systematic, and sustained change. Failure to implement proven innovations, from electronic health records to clinical practice guidelines and checklists, is a familiar complaint.[3] The lag between proof of efficacy and widespread industry adoption can be measured in decades.

Nonetheless, some organizations have managed a significant transformation. They are the subjects of numerous publications and talks and are well known to many, including Intermountain Healthcare, Salford Royal NHS Foundation Trust, and Virginia Mason Medical Center. Yet even the best institutions have failed to scale or spread. Kaiser Permanente, once the darling of health reformers, is a real presence in only a few markets. Many internationally recognized brands, such as the Mayo Clinic, Cleveland Clinic, Massachusetts General Hospital, and The Royal Marsden, have largely remained in their original markets or made only limited investments elsewhere.

Why, then, in the face of such clear advice and compelling exemplars, has change been so slow, localized, and inconsistent? Why have validated models and best practices failed to transfer? The structure of healthcare systems can certainly hinder spread. The balkanized nature of specialist medicine and nursing tends to fragment the organizational structure of delivery systems into independent institutions and departmental silos. Each usually has its own budget and revenue source, and consequently they tend to function as profit-maximizing independent businesses acting in their own interests, not the system's, with few incentives to collaborate.

Beyond this, the uncomfortable reality is that health care is obstinately local. Societal and community values, individual patient preferences, patterns of disease, capital and real estate resources, institutional history, and staff numbers, skill sets, and work preferences vary from one region to the next. Although leading organizations' methods or organizing principles may be taught, their foundational histories, organizational cultures, and passionate local change leaders are harder to transport across state or national boundaries. For example, Toyota gladly teaches its methods to other car companies, but many competitors trying to emulate Toyota have been challenged to replicate its success.

System transformation is ultimately effected through unit-level operational change. To transform, individual institutions and delivery systems must each select from among a diverse set of tools, exemplars, and approaches those that resonate most with their local communities of patients and staff. Lessons may surely be taken from innovations in other healthcare delivery organizations or imported from management models applied in other industries, but ultimately each must be implemented locally in the institution's own wards, operating rooms, clinics, and consulting rooms. Most important, these approaches must be adapted to meet local conditions. The questions each delivery organization must answer are not just, What should we do?, but also, How do we do it here?

Unfortunately, there is no magic bullet, no single dominant model that can be "rolled out" or franchised. On the contrary, transformation requires local redesign and change at each of its myriad delivery units: local change at global scale.

TWO KEY TRENDS DRIVING CHANGE IN DELIVERY ORGANIZATIONS

Short-term market pressures compel delivery organizations to address productivity and demand-supply mismatch by delivering care that is faster, better, cheaper, and, nowadays, remote. Beyond this, two longer-term trends are changing the fundamental nature of healthcare delivery. Both have a significant impact on the way professionals work together, and both are forcing delivery organizations to change.

The first is a continuing transition from an individual-based to an organization-based enterprise. For centuries, health outcomes were driven by individual clinician excellence. Accordingly, clinicians were trained, recruited, regulated, and managed as individuals. In the modern era, however, health outcome is equally a function of organizational and team excellence. To be sure, individual skill and training are still necessary, but they are now no longer a sufficient condition for the best patient outcome.

In some quarters, this transition is controversial. As healthcare becomes increasingly "corporatized" and doctors become employees, some argue that a consequent loss of physician independence not only contributes to burnout but also harms quality. This view holds that independent nursing and medical professionals who advocate in their patients' best interests are at the heart of high-quality care. Its advocates fear that individualized and compassionate care risks being lost in the organizational machine.

Nonetheless, the ascent of the organization and its dominance over the individual are the modern reality of healthcare, for good and bad. There is some advantage to a focus on the organization. Many of the most egregious failures in patient care have their roots not in the failure of individual professionals but in poor delivery system design and function. How we structure and manage groups of individual caregivers matters, in large part because of the key role now played by teams. The challenge of modern healthcare is to develop better organizations capable of delivering compassionate and individualized care on a grand scale while preserving the personal relationship between clinician and patient and clinicians' sense of control over their working environment.

The second trend is a more fundamental, science-driven change in the core processes of preventing, diagnosing, and curing disease. Advances in biology, analytics and machine learning, and communication technology are changing the way in which healthcare's core activities of disease finding, diagnosis, treatment, and prevention are undertaken. Wearable technologies, population analytics, and personal health record algorithms can identify at-risk patients long before disease is manifest and the patient typically presents. The Covid-19 pandemic has reinforced the way in which modern communication technologies and point-of-care and noninvasive testing can allow diagnostic hypotheses to be formulated and even tested at a distance, often without recourse to a specialist or the need for an in-person visit. Expert treatment advice is moderated by patient-to-patient interaction via social media and patients' and nonmedical professionals' access to digitized algorithms, and therapies are increasingly targeted to smaller populations based on genetic profile. Rules-based systems guide the activities of health coaches with no medical or nursing training. Many interventions, previously considered hospital only, can now be safely delivered in distant outpatient settings or the patient's own home.

These trends have the potential to fundamentally change the nature of healthcare delivery as technological advancement enables less expensively trained staff to make more sophisticated decisions. Those without medical training can now make decisions that used to wait for medical professionals. Technological advancement tends to distribute decision authority, and as a result teams become more diverse and geographically distributed.

The primary impact is on how we work. Better supported and easier decision-making changes who can or should perform the work of care, where and how that work can be undertaken, and what kind of organization is needed to support it. We are seeing this effect already. Teams now comprise individuals who are increasingly working across organizational boundaries in interprofessional groups that combine clinicians, managers, and, most important, the patient. Medical decision-making regarding an individual patient's care is increasingly based on large data sets, and expert systems make recommendations based on the aggregated experience of thousands of like patients.

However, traditional healthcare delivery organizations evolved to support an entirely different style of care. When general practitioners and hospital specialists treated patients with only one disease and when treatments were fewer and less well targeted, the independent, lone doctor was the primary decision maker. When consulted, he (and it was usually "he") saw the patient in person and was supported by a suite of nursing and technology services that were centralized around his work and overseen by a hierarchy of lower-status professional managers. The hospital and consulting room were the doctor's servants. In the modern era, this classical model of the delivery organization as the doctor's workshop is no longer fit-for-purpose. Increasing patient complexity and technological capability are mirrored by increasing size, diversity, and distribution of the care team, and previously stand-alone institutions are becoming part of integrated regional networks.

These two trends are forcing the widespread operational redesign of existing organizations to create institutions and systems better suited to new ways of working. Moreover, operational and organizational redesign is unlikely to be a one-time occurrence: more likely it will be an ongoing necessity because the nature of new technology is to constantly drive changes in the operations of healthcare delivery. As a result, we will always be rearranging the tasks and decisions of care, reallocating roles and decision rights, and resituating care as pharmaceutical, device, digital, and communication innovations make new alternatives feasible. To this extent, the ability to repeatedly transform—to restructure organizations and revise clinical and operational processes—is becoming an essential long-term organizational capability: a way of being rather than an event.

IMPACT OF THESE TRENDS ON DELIVERY ORGANIZATIONS

The new ways of working enabled and forced by technological evolution have two important and often underappreciated organizational implications. The first of these relates to the structure and operations of delivery organizations.

When task responsibilities and decision rights are redistributed among professionals and institutions, these groups are forced to redefine their relationships and ways of interacting. In practice, this means developing new ways of working within a team and smoothing patients' passage from one team, unit, or organization to the next as they traverse a system or network to receive their care. Smooth passages through complex systems are not accidental. Other industries devote substantial resources to ensuring that customers do not experience the complexity of the systems developed to serve them, but healthcare all too often makes the navigation of our complexity the patient's responsibility. The pathways that complex, multi-comorbid, or chronically ill patients take through delivery systems with multiple organizational boundaries need to be specifically designed to be simple and navigable.

In effect, this requires redesign in two dimensions: the configuration of people, technology, and routines within each unit and the relationship of multiple units and organizations that contribute to a patient's care. Complex patients interact with multiple organizational subunits, each delivering a portion of the care and contributing part of the value that patients receive from their care. Each ward, clinic, operating room, doctor's office, or pharmacy must be specifically configured internally to be capable of reliably delivering the portion of care for which it is responsible. At the same time, the transitions across the delivery system's multiple organizational and departmental boundaries must be redesigned to coordinate the patient's overall care.

The focus of this redesign is the local operating system: the fundamental unit of any delivery organization. An operating system is made up of the care process and its associated business processes, the staffing model used to implement these processes, the medical and information technologies and physical infrastructure that support staff in their work, and the data systems, metrics, and mechanisms of behavioral influence that are used to exercise operational control. These elements must be aligned and made fit-for-purpose at each of the many organizational and system units with which the patient comes in contact. The need for operating system redesign occurs whenever previously standalone institutions coalesce into networks, existing networks take on the challenge of population health, or organizations adopt new technologies that change work patterns. In all these situations individual and institutional roles and responsibilities may have to be redistributed and multiple local subsystems reconfigured.

Who is to do this work, and how? The second organizational implication of the changes described previously relates to the model of leadership and control within a delivery organization. Over the course of the twentieth century, the model of centralized hierarchical managerial control initially advocated by Frederick Taylor and the "scientific management" movement in the late nineteenth century has given way to a model of decentralized operational control and frontline leadership. This transition has already occurred in many service and production industries that have moved away from command-and-control hierarchies toward individual self-management and self-managing teams.[4]

Centralized expert problem-solving resources have been replaced by frontline staff who are skilled and authorized to identify and solve problems then and there and are empowered to redesign systems and structures in the longer term. Decentralized problem-solving authority was one factor that helped organizations successfully respond to the early challenges of the Covid-19 pandemic.

However, in healthcare, in spite of increased recognition of the importance of clinician engagement and leadership, key frontline workers, especially doctors, continue to hold themselves apart. They often view the delivery organization more as the context for their individual professional practice than as an essential part of the overall mechanism by which they achieve a positive patient outcome.

Yet transformation depends on the clinical staff. Structural, operational, and managerial change is required to bring organizations together at the highest level and to redefine operations, behavior, and working relationships at the lowest. This work needs the involvement of clinical staff and depends on clinicians and managers working together. It is the clinicians who have the scientific knowledge and operational control required to effect meaningful change at the unit level. Therefore, transformation is also the work of identifying, developing, and supporting a group of people within the delivery organization who understand the work of taking care of patients, can lead operating system redesign, and can undertake ongoing oversight and control of improved units and systems.

Unfortunately, those key frontline workers who are interested in transformation face an uphill battle. Healthcare delivery is a particularly difficult setting in which to bring about change, in part because of the difficulties of exercising operational control in this context.

THE CHALLENGE OF IMPLEMENTING LOCAL CHANGE

Why is changing the way we work within units and relationships among units so difficult? Three characteristics of healthcare make this work challenging and affect the way management principles developed in other settings can be applied in healthcare.

The first of these characteristics relates to the nature of the science underpinning healthcare delivery. Despite dramatic advances in our understanding, the medical science base is far from complete and care remains an uncertain business, a fact starkly demonstrated by the emergence of a novel disease in 2020. Unlike in many production industries, causal relationships in medicine are probabilistic, not deterministic. Medicine is based on biology, not Newtonian mechanics, and accordingly its "rules" and "standard operating procedures" are incomplete, evanescent, and rarely universally applicable.

As a result, many patient-clinician interactions are still empirical: we try something and see what happens. A "best practice" does not guarantee an outcome; it simply makes it more likely. Scientific advances improve our probability estimates, but even after the unwarranted variation resulting from inadequate systems is removed, a significant level of variability and uncertainty remains. Patients simply do not respond to therapy with the same reliability that metal forms in a press or that meat cooks on a grill.

Second, this uncertain science is in the hands of a group of independent professionals. Physicians remain highly autonomous, largely a result of the way they are recruited and trained. As the volume of medical knowledge has increased, training programs have become more specialized. This has resulted in a generation of doctors trained to focus on that component of the patient's care for which they are responsible, not the broader system of care of which that component is a part. Other health professions are equally independently minded. Because it takes a wide and sophisticated skill set to cure disease and relieve suffering, nurses, doctors, therapists, and social workers have each been deliberately trained to focus on a different aspect of the overall value the health system creates for the patient. Although they share the same broad goals of preventing disease and returning ill patients to health, they legitimately differ in their approaches to achieving them.

Even when they are paid employees of a healthcare delivery organization, doctors and nurses maintain a strong allegiance to their professions, professional organizations, and professional peers. Correspondingly, they identify less with the delivery organization and its managerial staff. This is particularly true for doctors who have an independent revenue source, as under the fee-for-service reimbursement system in the United States or from private practice in the United Kingdom or other national health systems. The strong value set already in place before joining a delivery organization only further supports their independence. Professionals will rebel if an organization's goals are not perceived to be consistent with these values, a discrepancy often at the heart of the persisting conflict between clinicians and managers.

Third, patients are equally autonomous. In most service industries, customers interact with a service "wrapper" that is highly responsive to their preferences, but the creation of the core product, such as the cooking of the fast food or the safe piloting of a plane, remains exclusively in the hands of the professional. Customers are excluded from these operations. But in healthcare, patients genuinely are "coproducers." They are constantly making medical decisions—if, when, and how to intervene—often over long periods of time. These choices have a significant impact on exactly the same outcome the professionals and delivery organization are trying to influence (and for which they are being held accountable). In few other settings are service providers as vulnerable to the customer's failure to use that service appropriately or correctly. In other words, if you miss your flight, it is your problem, not the pilot's, but in healthcare, if the patient does not take the medication, the system is nonetheless accountable. The patient is, in effect, part of the professional team.

What these three factors—an incomplete and dynamic knowledge base and the pivotal roles played by independently minded doctors and patients—have in common is the behavioral variability they create at the front line of care. They make it challenging to exercise operational control and implement innovations and operational change. These factors help to explain why inflexible mandates from the top often tend to be controversial and unsuccessful.

These characteristics also mean that clinicians and patients necessarily have a central role in the transformation of care systems. Only they have the requisite knowledge to confront the complex interaction between personal and community values and the nature of a disease, the current state of medical knowledge and technological capability, and the ideal local and regional organizational arrangements for delivering care to patients suffering from that disease. Only they have the final control over care choices and how they are executed.

In sum, clinicians at the front line need to be involved in unit-level operational redesign for instrumental reasons. It is they who have the knowledge and ability to exercise control. But they also need to be involved for therapeutic purposes. Returning to clinicians' control over their local environment is a way of addressing one of the causes of burnout, what Eisenstein has called "an act of self-care."[5]

LEADING FROM THE MIDDLE

The idea that clinicians should have an enhanced role in the design and management of delivery organizations is by no means a new one. There are numerous papers, talks, and blogs on clinician engagement and leadership. However, the now-popular term "physician leadership" is often used to refer to leadership at the chief executive and senior decision-maker level. By "clinical leaders," we usually mean those in named leadership positions. But the need for reform at the unit level—the ward, operating room, clinic, or practice—requires the engagement of a larger group of practitioners working with patients day to day. These are leaders in the middle of the organization working in patient-facing operating systems several layers below the senior leadership. It has become increasingly clear that, despite well-intentioned efforts, top-down implementation of the rules and protocols of "evidence-based medicine" is not sufficient to transform a system of care or practice at the unit level. MIT's Ed Schein is popularly quoted as observing that "you can't impose anything on anyone and expect them to be committed to it." Nowhere is this truer than in healthcare, where no one can impose a course of action related to patient care on the professionals who provide that care.

Unfortunately, clinicians are often schooled in perspectives and skills that run directly counter to those that are needed to effectively lead change and exercise control of the local operating system in which they also practice. They are not well prepared for a change leadership role. Both the new ways of working in the future, enabled by new technology, and the leadership skills to help a team learn and implement them (that is, to lead their colleagues in a clinical team through change) are unfamiliar to many clinicians. The approaches and language common to the management models drawn from other industries can clash with core values and behaviors of clinical practice.

What appears obvious to management consultants and academics is foreign to clinicians for at least four reasons. First, doctors in particular often have limited experience operating in a team of equals that includes those skilled in management, finance, or process engineering. Clinical training is still based on the presumption that individual action "causes" a good (or bad) patient outcome. It emphasizes individualism and a strong ethos of personal accountability that is reinforced by the medicolegal code. In usual group settings, such as the emergency room, operating room, or catheterization lab, the doctor is typically the high-status content expert in a hierarchical team. Even in those multidisciplinary meetings where the status differentials are not so overt, participants are frequently all health professionals who share some core values and perspectives.

Second, they are not trained to have an enterprise focus or mindset needed to design patients' paths through complex organizations or regional systems. One effect of increasing sub-specialization is that individual clinicians increasingly focus on the small portion of the patient's overall care that is their responsibility (and specialty), a focus that is reinforced by the transactional way in which their activities are measured and reimbursed. In other words they preferentially concern themselves with their portion of the overall value chain, not the wider chain or longer patient journey.

Third, clinicians are often naturally averse to risk. The principle of primum non nocere (first do no harm) makes clinicians reluctant to perturb the current system without strong evidence that to do so would be safe and effective, even when that system is clearly underperforming. Such a mindset not only tends to preserve the status quo but also makes clinicians suspicious of the kind of rapid cycle experimentation that is at the heart of modern approaches to improvement and innovation. Interestingly, clinicians and organizations did, at least temporarily, embrace rapid experimentation as they responded to the 2020 Covid-19 crisis.

Finally, clinicians are only too aware of the uncertainty that underlies much day-to-day clinical practice. This tends to make them prefer to maintain flexibility and unwilling to "lock in" practices lest they be inflexible later. It makes them wary of any standardization that could limit their ability to respond rapidly to evolving clinical situations. Standard care is frequently dismissed as "cookbook medicine."

These aspects of clinical practice do not align well with the recommendations of the formalized approaches to management and performance improvement common in other industries. In fact, those approaches are typically based on completely opposite behaviors. Other industries measure performance through compliance with an invariant standard. They aim to reduce ambiguity through high degrees of specification and standardization and exploit any remaining variance as a mechanism of learning. Such industries encourage innovation by exploiting the diversity in team skills, and to this end they deliberately flatten hierarchies and create groups of equals with unusual skill combinations. Notably, nonmedical industries promote experimentation, not in the controlled environment of a lab or under the oversight of a rigorous clinical trial review process, but in real time, on the shop floor, with live customers and small sample sizes.

Given the clash between the culture and practices of healthcare delivery and those approaches to improvement and innovation that are common in other industries, it is little wonder clinicians are often slow to adopt well-accepted management methodologies into healthcare and are thus dismissed as impediments to change.

Herein, then, is the challenge. The changes healthcare delivery organizations must make to accommodate current demands and future innovations require rebuilding unit-level operating systems and developing new relationships among individuals, units, and organizations working together in a wider system or regional network. This requires engagement of frontline clinicians who have both the local knowledge and access to the levers of control over unit-level operating systems that are necessary to make change. To effectively exercise this control and develop systems that are more fit-for-purpose, however, clinicians and managers have to learn new behaviors and skills. They must work together within and across organizational boundaries in interprofessional and multidisciplinary teams, planning systems to support the management of at-risk patient populations as well as individual patients, overseeing the day-to-day performance of these systems, conducting experiments and making necessary midcourse corrections, and, of course, leading change among their colleagues. Yet the very people needed to lead local change in their units and organizations are not just ill prepared for the task, they are likely trained in a set of skills that are contrary to the ones they will need to bring about these necessary changes. On top of that, the management principles and tools they are offered seem insensitive to the clinical context with which they are familiar. If we are to engage clinicians in change leadership at the front lines of care, we will need a model of management and innovation that addresses these clashes in perspective and accommodates the particularities of the healthcare context.

This book aims to do just that. Chapter 2 begins a discussion of what the work of managing care is and how leaders in the middle of delivery organizations can do it: how they can establish its goals, design the necessary operating systems, lead change, exercise daily oversight, and routinize ongoing refinement and constant innovation. It starts with identifying the purpose of the enterprise. Care is managed to achieve a goal, and the nature of that goal will shape how we manage care. Chapter 2 considers that guiding goal.

CHAPTER 2

Identifying Value and Defining Purpose

C are delivery units and organizations worldwide are currently under growing pressure to do more with less. However, the short-term goal of increasing efficiency often competes with other longer-term goals such as improving the health of populations and the quality of care and responding to changing technology and public expectations. The way these priorities are balanced and goals are set will shape the future form of existing organizations. Before those in the middle of delivery organizations can exercise greater control over their working environments and lead transformative change, they must first choose how to frame the purpose of any proposed change. What is the change intended to achieve, how will this contribute to my, and our, broader goals, and how will it affect my work?

The possibly apocryphal anecdote of President Kennedy's visit to the space center makes a popular management consultant point. In reply to the question "What do you do here?" a janitor supposedly replied, "I'm helping put a man on the moon." Successful organizations have a clear sense of purpose, shared by employees throughout the organization, which focuses corporate action, motivates staff, and orchestrates their collective work. A mission statement describes why the organization exists, what its goal is, how it contributes to its customers, and what makes it special. A clear purpose helps individuals make a direct connection between their work and the direction of the overall enterprise. In the context of organizational transformation and operating system redesign a shared purpose focuses the proposed changes. Resolving fragmentation in current care systems is unlikely without first addressing the fragmentation of both organizational and caregivers' goals.

We might assume that developing such a sense of purpose in healthcare would be particularly straightforward. Just like the space program of the early 1960s, healthcare has a single, compelling, and widely shared goal. Surely all clinicians are committed to healing the sick and saving lives? This is a purpose that all—nurses, doctors, managers, therapists, secretaries, orderlies, lab staff, and cleaners—can buy into, not least because those individuals self-selected a healthcare career and were then subject to a particularly strong socialization during their professional training and work experience.

Unfortunately, the organizational and professional complexity of healthcare means it is not so easy. Healthcare systems are made up of multiple stakeholders. Regulators; insurers; inpatient, primary, and community care providers; and patients have their own goals and agendas. Confusion about the purpose of health care is endemic, both coloring national debates and confounding individual delivery organizations. Each professional group focuses on a different aspect of the patient's well-being, and each organization in a system has a different mission. Many organizations have several potentially conflicting missions. Even if nurses, surgeons, therapists, and social workers were to all share the same purpose, the organizations of which they are a part may not.

On the national stage, notions of cost, quality, and access are often pitted against each other. Within organizations, things are no less confused. Goals relating to the health of populations, the care of individuals, teaching, and research often compete for limited resources. Despite protestations that "the patient is at the center of everything we do," the various healthcare professions often provide care without reference to, or coordination with, each other. Many delivery organizations implicitly give top priority to the needs and actions of a small group of staff. (A colleague once noted that his way to test a hospital's "patient-centeredness" was to ask where the chief of surgery parked: if in a reserved space near the front entrance, it suggested this may not be such a patient-centered organization.) The shared sense of purpose that unifies the actions of a group of independent and autonomous professionals working within a clinical service is often not immediately obvious.

Yet the patient's overall outcome critically depends on their unified action. It is the combined impact of individual skill, team performance, and operating system functioning that determines quality of care. Only when these are acting in concert will delivery organizations—whatever their size, nature, or target population—succeed in providing high-value care.

For this reason, any effort to bring about change or exercise control over regional, institutional, or unit-level operating systems must begin with an understanding of purpose. Undertaking a transformation without first clearly identifying what the renewed organization or unit is to become, and why, risks squandering both institutional resources and staff energy and commitment. For what purpose is operational control being exercised? What is the goal of change? In effect, purpose is the "why" of an organization:[1] why are we doing the work we do?

The best commercial enterprises have clear answers to questions such as these. In a competitive market, an organization's purpose is to deliver a unique value to its customers, one for which they are willing to pay. Commercial organizations are lucky enough to have a unitary metric, profit, by which progress toward this goal can easily be assessed. Healthcare organizations are not so advantaged.

Effective commercial organizations are distinguished by having a clear strategy which defines how they will deliver value in a competitive market. A strategy is a response to external environmental conditions and the current and expected competitive landscape. It is primarily about the organization's positioning within its market: to this extent it is outward looking. The strategy defines the basis on which the organization has chosen to compete and how it is to be distinguished from its competitors. In a highly influential paper, Professor Michael Porter argued that competitive strategy is about being different. "It means deliberately choosing a different set of activities to deliver a unique mix of value,"[2] ideally a value that others cannot deliver. To the chagrin of proponents of Japanese improvement methodologies, he further argued that neither quality nor quality improvement is a strategy. Being good is necessary but is insufficient grounds on which to compete. It is too easy for competitors to improve their quality. It cannot be unique.

A clear strategy gives a commercial organization as a whole its purpose. Purpose looks inward to unify its component parts and the actions of a diverse staff. Strategy and purpose are unified by value. The unique value the organization delivers to its customers gives it its strategy in the marketplace and shapes its workers' purpose. The best organizations offer an identifiable unique value that both attracts their customers and unites their employees around creating and delivering it. They are instantly recognizable: we return to these banks, airlines, restaurants, and hairdressers again and again, not because we have to but because we choose to as we have previously received something we value. The organization also has a choice: what value to deliver its customers and what value not to. Of all the ways to provide value to our customers, on which do we choose to focus? The value the enterprise chooses to deliver is sometimes called the "value proposition."

So strategy, purpose, and value are closely linked. The organization's strategy is defined by the unique value it chooses to deliver to its customers, and this gives its workers a unifying sense of purpose that serves as the common goal for their work and gives meaning to their jobs.

PURPOSE OF PURPOSE

To a large degree healthcare delivery organizations are no different from commercial enterprises in their need to agree on a purpose. For them the need to establish a clear sense of purpose that focuses professionals' actions and guides transformation efforts is made all the more urgent by three interrelated problems: disagreement, uncertainty, and noise.

Disagreement

A powerful yet often unspoken assumption among clinicians of different professions and disciplines is that we are all working to achieve the same goals. In fact, evidence suggests that staff from different professions and disciplines differ substantially in what they see as the goals of the enterprise and the best mechanisms for reaching those goals. As already noted, this is in part by design: each discipline was established to optimize a different aspect of a patient's overall care. Nurses, therapists, and doctors have distinct roles and have been explicitly trained to address different components of a patient's needs. Each profession has its own body of science, mental models, practices, and specialist therapeutic interventions, so it is not surprising that those from different professions disagree about the intended outcome or the most appropriate mechanism for achieving it.

Interspecialty and interprofessional disagreement abounds: nurses versus doctors, oncologists versus surgeons, orthopedic surgeons versus neurosurgeons, and managers versus clinicians. Wherever we look for discordance we find it—we simply cannot presume unity of goals and perspectives. Of all the potential clashes, three in particular pose an important risk for patients: among the caregiving professions ("What are we trying to achieve with and for this patient?"), between doctors ("What is the best therapeutic course of action in these circumstances?"), and, of course, between the patient and their family and the clinical staff responsible for their care ("What do I want from my care?").

These differences were well illustrated by a study that each day asked a deceptively simple question about each patient of every doctor, nurse, and allied health professional treating patients on a group of adult medicine wards: "Why is this patient here *today*?" Respondents were given four simple options from which to choose: active medical problem, patient receiving palliative care, social problem, or waiting for rehabilitation. Concordance between pairs among the three role groups ranged from 63 percent to 67 percent. In only 50 percent of cases did all three disciplines concur.[3] Similar discordance is found among specialties within a profession: in another study, for example, urologists and radiation oncologists presented with the same patient vignette recommended very different courses of action.[4]

Clashing views of which goal should take priority has colored relationships between clinical and managerial staff for decades, and the gap between clinicians and managers does not seem to be improving. In a 2003 survey in the United Kingdom 78 percent of chief executives agreed that management was driven more by clinical than financial priorities, but only 24 percent of clinical directors came to the same conclusion.[5] Respondents to the same survey in the United States were even more negative.[6] The gap between them was similar when the survey was repeated in the United Kingdom in 2016: 96 percent and 43 percent, respectively.[7]

To a large degree such differences represent clashing professional cultures, suggesting that the gap is hard to bridge. Research finds significant differences in perspective among doctors, nurses, and managers. Doctors conceptualize clinical work in individualistic terms, whereas nurses' and managers' view is more system oriented. In contrast to managers, neither nurses nor doctors support constraining clinical autonomy with transparent financial accountability.[8]

Different professional perspectives are often reflected in and reinforced by differences in language with distressing impact. Some differences are subtle but can have disastrous consequences. One such was the difference that led to the 1994 death from a cyclophosphamide overdose of a patient being treated at Boston's Dana-Farber Cancer Institute. The error resulted, in part, from competing interpretations of the word "dose." Whereas nursing staff interpreted the term to mean a single dose delivered during a shift, medical staff used the term to mean the total course dose to be delivered over four days. The patient died after receiving the course dose daily for four days. Medical and nursing staff framed their work in different units of analysis.

Other differences are less subtle. Physicians often hear the business language of "cost containment," "value," "performance," and "efficiency" as "an indiscriminate call for reduction in services across the board and a clear prioritization of dollars over patients,"[9] causing them to withdraw from the activities of system redesign and improvement and resist system change. To them this language goes against deeply held professional values.

The process of jointly agreeing on a collective purpose can resolve these disagreements by exposing them: shared purpose can be created only by making profession- and service-specific goals and mental models explicit. Ultimately, finding a common purpose will require reconciling differences in professional models and collectively defining a common lexicon.

Uncertainty

An important contributor to such disagreement among members of a multidisciplinary team is the uncertainty that bedevils the practice of health professionals of all disciplines. If the care needed by each individual patient were clear, certain, and unchanging, then aligning the actions of the various caregivers in a delivery organization or system would be much less challenging. However, where the care necessary is uncertain (and therefore variant and emergent), creating unity of action is more difficult.

The uncertainty surrounding daily practice comes from three basic sources: incomplete medical knowledge, unreliable execution by inherently unstable organizational processes and systems, and individual variation among patients, each of whom has their own biology, values, and preferences.[10] Those unfamiliar with the daily workings of delivery organizations often speak, act, and make recommendations as if health care is, or could be, more production-like than practicing clinicians know to be possible. Even before the Covid-19 pandemic, the daily reality for those in practice was that in many clinical situations it was clear neither what to do nor how to do it.

In the past, delivery organization leaders and managers have used protocols and pathways as a mechanism of at least reducing, if not removing, the uncertainty in clinical practice. By prospectively writing down and promulgating "the right thing to do" (i.e., the "evidence-based best practice"), they have tried to create consistency, stability, and reproducibility in team-based patient care and operational processes.

However, this is not so easy when there is no best practice or any clear way of implementing a known best practice. In the absence of an externally defined decision rule, expert clinicians make decisions by referring to their own internal rules of thumb (heuristics), developed over years of experience by making thousands of observations of the complicated interactions between cause and effect in patient care. By their nature, these heuristics are implicit and unique to each individual clinician and, as such, cannot be used to guide group decision-making. Often expert clinicians have difficulty even articulating them and thus cannot reduce the uncertainty for their colleagues.

A clearly stated shared purpose helps direct joint action in the face of this uncertainty. It provides a guide where there is no clear decision rule by structuring the uncertainty as the question, "Of several possible courses of action, which is most in line with our purpose?" The joint purpose in not in itself clinical advice. Rather, it creates a standard and set of shared measures by which competing clinical advice can be analyzed and judged.

Noise

The external noise that often surrounds working clinicians can make focusing a team's actions even more difficult. Myriad external influences on their decision-making and action vie for clinicians' attention. These include externally set productivity targets (such as minimum waiting times), report cards and league tables, financial incentives, and a constant flow of commentary from local and national media outlets. All bring with them a risk of taking an organization's attention away from its goals.

The purpose of purpose, therefore, is to create an agreed-upon reason for working together that aligns professionals, provides a decision rule when there is no other, and focuses attention in the face of external noise and distractions (Table 2.1).

Most important, the healthcare organization's or unit's purpose must provide guidance and a standard against which individual and organizational actions can be tested. Individuals and teams need to be able to ask of themselves, "Does this decision or action advance our purpose?" To be most useful, the

Table 2.1. The purpose of purpose

Issue	Goal	Example
Disagreement	**Promote alignment and unify action**	• Align individuals and the organization with the patients they serve. • Align individuals with the organization (i.e., promote staff engagement). • Align the organization with individuals (i.e., attract and retain desired staff). • Align within a team (i.e., create shared goals and unity of action). • Align multiple teams (i.e., promote coordination and integration). • Align clinicians and management.
Uncertainty	**Provide a decision rule**	• Guide action in the absence of a clear clinical rule or organizational policy. • Aid in making trade-offs in allocation of scarce resources (prioritization of action).
Noise	**Create focus**	• Retain focus in the face of noise. • Inform the choice of metrics, the design of the measurement strategy, and the configuration of internal operational controls.

agreed purpose must be connected to the advancement of patient well-being: does this decision or action advance patient well-being, of individuals or of a population? For leaders embarking on system reform, clarity of purpose serves as a guide for future redesign.

Recent years have seen the emergence of two primary candidates for the common purpose for delivery organizations that would address the three needs in Table 2.1: the triple aim and value-based health care.

TRIPLE AIM

In 2008 Don Berwick and colleagues tried to address the problem of conflicting perspectives by identifying a common purpose
that could guide transformation efforts. They argued that in
order for the United States to achieve high-value health care, improvement efforts needed to pursue three goals simultaneously:
"improving the individual experience of care; improving the
health of populations; and reducing the per capita costs of care
for populations."[11] Since then, this "triple aim" has influenced
health policies worldwide. Although these three aims are still
potentially in conflict—for example, using a new, more effective
but more expensive treatment can improve outcomes but raise
cost—the triple aim has clarified what national-level care system
redesign is trying to achieve. More recently, in recognition of the
risks of burnout, a fourth aim has been added: "improving the
work life of health care providers, including clinicians and [non-
clinical] staff."[12]

However, for individual organizations, the potential conflict
is more challenging. As Berwick and colleagues noted, "from
the viewpoint of individual actors responding to current market forces, pursuing the three aims at once is not in their
immediate self-interest." Most commonly, organizations (and
individual clinicians, especially when paid fee-for-service) find
that when they are successful at improving quality of care—fewer
errors, greater safety, fewer complications, lower readmission
rates, better secondary prevention, and so on—they are rewarded
for their efforts with more work and lower overall reimbursement. Improved quality can have both positive and negative
economic effects for delivery organizations. It can reduce volume
and income by reducing the additional demand created through
failing to get it right the first time. It can also, by improving an
institution's reputation, increase referral rate while creating

the spare capacity in which those additional patients can be treated. Despite these limitations, the triple aim has remained a helpful construct for delivery organizations because it has articulated a clear set of goals.

However, as a central rallying point for independent professionals, the triple aim faces a more fundamental challenge because clinicians often find the goal of cost constraint problematic. Healthcare professionals were trained to put the needs of the patient first, without reference to cost. In previous generations, the situation was simpler: governments worried about cost and accordingly chose which societal resources to make available, and clinicians worried about patients and mobilized those available resources in whatever way they thought would benefit the patient most. The triple aim has had the unintended effect of making clinicians responsible for cost, burdening them with a concern that many feel conflicts with their commitment to patient well-being. Moreover, as Davies' surveys of clinician-manager relationships attest, the issue of cost constraint has divided clinicians from managers for many years.

On a more practical level, the "health of populations" draws heavily on the discipline of public health, whereas the "individual experience of care" depends more on the work of acute care clinicians, and these two groups tend not to interact with each other in most delivery organizations. Each component of the triple aim is more likely to be achieved by a different part of an organization or health system than together by an individual team. This reduces its utility as a mechanism of unifying action and promoting integration and collectivism within an individual delivery organization or one of its teams or as a mechanism of guiding transformation efforts.

Hence healthcare delivery organization leaders needed something else to unify actions within teams and to focus the work of individuals. To address these issues, Porter and colleagues proposed a possible way of reconciling the perceived conflict between cost and quality and uniting the often-conflicting interests of healthcare's myriad stakeholders by making the goal of care "value."[13] The benefit of this framing would be that it would subtly shift the discussion from cost as a stand-alone consideration to the benefit realized for the cost incurred. It put quality back in the center.

DEFINING VALUE IN HEALTH CARE

Over the last decade "value-based health care" has become the common organizing construct in many national health systems, delivery networks, and organizations. These have defined value in several ways, although all with the same basic intent. The simplest definition is expressed in the equation

$$value = \frac{quality}{cost}$$

or $V = Q/C$.

More complex definitions, such as Virginia Mason Medical Center's, incorporate safety, appropriateness, and waste into the definition of quality:

$$quality = appropriateness \times \frac{(outcomes + service)}{waste}$$

The goal implied by the $V = Q/C$ equation is either to achieve the maximum amount of quality for a given amount of cost, or the minimum amount of cost for a given amount of quality. Proponents of value as the goal have argued that this concept resolves the conflict between cost and quality and therefore facilitates clinician engagement in a productive conversation about resource use. As Lee puts it, "The value framework thus offers a unifying orientation for provider organizations that might otherwise be paralyzed by constituents' fighting for bigger pieces of a shrinking pie."[14] After all, "health outcomes per dollar spent"[15] has an intuitive appeal. As Lee further argues, "No one can oppose this goal and expect long-term success."

Unfortunately, as with other externally derived delivery organization goals, "value" has not been without its problems. One of these is that some clinicians view the pursuit of "value" as nothing more than cost reduction in disguise. After all, health outcome per dollar spent, effectively output per unit of input, does have the ring of impersonal mass production and economic efficiency about it.[16]

Another challenge relates to the question of how quality is defined. None of healthcare's many stakeholders disagrees that value should first and foremost be created for the patient. But how do patients experience that value? It was originally proposed that value center on a hierarchy of patient outcomes, ranging from survival and recovery to avoidance of treatment-related illness.[17] Since then the International Consortium for Health Outcomes Measurement (ICHOM) has created disease-specific standard outcome measure sets focusing on categories of measures such as "survival and disease control," "burden of disease," "functioning," and "complications of treatment."[18]

However, outcome hierarchies by their very nature make implicit trade-offs by prioritizing some outcomes over others. Not all patients rate survival over avoiding severe disability or value outcome over process. In the past, measure sets tended to downplay process of care and patient experience of care, although this is changing. ICHOM's pregnancy and childbirth measure set includes measures of "birth experience" as one of its measures of patient satisfaction with care, for instance.

Defining value as outcome per unit cost has been a significant step forward in that it has helped to resolve the perceived conflict between cost and quality, unify healthcare's disparate participants, and placed the patient at the center of the debate.

However, the controversy has not been completely settled. By focusing solely on quality as outcome, delivery organizations risk hardwiring some assumptions about patient preferences and priorities into the way they design protocols and measures or make investments in future services.

As used in routine practice, the term "value" has unfortunately more often been interpreted to mean cost reduction and productivity enhancement than quality improvement. This is in part because "value-based health care" tends to be thought of at the institutional, not patient, level. Value-based contracts between hospitals and physician groups and their insurers tend to measure cost and quality in the aggregate. The result is that increases in value are most easily achieved by increasing the number of interactions provided and patients seen per doctor, ensuring routine processes are followed (such as the number of eligible patients offered smoking cessation counseling), or by decreasing utilization of expensive tests and therapies per patient, not necessarily by delivering more of what patients want. Delivering value in economic terms has not turned out to be the same as delivering what patients value.

Value-based contracts also require increased documentation of costs and quality. As a result, doctors have suffered doubly through increases in both clinical workload and administrative burden. In the United States physicians bear the primary responsibility for recording and certifying clinical data and interactions. One study found that doctors spend two additional hours on administrative and computer work for every one hour spent in face-to-face contact with patients.[19] Should doctors succeed in reducing this burden, either through developing creative labor-saving apps or employing scribes to free them up from the computer work, they are rewarded not with more time per patient, but more patients per unit time as their employers or groups strive to increase productivity.[20]

Thus, ironically, value-based health care may be contributing to the sense of depersonalization and personal ineffectiveness that characterizes burnout.* This raises the possibility that burnout risk might be reduced by returning to a focus on what the individual patient values and to what gives clinicians pleasure in, and a sense of control over, their work. But if clinicians' shared purpose is to deliver value not to the institution but to the patient, and unit-level operating systems are to be redesigned to support that goal, it will be important to be clear about what patients really do value.

WHAT DO PATIENTS VALUE?

It is not surprising that price does not figure in patients' assessments of the value delivery organizations provide. Patients have little interest in cost beyond their own out-of-pocket expenses, and budget deficits and the percentage of gross domestic product (GDP) spent by their nation's healthcare system hold no sway. However, surveys of patient preferences and studies of their actual choices reveal a greater complexity than is typically captured by outcome hierarchies[21] or is often understood by doctors.

Clinicians tend to presume that, because of their unique relationship with the patient, they know what patients value. But they can be wrong. For instance, one group of pediatricians was surprised to find that parents of children who were evaluated for deep brain stimulation but not offered the procedure still derived value from the interaction. In this national referral service for children with abnormal muscle movements (dystonia)— arising either from a congenital condition or a brain injury—the majority (75 percent) of children referred to be evaluated for an

---

* Interestingly, burnout rates are lower in those specialties less tied to a computer, such as surgeons.

implantable device were deemed ineligible for the procedure. The doctors' presumption was that it was the treatment—the implanted stimulator—that added value. However, the families rejected for the procedure in fact highly valued the assessment process. For them, having all the options for their child explored by a group of experts and the opportunity to process the results with the specialist brought a sense of having done the best they could for their child: for them the detailed assessment was as much the treatment as the procedure. As a result, the service chose not to target its referral criteria (in effect, "head hunting" eligible children) but instead maintain very open referral criteria.[22] In other words, patients place great weight on the process of their care and can value process over outcome or some outcomes over others, both of which can reduce the relative importance of those outcomes included in standard hierarchies.

Several common themes emerge from patients' responses to questions about what they want their healthcare services to deliver. Patient surveys and focus groups have found that patients place importance on factors such as the following:

- **Relationships:** Responses to many surveys confirm the extent to which patients accord great importance to the nature of their relationship with their caregivers and related delivery organizations. In practice, for many patients, "continuity" means seeing the same individual caregiver or team over long periods of time. It means knowing and being known. Patients may even preferentially select services that have been publicly rated as "lower quality" but that are local and familiar.
- **Trust:** Trust is central to patients' expectations of their therapeutic relationship. Patients need to trust that their caregivers are nonjudgmental, skilled, and appropriately well trained, and that the choices they recom-

mended have been made with that patient's best interests in mind, not the system's. In fact, confidence and trust in their caregivers is rated as more important than personal involvement in decision-making.[23] Patients also want to be trusted: something that is not always the case in paternalistic systems.

- **Control:** In spite of this, patients do want to be involved in making decisions about their own care. They want their input invited and their choices respected. Closely tied to this is the notion of respect, not only for their autonomous choices but also for their culture, individuality, and personal narratives. This value often conflicts with modern systems' needs for efficiency, which risk leading to patients being treated as the vessel in which the disease is contained.

- **Insight:** The experience of illness is one of loss of control. Illness is a time of great uncertainty and ambiguity. Patients express a need for hindsight ("Why did this happen to me?") and foresight ("What will happen to me in the future?"). Hence they accord importance to caregiver communication skills, the quality of information they receive, and comprehensible answers to their questions.

- **Compassion:** Kindness and compassion are central to patients' expectations of their health services. Empathy, respect for their privacy and dignity, and a balance of hope and realism are routinely rated as important.

- **Kindness:** Perhaps as a reaction to the economic framing of value, interest has grown in the idea of kindness in care.[24] One group of authors identifies six types of kindness in cancer care—deep listening to what really matters to patients, empathy, generous acts of discretionary extra effort, timely care that reduces the

anxiety that comes from uncertainty, gentle honesty,
and support for family caregivers—which
"complement[s] the wonders of high-tech care with the
humanity of high-touch care," thereby creating value in
addition to the technical aspects of the care.[25]

In sum, what patients value is a complex amalgam of factors
relating to the process, content, and outcome of their interactions with their caregivers and the healthcare system, something that is not easily captured by a single set of metrics.
Moreover, different patients weigh these factors differently and
make trade-offs in unexpected ways. The people who write the
guidelines or create systems of care are often younger, healthier,
and from different cultures than many of the people to whom
the guidelines apply. Contrary to the choices that the designers
and managers might make, patients may prefer death to life
with disability, a shorter period of relative wellness over a longer
period laboring under a heroic chemotherapy regimen, or a better process of care leading to a less-than-perfect outcome (which
is, after all, is what good palliative care provides).

Patients also vary in their ability to take control or develop
trust. The UK Department of Health's "Life Stage Segmentation
Model" identified five distinct population segments, each differ-
ing in their health attitudes and behaviors. Whereas "health-
conscious realists" (estimated to be 21 percent of the population,
weighted toward females and older people) felt in control of their
health and were highly motivated, the "unconfident fatalists" (estimated to be 18 percent of the population and tending to be
older people and those living in the most deprived areas) were
more accepting of their current poor health and did not think
that a healthy lifestyle was within their control.[26]

Hence, patients may define value in ways their health professionals may not, such as accepting demonstrably lower-quality

care from an organization that is familiar and close by. And the value that those who refer patients to a unit or organization are seeking may differ from what the patient wants. In many circumstances the referrer is as much a "customer" as the patient. Finally, factors such as a lack of insurance or accessible high-quality services, which are outside patients' control, may shape how they think about value. Hence, although it is attractive to make value the centerpiece of an organization's or unit's strategy and the shared purpose that unifies staff, it can be risky to treat value as a single and uniform concept and make assumptions about what patients value.

VALUE AND VALUE CREATION

Using the concept of value to focus staff and operations is further complicated by the fact that value has many different aspects. Which aspect of value patients prioritize varies among individuals in a population, within an individual at different points in time, and across the different parts of a delivery system.

The aspects of value patients prioritize early in a disease process may not be the same as those later on. For example, patients suffering a stroke are treated aggressively with thrombolysis or thrombectomy acutely to minimize the risk of neurological damage and lasting deficit. Only later do they enter rehabilitation to help address any remaining deficit. Although patients may happily cede personal control and a familiar relationship with caregivers in the first few hours of emergency care, they are not willing to do so in the weeks of the rehabilitation phase. Because the preferred aspects of value evolve with the disease and the treatment, so too must the healthcare services that deliver them. For instance, the tertiary dermatology service at Guy's and St. Thomas' NHS Foundation Trust in London asked patients in its psoriasis clinic what they valued from their care services. Patients early in the course of their treatment valued personal care from their specialist in person and at the referral hospital. Those further along in their treatment, who were now stable on a monoclonal antibody therapy and only needed periodic monitoring, saw no benefit in traveling into central London. The department responded by establishing in-person and virtual outpatient services that ran in parallel.

As this example demonstrates, care delivery systems are made up of many processes, units, and organizations. Each contributes to creating patient value in different ways and at different points in time. The "hub-and-spoke" design of modern stroke services, in which high-acuity stroke services centralize patients and deliver care for the first 24 to 72 hours, and lower-acuity facilities deliver the subsequent rehabilitation care closer to home, reflects the nature of this disease, its treatment, and the nuanced nature of patient value. The overall value the patient ultimately receives is an output of the system as a whole, but each institution or site of care addresses a different aspect of that overall value: highly technical and possibly impersonal diagnostic and therapeutic services in the former, and compassionate interactive care in the latter. In effect, each component of a larger system has a different value proposition for the patient at each stage of the patient's journey.

Where do these considerations leave us? It is clear that the terms "value" and "value creation" mask a wealth of subtleties, but what does this imply for practice? First, it may simply not be possible to identify a single definition of value for a heterogeneous group. Patients interacting with different parts of a larger health system likely have very different notions of value: varying according to health problem and stage in the disease process. Other industries do not face this problem. Elsewhere, organizations can focus on delivering one kind of value to one market segment. Their customer interactions are often short lived or oc-cur over a well-defined period of time. If they do have multiple interactions with the same customer, it is usually to repeatedly deliver the same kind of value. When you book your second trip on an airline, you are expecting the company to deliver the same value you received the last time you flew with it. In contrast, in-creasing numbers of patients living with multiple comorbid con-ditions and therapies that put conditions into remission but still require ongoing surveillance make long-term relationships and evolving definitions of value the new norm in health care. The same organization or system has to deliver different value to the same patient and different points in time. Any planning to deliver value-based health care must treat the term "value" as a plural.

Second, it is difficult to understand all the subtlety of what patients value as they interact with different parts of a larger system without asking these patients directly. To understand what patients want, many delivery organizations are tempted to look at the results of standardized, closed-response patient sat-isfaction surveys. However, such surveys often provide insuffi-cient insight into what patients really value and seek from their caregivers and delivery organization and may miss important cultural variations. Their results can be too general to guide spe-cific actions. Focus groups and individual interviews tend to give caregivers more insight into what patients value and the ways in which they make trade-offs at different points in time. When leaders form their beliefs about patient values, preferences, and abilities in the rarified atmosphere of a boardroom or solely with reference to large-scale clinical or patient satisfaction data sets, it is possible to completely misspecify the value patients are really seeking from their caregivers and healthcare system. They may set goals and design services that fail to deliver what their pa-tients actually value.

Third, as Chapter 5 discusses, one organization, service, or unit may not be able to deliver everything that patients value. As in other industries, different operating models are needed for different aspects of customer value. Online and in-person services deliver different value differently. Larger healthcare systems have to be deliberately designed so that their different units deliver different aspects of value in a coordinated way.

Taken together, these considerations imply that various organizations or units serving distinct patient subpopulations at different points in their disease processes will each have to define for themselves what value they should be designed to deliver. In effect each unit needs its own strategy that positions it in a wider system and differentiates the value it provides from the value to be provided by other units or delivery organizations. To do this they may certainly make use of well-researched and validated, publicly available metrics such as those developed by ICHOM, but this does not absolve each organization or unit from the hard work of first understanding what makes the particular populations they serve unique and what these patients value and then designing their systems to specifically deliver that value.*

This can be harder than it sounds. Clinicians often express value and purpose as some version of providing high-quality services to their local communities, but quality in itself is neither strategy nor purpose. Nor is excellence, safety, nor the practice of evidence-based medicine. Patients take these aspects of care for granted. They do not create a unique position in a marketplace but are instead simply price of entry: what any delivery

---

* "Goal-oriented" care is the application of this thinking to individual clinician-patient interactions. For each interaction the practitioner develops an understanding of the patient's goals and what dimensions of value they give priority. (Mold J, Blake G, Becker L. Goal-oriented medical care. *Fam Med.* 1991;23[1]:46–51.)

organization has to be capable of to deliver value. In this sense, quality and safety and services provided are not the purpose, but mechanisms for achieving purpose.

PUTTING IT TOGETHER: CONNECTING VALUE, PURPOSE, AND ACTION

Modern health care demands coordinated, focused action of its myriad component parts. Because what patients value varies, healthcare transformation requires redesign of each patient-facing care unit and of the way these units are integrated into a larger system of care (in other words, localized change at enterprise scale). This means developing both a local and a system understanding of value, in which each unit provides some aspect of value, and these add in a coherent way to the overall value delivered by the larger system (Figure 2.1). Each unit that delivers a portion of a patient's care must develop its own understanding of what the patient values at this point, and thus its value proposition. But this cannot be in isolation from the rest of the value chain and delivery system. Instead, each unit's value proposition should fit into the overall purpose of the wider organization. Each point in the value chain also needs an understanding of what aspects of value other units will be providing, if only to help inform the decision of what aspects of value not to provide here. This is as true within a single hospital where a patient passes across multiple departmental boundaries as it is in a larger system when patients' journeys take them from one delivery organization to another. Determining which aspect of value will be provided where and by whom is an essential antecedent to delivering integrated care.

The implication here is that the precursor to any program of transformation is a widespread organizational conversation about patient value. This is much more than simply listing the

Figure 2.1. The distribution of value

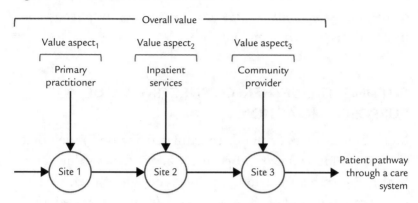

organization's values on its screensavers or on posters on the walls in the hope that these will serve as the core around which local operating systems are redesigned. It must be an explicit conversation at both the organizational and unit level focusing on the question, "What are we trying to achieve with and for the patients we serve?"

Important as it is, the identification of patient value is just the starting point for a longer and deeper analysis. An operating system's design will depend on the nature of the care it is to support and the outcomes it is intended to achieve. The ability to deliver value depends on an understanding of which activities create that value and thus achieve our purpose. In the TPS defining value is followed by identifying those specific production process steps that add value. The rationale for seeking greater specificity in value definition is to enable deeper understanding of causation in the value creation system and thus enable better operating system design and management.

In effect there is a hierarchy of design choices that must be made to create delivery units, organizations, and systems capable of achieving a value-based purpose. These choices will shape the nature of the operating system design and the approach to managing the change process required to implement it.

The first of these is to determine what value the overall system will deliver. In competitive markets organizations are constantly determining which element of customer value to deliver on and which to not. Some airlines choose to deliver on a customer value dimension of low cost, prioritizing this over other aspects of value such as physical comfort. Other airlines have made the exact opposite choice. Of course, in choosing to focus on only some aspects of value, each company has deliberately chosen not to serve some customer segments. In healthcare we are committed to providing care for all, and not denying care to one patient segment. But this does not prevent an organization or system from choosing which dimensions of patient value will be delivered at different points in the wider system. Hence a second set of choices is to determine which aspects of value each unit in the wider system will deliver and, by implication, what will not be delivered by that unit or in that location. In healthcare the design question is not "Which aspects of customer value do we deliver?" but "Which aspects do we deliver *here* and which elsewhere in our system?"

The next set of choices relates to the activities that create value. Each unit has to identify, and then undertake, the activities that deliver on the chosen value proposition. It has to answer the question "What is it that we do that creates value for our patients?" The unit's answer depends on clinical professionals' understanding of cause and effect in the creation of value and melds the science of medicine with the humanity of caregiving and the practicalities of designing and running a complex delivery organization. It defines the staff's specific clinical and managerial activities and sets the priorities for action and for investment. This choice ultimately finds expression in the organization's protocols, pathways, recruiting policies, and resource investments.

The fourth and final set of choices relates to the design of the operating system that is the context for the clinical and managerial professionals' practice. These choices define the staffing model and the organization's culture and shape the way staff behave toward the patient and one another.

In sum, the way we frame what patients value and thus the nature and purpose of our shared enterprise determines so many subsequent decisions, including the processes we use, the staff we hire, the behaviors we encourage, the technology we acquire, the way we deploy it, and what we measure and track. Decisions about each of these will influence the design and therefore performance of unit-level care systems. Operating systems should not be redesigned, and healthcare delivery organizations cannot be transformed, without clarity about the patient value each is intended to create. A value-based purpose is a decision heuristic in two senses. It shapes individual professionals' behavior and clinical choices in the absence of a clear and prespecified decision rule or protocol, and it shapes the design of the operating system in which these individuals practice their professions.

EXAMPLE OF AN ALTERNATIVE FRAMING OF PURPOSE

New Zealand's Waitemata District Health Board (WDHB) provides an example of an alternative expression of organizational purpose that serves as a reference point for the creation of unit-level value propositions. After wide consultation, WDHB's senior leadership explicitly framed its purpose in a way that it hoped would resonate with staff. It chose three interrelated concepts: to relieve suffering; to prevent, cure, and ameliorate ill health; and to promote wellness.[27] The key principle is the first of these. The organization exists to relieve suffering from ill health, either through direct actions to reduce the physical and psychological burdens of those afflicted with ill health or secondarily by removing the underlying causes of this suffering.

Expressing the organization's purpose in this way has several advantages. First, it directly connects the organization's purpose with caregivers' core value sets (and the spirit of their oaths of professional dedication). Second, many of today's most pressing healthcare issues—such as safety, variability, poor access, and inequality—can be seen through the lens of their potential to cause further suffering in those the organization is committed to helping. Providing safe, effective, efficient, and reliable healthcare services is necessary to relieve (and cause no further) suffering. Hence, as Table 2.2 shows, although it differs from the conven-

Table 2.2. Comparing two ways of framing purpose

Triple aim		Waitemata purpose	
Improving the individual experience of care	• IOM six aims of care: safe, effective, patient-centered, timely, efficient, and equitable	**Relieve suffering**	• Compassionate care • Error-free care • Timely care • Effective communication • Pain management
Improving the health of populations	• Public health aims: improving nutrition, poverty reduction, violence reduction, etc.	**Promote wellness**	• Primary and secondary prevention
Reducing the per-capita costs of care for populations	• Per capita spend • Percent GDP on health care • Growth rate	**Prevent, cure, and ameliorate ill health**	• Effective care • Appropriate care • Rapid access • Smooth transitions

tional triple aim, this expression of purpose nonetheless enables WDHB's leaders to keep the important elements of the triple aim in staff's focus. But it was framed in a way that WDHB believed would be more congruent with the professional values and goals of clinical staff and the values of the patients it served. Expressing its purpose as "to relieve suffering" allowed WDHB to pursue its performance improvement agenda in a way that resonated with its clinicians and did not alienate them the way that a purely efficiency-driven agenda might have. It also allowed each unit to develop its own value proposition that was connected to the enterprise as a whole.

Finally, WDHB has connected this purpose directly with its corporate values and with specific observable actions. So "purpose" is no longer a theoretical construct: it is something that is visible in the everyday performance improvement programs to which staff are exposed. Figure 2.2 shows how WDHB links its "promise" (to its patients) to its "purpose" (that unifies staff action and connects that action to patients) and its "priorities" (clarifying key actions will be pursued at an organizational, unit, and individual level). By connecting promise, purpose, and priorities, WDHB hopes to liberate clinical and managerial staff to innovate while ensuring that all actions are in the pursuit of patients' best interests. Gulati calls this "freedom within a framework."[28] In this way the organization's myriad internal initiatives, some linked to day-to-day performance management and others linked to longer-term innovation and performance improvement, are all elements in the execution of its overall approach and related to the organization's core values (the bottom row in Figure 2.2).[29]

Many organizations rely on a shared understanding of medical science and staff's professional codes of conduct to provide common purpose and connect organizational priorities and staff behavior. Although they specify their corporate values—you can see them written in colorful font on posters in the

Figure 2.2. Waitemata DHB purpose and actions

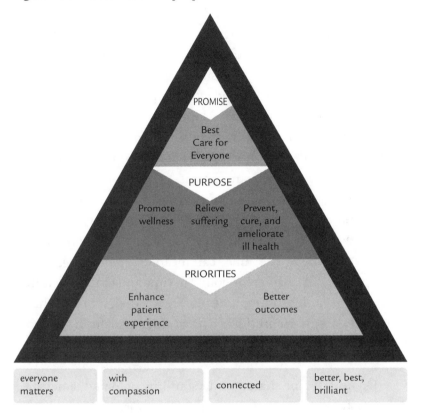

hallways—the purpose, actions, and behaviors required to make such values real are often left unspoken and implied. WDHB, in contrast, has taken an approach that is less common—it instead specified these in great detail and ensured that staff were exposed to them regularly.

IDENTIFYING VALUE AND DEFINING PURPOSE: IMPLICATIONS FOR ACTION

WDHB has chosen a particular expression of its purpose to meet its needs for creating unity among its staff and focus in its actions.

However, this is not the only framing of purpose that can do this. The important principle is that each delivery organization, unit, team, and practice needs to agree on an expression of its purpose so that it can guide its staff toward unified action. Individual professionalism alone may not suffice, as it tends to motivate individual more than interdependent action. In the case of WDHB, the organization as a whole developed a shared expression of its purpose through a protracted consultation among staff. At a much smaller scale, establishing purpose may only require a brief conversation among the team. This is, of course, one of the goals that the surgical checklist, reviewed by the team at the commencement of each procedure, is intended to achieve.

Discussions of value-based health care are often confused by the facts that the word "value" can mean different things to different people and at different points in time and that these differences have meaningful implications for the design of healthcare units and systems. Hence, identifying value and defining purpose for healthcare delivery systems involves specific steps:

- Do not assume shared understanding of, or agreement on, the purpose and goals of the activities within a multidisciplinary team, unit, or organization.
- Open an explicit conversation among team members or across the organization about what "we are collectively trying to achieve in our personal practice and our system design."
- Make the debate explicit.
  - What do our patients value? How does what patients value vary over time or by location of service? How do our patients make trade-offs among competing dimensions of value? What are we trying to achieve?
  - How do we know this to be so? How will we know we are successful?

- ○ Why are we doing it this way? What cause-and-effect relationships do we think are at play?
- Consider the aspects of value delivered to the patient by other parts of the wider delivery system and how these relate to the aspects of value your unit chooses to deliver.
- Ensure all stakeholders have an opportunity to contribute to this conversation (actively seek out the quieter members of the team and ask them for their thoughts).
- Explicitly articulate the connection between your value proposition to patients and your purpose, the actions required to execute this purpose, and the behaviors needed of staff.
- Create a process and forum for regularly reviewing the previous questions (especially as redesigned operating systems are being put in place and implementation experience is accruing) and for regularly reviewing progress toward achieving this purpose.

Chapter 3 considers some of the design decisions needed to build a system for effectively delivering the intended patient value.

PART TWO

Designing Systems that Deliver Value to Patients

Principles of Operations

Having a clear understanding of the value the unit or organization intends to deliver to the patient or referrer is only the start. A value proposition is only as good as the ability to execute it. Clinicians tend to focus on their own role in creating value, but the reality in the modern era is that it takes a system, not an individual, to effectively implement a value proposition. Although individuals are essential contributors, organizational performance is now as important as individual skill and excellence in creating a health outcome.

Commercial organizations have long recognized that performance is a function of not only resources but also how those resources are deployed. The same is true in healthcare: the effectiveness with which a healthcare delivery organization is managed is an independent determinant of patients' clinical outcomes. Researchers in one study sought to define the essential characteristics of good management along three operations-focused dimensions: performance monitoring, target setting, and incentives/people management.[1] They defined 18 management practices and rated each from worst to best to create an organization's "management practice score." In a large sample of hospitals, a one-point rise in management practice score was associated with a 6.5 percent reduction in a delivery organization's 30-day risk-adjusted acute myocardial infarction (AMI) mortality rate in the United Kingdom, and a 7 percent reduction in the United States.[2]

Of course, although such associations do not prove causation, they do suggest that the way that key resources such as professional staff and technology are configured can have an impact on how effective those resources will be in achieving their desired outcome. We expect the design and management of healthcare delivery organizations to have financial implications: we now know that it also has clinical significance as well. Of note in this study was the observation that more managers had clinical training in those hospitals with higher management practice scores, lending credence to recent interest in clinician leadership. Clinicians aiming to have an impact on their patients' well-being increasingly need to concern themselves not only with the quality of their own practice but also with the functioning of the organizational context that is its setting.

The organizational entity primarily responsible for creating patient value is the local operating system. An operating system is the basic unit of an organization. It is made up of the care process, which defines the sequence of decisions and tasks needed to address a health problem, and the set of staff, physical, and information resources needed to implement those decisions and tasks into practice. The term "operating system" describes a larger organizational subunit than that described by the term "clinical micro-system," defined originally by researchers at the Dartmouth Institute as the "small group of people who work together on a regular basis to provide care to discrete subpopulations of patients."[3] In effect, the clinical micro-system is the team and the operating system is the broader organizational subunit in which they work.

Because most delivery organizations and systems are made up of many small-scale operating systems, any large-scale transformation of a delivery organization will require multiple operating system redesigns. Operating system change is needed to accommodate and support new technologies and ways of working. Change at this level is the ultimate mechanism by which national policy or organizational strategy is executed. Importantly, this is the level at which leaders in the middle can most effectively exert their influence: by redesigning their local operating system and participating in its day-to-day oversight and control.

Operating systems are made up of four key components: the care process itself, the workforce that undertakes the clinical and managerial work of care delivery, the supporting infrastructure (including digital, communication, and medical technology and the physical space in which care is delivered), and, finally, the mechanisms by which operational control is exercised over the system. Through redesigning these four components and then taking control over them, clinicians can lead transformative change from the middle of the delivery organization by creating operating systems that more reliably deliver value to their patients and better support their professional practices. The goal of defining patient value and staff purpose at the unit level is to enable local leaders to focus that redesign.

How, then, should healthcare delivery organizations and unit-level operating systems be designed and managed? If care is the organized delivery of science, how should we organize it? What are the options available for system design, and what principles should we apply to choose among them? Clearly, something more than simply aggregating essential staff and technology, either physically or virtually, is required.

Other industries such as airlines, food services, banks, and hotels have been guided by some basic principles of operations design and management as they have improved their quality and efficiency. Although clinicians are sometimes wary of management principles drawn from other industries, particularly manufacturing, the concerns about safety, uncertainty, risk, reliability, and the costs of failure in sectors such as nuclear power, airline travel, and high-tech manufacturing parallel those in healthcare.

Healthcare equally can be guided by insights from operations research. In fact, some are already applied to healthcare delivery: for example, queuing and flow modeling to increase efficiency and decrease costs. Several other findings from operations research have particular relevance to healthcare delivery organizations. The first of these relates to the overall architecture of a system for production.

SYSTEMS OF PRODUCTION

The history of manufacturing is one of evolving approaches to production.[4] Before the industrial era artisans created most products (e.g., bowls, bows, adzes) one at a time. The craftspeople undertook all the required tasks: they created the design, sourced the right materials, made the product, and then found a way to sell it (Table 3.1). The quality of the product was solely a function of the quality of the materials available and the craftsperson's skill in these various tasks.

Such a system had much to recommend it: products could be uniquely configured to account for variations in the available raw materials and the needs and desires of each customer. Nonetheless, it was also a slow and expensive way of making a product. Products tended to unintentionally vary in more or less subtle ways, and the whole model depended entirely on a supply of skilled craftspeople.

A foundation of the industrial revolution was the invention of other systems of manufacture. Higher product volumes could be made if the various manufacturing tasks were divided among more than one maker in a system called a "job shop." In this model, the partially completed product (termed "work-in-progress," or WIP) moved from one worker to the next, and each worker performed some important part of the overall production process in sequence. Because workers were somewhat specialized in their

Table 3.1. Summary of production systems for low-volume products

Craft shop	Job shop	Batch model
Basic structure		
A single operator makes the entire product, undertaking all of the necessary tasks	Products made one-at-a-time, each fabrication stage may be undertaken by a different worker	Products made in groups
Example		
Artist, potter, gun maker	Custom printing wedding invitations	Heavy equipment manufacture
Healthcare example		
Dentistry (dentist takes x-rays, gives anesthetic, and treats)	Most acute medicine	Some psychiatry (e.g., group visits), antenatal groups
Flow		
No flow: product stays with the worker, who may move from machine to machine	Wandering flow: product moves from one workstation to the next, different products may flow in differing sequences	Wandering flow: products move from one workstation to the next, waiting at each stage for the previous to be completed
Resources		
Highly skilled individual	General purpose machinery, widely skilled workers	Machinery and workers more specialized
Advantages		
Products unique or highly customized to customer's exact needs	Unique products	Lower costs because it can accommodate higher product volume while retaining some flexibility in product type and schedule
Flexible to changes in customer's requirements	Can respond to emergency demand	
Disadvantages		
High costs of production	High costs of production	Scheduling is hard and it may not be known where any one product is at any one time
Quality dependent on operator	Lots of machine down time; machines need recalibrating for each new product type	

own tasks and repeated them frequently, the quality and consistency of the products could be increased. While increasing efficiency relative to a single craftsman, the job shop production system nonetheless preserved the ability to make many different kinds of product using the same workers and machinery and to make mid-production changes to the design or fabrication of an individual product to respond to changing customer demand.

Batch processing is a variant of the job shop model, in which multiple products are made at once. Products follow a less jumbled pathway through the production facility than one-off products: their route through is more planned. Making many products at the same time increases production volumes and reduces the cost per product while preserving the job shop's flexibility.

Healthcare organizations continue to employ exactly the same nineteenth-century production models to structure the work of care delivery. Most modern health care is still produced using the first two systems. Dentistry is often organized like a craft shop, especially where the dentist takes the x-rays, interprets them, mixes the amalgam, delivers the anesthesia, and performs the therapeutic procedure. For much of the nineteenth and twentieth centuries the solo primary care practitioner also used the craftsman model. He or she typically undertook all the steps of an episode of care: evaluation, diagnosis, treatment planning, and treatment delivery. The primary practitioner also performed much of whatever diagnostic laboratory or radiological testing was necessary: every practice had its microscope.

Inpatient and specialist care is usually organized like a job shop. Patients move from one "workstation" to the next—for example, emergency department, radiology, operating room, intensive care, and ward—in a sequence determined by their clinical need. Each workstation specializes in a different component of the overall care process, and different patients may flow in a different sequence through some or all of the workstations depending on their clinical condition.

Modern primary care has also become more like a job shop, in which the "workstations" are the many different community-based organizations and outpatient services that make up the primary care system, such as home nursing, community social services, outpatient laboratories, and independent specialists and primary care practitioners. The complexity of such care was recently detailed by one primary practitioner who described an episode of care of a single complex elderly patient that required 40 communications among 12 clinicians, and 11 office visits (none of them with his primary care provider) and 5 procedures, all over an 80-day period.[5] The closest healthcare comes to "batch processing" is probably group counseling, when care is provided to multiple patients at once.

Many despair at the extent that modern healthcare remains a "cottage industry" (a term used to describe industries based on the craft and job shop production systems). One group of authors recently wrote that "our current health care system is essentially a cottage industry of nonintegrated, dedicated artisans who eschew standardization. Services are often highly variable, performance is largely unmeasured, care is customized to individual patients, and standardized processes are regarded skeptically. Autonomy is hard-wired into the system, because most physicians practice in small groups with limited oversight or coordination."[6]

However, historically the craft and job shop models have in fact served medicine well. Even in modern times there are situations not only when patient requirements vary but also what ails the patient and what needs to be done about it are not immediately obvious. In such circumstances the flexibility afforded by the job shop model is a great advantage, allowing clinicians to create a customized care plan for each patient and make use of a wide range of diagnostic and therapeutic resources. The job shop maximizes the use of the expert's time, an increasingly scarce resource, while allowing staff to be interrupted to deal with urgent situations.

Unfortunately, the job shop model's flexibility and ease of customization come at a price. Less complex patients tend to wait at each workstation, elongating their passage through the whole system, and care tends to vary inappropriately from patient one to the next. The model does not necessarily lend itself to the levels of standardization associated with improved quality and enhanced patient safety in the modern era. Whereas in a manufacturing setting someone takes responsibility for moving the partially completed work product from one workstation to the next, in healthcare it is typically up to each patient to navigate his or her path through the system. Finally, it is an inherently expensive way to care for large numbers of similar patients and, because flow in a job shop is jumbled by its nature, it is hard to plan service volumes and realize volume-based efficiencies.

HIGH-VOLUME PRODUCTION SYSTEMS

Growing markets in the nineteenth century necessitated production in greater volume, and new science and technology allowed modern production processes that supported mass production (Table 3.2). Of course, the greatest revolution in production came with the development of the assembly line. Products flow singly, but continuously, along a line and each worker undertakes a highly standardized set of tasks over and over again as each new partially assembled product flows by. The assembly line model depends on the product's component parts being made with such precision that any one is interchangeable with another. Regardless of which part the worker takes from the parts supply, it will fit into the product being assembled, and the product and production process used to make it are so highly standardized that a process step can be undertaken over and over again without requiring variation.

Such high-volume models are less prominent in healthcare, although elective surgery has some of the characteristics of an assembly line. However, there are few examples of the extreme standardization and interchangeability seen in production industries. One rare healthcare example is an assembly line for cataract surgery created by Russia's eminent eye surgeon, Svyatoslav Fyodorov at the Research Institute of Eye Microsurgery. In this model the patients and their beds moved on a production line and the surgeons stayed still.[7]

The key strength of these systems is that products can be manufactured in very high volumes and thus the price per product can be dramatically reduced. In the past the interchangeability of parts also made repair cheap. A broken product could be repaired by simply swapping out the defective part (although this seems to be progressively more difficult in the modern world because it can be cheaper to discard than repair a broken product). Most important, product quality is high because the volume justifies investments in specialized technology and staff and because "practice makes perfect." The same is true in healthcare, where the relationship between volume and outcome is well recognized.

Table 3.2. Summary of flow production systems for high-volume products

	Assembly line
Basic structure	Products made on a production line by assembling interchangeable parts in a standard sequence
Example	Car assembly
Healthcare example	Some elective surgery
Flow	Connected linear sequence
Resources	Highly specialized machinery and workers
Advantages	Very low unit cost because of high volumes
Disadvantages	Large initial capital outlay

However, assembly line systems are highly inflexible. They are built for a limited range of products. A television cannot be manufactured on an automotive assembly line. In the extreme case of high-volume production, such as an oil refinery, the production line often cannot even be shut down without causing major disruption.

PRODUCT PROCESS MATCHING

Why study this history? The answer lies in a key lesson from production system design: different products lend themselves to being produced using different systems. Products evolve over a life cycle; from a single research prototype to a small test batch to a larger production run of the final design and then, finally, back to a smaller volume of replacement parts for a product that has been supplanted by a newer model. Each stage suits a different manufacturing model, from job shop to assembly line, in part based on volume required and the amount of product-to-product variation needed by the customer or forced by the nature of the materials and technology used to make it.

Hayes and Wheelwright proposed a "product-process matrix," shown in Figure 3.1,[8] to represent the ideal match between the product type, or life cycle stage, and the production system used for manufacture.[9] As the matrix implies, employing the "wrong" production model—one misspecified for the nature of the product—can result in inefficiency and poor quality. For example, car manufacturers build their Formula 1 racing cars in a highly customized job shop, not on their commercial car assembly lines. As a company develops a new product for manufacturing in higher volume, it usually has to make investments in specialized facilities, staff, and machinery and, of course, make a commitment to a limited product range. This makes updating its product range expensive.

Figure 3.1. Product-process matrix

	One of a kind	Multiple products, low volume	Fewer products, higher volume	Commodities
Job shop	Commercial printer			No companies
Batch		Heavy equipment		
Assembly line			Automobile assembly	
Continuous flow	No companies			Sugar refinery

Apart from the product volume required, a number of factors determine the ability to manufacture a product using a particular production system, including the nature of the raw materials available, the skill of the available workforce, and our technical ability to standardize and refine products and minimize variation among multiple copies of the same part. Underpinning all of these is the level of scientific understanding of the determinants of high quality and the ability to exercise control over these factors.

Not all production processes are equally well understood. For centuries, we have made products (and, frankly, treated patients) without fully understanding all the nuances of the underlying biology or chemistry. But the more we understand, the more control we can exercise over the production process. Bohn proposed a classification of process knowledge for production processes, arguing that technical knowledge could be measured, at least qualitatively (Table 3.3).[10]

This insight echoes an observation made by Lord Kelvin, the famous Scottish physicist, more than a century before:

> I often say that when you can measure what you are speaking about, and express it in numbers, you know something about it; but when you cannot measure it, when you cannot express it in numbers, your knowledge is of a meagre and unsatisfactory kind; it may be the beginning of knowledge, but you have scarcely, in your thoughts, advanced to the stage of science, whatever the matter may be.
>
> Lecture on "Electrical Units of Measurement" (May 3, 1883)

With increasing stages of knowledge (see Table 3.3) the manufacturing process can be more highly specified and more tightly controlled. You have to understand your process to control it. Moreover, higher stage knowledge allows control of the outcome through control of the antecedent process because we can exactly define which process steps will reliably create the intended outcome.

A similar lesson—product-process matching—applies to healthcare delivery. Different conditions and procedures lend themselves to different production models. In the case of the psoriasis clinic at Guy's and St. Thomas', discussed in Chapter 2, clinicians concluded that the care of stable patients in remission lent itself to standardized care delivered in a more assembly line fashion, and new unstable patients were more suited to a job shop model.

Although most processes in healthcare could certainly benefit from standardization—using protocols, pathways, or decision criteria sets—standardization's benefits differ depending on whether the stage of knowledge is high or low. When the stage of knowledge about the disease and its treatment is high, imple-

Table 3.3. Stages of process knowledge

Stage	Name	Description
1	**Ignorance**	Phenomenon not recognized or the variable's effects seem random
2	**Awareness**	Variable known to be influential but can be neither measured nor controlled
3	**Measure**	Variable can be measured but not controlled
4	**Control of the mean**	Control of the variable possible but not precise, control of variance around the mean not possible
5	**Process capability**	Variable can be controlled across its whole range
6	**Process characterization**	Know how small changes in the variable will affect the result
7	**Know why**	Fully characterized scientific model of causes and effects, including secondary variables
8	**Complete knowledge**	Knowledge of all interactions such that problems can be prevented by feed forward control

menting the standard process is more likely to generate the desired outcome. When the stage of knowledge is low, although it is still possible to standardize the care process, implementing the process steps may not so precisely determine the patient's outcome. But this does not make standardization useless in a low-knowledge-stage disease or process. The purpose of standardizing a low-knowledge-stage care process is not so much to control the outcome but to create stability and reduce variation to promote learning.

Three other observations about the stage of knowledge in healthcare are important. First, for many diseases, our current understanding does not put us at the top end of the scale of knowledge in Table 3.3. In few diseases are all the secondary variables and their interactions fully characterized and controllable. In the extreme case of a new disease, for example AIDS and Covid-19, many of the most important variables may not be appreciated early on. When Covid-19 emerged it was initially conceived of as a predominantly respiratory illness and only later was its multisystem nature (the neurological, hematological, and gastroenterological manifestations) recognized. Second, the current stage of knowledge varies from one disease to the next, so different diseases need different approaches within the same delivery organization. Finally, the stage of knowledge for a given disease changes over time. Diseases that were once poorly understood are now well characterized, and thus the ideal organizational approach to the management of a given disease will change over time.[11] Many acute diseases have become chronic conditions as medical knowledge has improved.

OPERATIONAL FOCUS

With different diseases at different stages of knowledge, how many different production models should a delivery organization maintain? Again, we can look to manufacturing for an analogy. Reflecting on the relative decline in the labor productivity of American manufacturing facing increasingly highly performing foreign competitors, Wick Skinner observed that "a factory that focuses on a narrow product mix for a particular market niche will outperform the conventional plant, which attempts a broader mission."[12] Producing many different products in the same production setting can reduce quality and efficiency. Less is more.

The performance advantage of focused manufacturing is rooted in the ability to invest in specialized machinery and staff and configure these resources to ensure that the "entire apparatus is focused to accomplish the particular manufacturing task demanded by the company's overall strategy."[13] These plants can build a singular system for one task. Focused operations enable staff to develop deep expertise with a limited range of tasks ("practice makes perfect"). Skinner noted that "focused manufacturing is based on the concept that simplicity, repetition, experience, and homogeneity of tasks breed competence." Finally, because focused plants tend to produce a larger volume of fewer products, per-product costs are often lower than they would be if the same product were produced in a diversified plant.

The notion of the "focused factory" has been a central construct in much recent thinking about the optimal design of healthcare organizations. Focus has been recommended at both the organizational level[14] and the unit level.[15] The model is now common: examples include elective surgical centers, day surgical units, geriatric emergency rooms, and breast or headache centers (the latter are sometimes called disease- or condition-specific "integrated practice units"). The prototypical focused factory, beloved of management academics, is Canada's Shouldice Hospital, an 89-bed hospital that exclusively treats inguinal hernias.

In all these examples the intent is to reduce the heterogeneity of patients treated and therapies delivered to reduce per-patient cost, increase safety and reliability, and improve outcomes. Focused factories by their nature tend to see higher volumes of a particular patient type or deliver higher volumes of a specific therapy, thereby leveraging the volume-outcome relationship.

MODULARITY

One way to create focus is to break a product up into its parts and distribute manufacturing across a number of specialist facilities so that each is focused on producing a limited range of parts. A modular product or process is one that can be made by assembling component parts that were fabricated separately. A computer's components (e.g., processor, memory, software) are produced separately, often by a separate manufacturer, and then reassembled in the final stages of production. The advantage of modularity is that it enables each component supplier to a computer assembler, such as Dell, to run a focused plant and leverage all the associated benefits. But, to achieve this benefit it must be possible to disaggregate a product into component parts, to define in advance how each component will fit together and interact with the others, to create parts that are truly interchangeable, and to segment the production line.

The opposite of a modular product is one that is integral, in which components are not interchangeable. Each is designed and built specifically to work only with the other components in the product and may not function as well, or even at all, when coupled with components for which it was not designed. Apple uses this approach. Its computers are optimized for Apple software. Each element of Apple's "ecosystem" is designed specifically to work with the others: laptops, phones, tablets, and peripherals.

Modular products are not "better" than integral, or vice versa. Each has advantages and disadvantages. When the work of producing a modular product is spread across multiple specialized companies, each can exploit the advantages of focus. Functionality (and uniqueness) is often increased when products are integral because all components are uniquely created and optimized to only work with each other.

These design considerations also apply to healthcare processes. When diagnosis can be completely separated from the treatment, the care process can be treated as modular. For example, cancer diagnosis and treatment planning can occur at a separate time and place from chemotherapy infusion. Similarly, the workup for elective surgery need not occur in the same place, or with the same team, as the surgery. In these situations, diagnosis and treatment can be specialized activities in separate, focused sub-units of a larger delivery organization, potentially yielding the expected improvements in quality and efficiency of a modular production process. Regional "hub-and-spoke" delivery models (e.g., stroke networks) exploit this fact.

In contrast, other care processes are fundamentally integral. Where treatment has the potential to yield key diagnostic infor-mation that could change the treatment process midstream—as in an exploratory laparotomy or mid-procedure frozen section—these two phases of care may not so easily be separated in time, place, or team. For such care processes an integrated care deliv-ery unit is more appropriate.

IMPLICATIONS FOR THE DESIGN OF HEALTHCARE DELIVERY SYSTEMS

What do all these product design and manufacturing insights mean for healthcare delivery? For generations the mainstays of healthcare delivery have been, along with community social and nursing services, the community medical center and primary care practitioner (respectively, the district general hospital and the general practitioner in the United Kingdom). These are what their names imply: highly flexible and adaptable, generalized re-sources for caring for a very heterogeneous population of patients and health problems. However, increasing patient numbers and complexity have revealed the limitations of the craft and job shop models. High volumes of complex patients with variable needs have contributed to delays, failures, and costs.

The insights from operations theory—product-process match-ing, focus, and modularity—have two direct implications for the design of the next generation of healthcare delivery systems.

First, operating systems should match the nature of the patient care they are intended to deliver, and second, organizations will need to support multiple operating systems to meet the needs of a heterogeneous population. Leaders in the middle of delivery organizations are crucial to making both of these happen.

Current delivery organizations are already moving in this direction. Institutions that specifically focus on the needs of major subpopulations, such as women and children, have long been a feature of delivery systems. Facilities focusing on specific procedures or disease groups, such as elective surgical and cardiac centers, are also now common.

Researchers in healthcare delivery tend to parse health care even more finely than at the population level, focusing on the details of the care process. They have distinguished "care" from "cure," or interventions that are "interpretive" (evaluation and management) from those more "intrusive" (procedures).[16] They have differentiated care processes that are linear and sequential from those that are more experimental and iterative,[17] or routine operations from problem-solving and innovative operations.[18] And they have characterized different care delivery organizations, for example, "value added processing units" and "solution shops."[19]

All these distinctions make the same basic point: from an operational point of view, not all care is the same. The care within a population varies. Put simply, vaccination against the communicable diseases of childhood, isolated knee replacement in an otherwise well middle-aged patient suffering from osteoarthritis, and the community-based management of frail elderly patients with multiple comorbid conditions all require different clinical processes and operations and, potentially, organizational structures.

So how should care be divided? What kinds of care suit different production systems? When would better matching of the care to the operational model result in safer, more effective, and efficient care than our current general services platforms can deliver? What is the healthcare equivalent of product type?

THREE TYPES OF CARE

The care of different patients and for different conditions varies in a number of ways that have operational significance: the extent to which activities are repeated; potential for care to be planned in advance or after an initial diagnostic and triage phase; the variability of necessary decisions and tasks and their propensity for standardization; and the number of diagnostic and therapeutic iterations needed to reach an outcome. Variance on any of these dimensions will influence the design of the preferred production system. In part, this reflects the extent of underlying clinical uncertainty about the causes of patients' conditions and therapy, and the tightness of cause-and-effect relationships (i.e., the stage of knowledge). Within the heterogeneous populations served by most health systems are at least three operationally significant subtypes of care (Table 3.4).

The first of these could be called "repetitive care." When a disease and its treatment are well understood, decision-making is often dichotomous. If the single test is positive, then the patient has the disease. Similarly, the outcomes of interventions are highly predictable; either the therapy is effective in all patients or we are able to identify a subpopulation in which the treatment will have its desired effect ex ante (sometimes called "precision medicine"). This level of diagnostic and therapeutic certainty allows patient pathways and care processes to be quite linear— highly standardized and prespecified—and organizational subsystems to be specifically configured to support this care process (i.e., focused). Instructions to caregivers can be specified in great detail and prescribed when the connection between process and outcome is tight. Quality (and outcome) of care can therefore be assured by ensuring and measuring adherence to the process.

Many aspects of modern medical care fall into this category. The most obvious examples are those with well-recognized patient pathways and provider protocols: chronic diseases such as diabetes and emergencies such as acute stroke or acute myocardial infarction (AMI). Testing usually allows rapid and precise treatment planning and the key determinants of a positive outcome—such as rapid transfer to catheterization—are described by a well-defined pathway. Furthermore, how to organize urgent care teams and systems to reduce the wait for definitive treatment is well known. Many interventions not specific to a particular disease, such as central line placement, can also be standardized and routinized to improve outcomes and reduce risk. Repetitive care conditions are distinguished by a known single best way of doing things, and processes and systems can be structured in advance of the patient's arrival to reliably deliver this best practice.

For the conditions in the "menu-based care" group, there is no linear and invariant pathway, and a single optimal intervention is not immediately apparent. However, the options are both well known and limited in number. Caregivers and patients must choose among several viable treatments, including no treatment at all. To this extent, problem-solving is constrained; there is a finite solution set and maybe even well-validated criteria for choosing one course of action over another. But the association between an action and an outcome is not so tight that the "right thing to do" can be specified in advance. No one treatment trumps all others. Knowledge stage is lower than in repetitive care. Without a sequence of highly specified steps the care process will involve iterations, feedback loops, and midcourse cor-

Table 3.4. Three types of care

Repetitive care	Menu-based care	Exploratory care
Cause-effect relationships		
Predictable outcomes	Probable outcomes	Unpredictable outcomes
• Well understood or tight cause-effect relationships	• Outcomes predictable within a probability range	• Poorly understood or loose cause-effect relationships
Stage of knowledge		
High	Medium	Low
Decisions and tasks of care		
Dichotomous decisions (if-then statements)	Defined choice set (validated decision criteria)	Untested heuristics (personal experience)
Standardized, repetitive tasks	Uniform tasks	Customized tasks
Example		
Diabetes care path	Breast cancer	Orphan diseases
Knee replacement	Long-term conditions	Multiple interacting chronic conditions
Central line insertion		Novel diseases (e.g., Covid-19)

rections. Nonetheless, patient pathways or clinical approaches can be broadly defined, and well-known unexpected events can be planned for.

In menu-based care choice among the available options is typically governed more by a patient's individual values and preferences than by a clinical decision rule. When no option clearly dominates and tests or treatments may involve a trade-off on such dimensions as experience of care, short- and long-term outcome, or side effects, patients must be supported to choose for themselves. Quality of care is judged by how well the care delivered matches the patient's preferences (what Mulley has called "decision quality"[20]). Breast cancer is a good example of a condition in this category. In repetitive care, process variation is unwarranted and often represents a failure of system design or control. In menu-based care, by contrast, much variation is warranted because it represents legitimate differences in patients' preferences.[21]

The final type of care is "exploratory care." The diagnosis or the treatment choice is opaque, and there is no well-defined solution set from which to draw. Clinicians must search for an explanation for the health problem or craft a solution to it one patient at a time. In exploratory care, the process is truly customized, although, as in menu-based care, it may draw upon standardized components. Each intervention—either diagnostic test or therapy—is effectively an experiment. Unexpected events truly cannot be planned for.

Patient care for some rare diseases or orphan conditions without an effective therapy falls into this category (and, in its early days, so did Covid-19). A more common occurrence is patients with multiple interacting diseases or drug regimens. Although each may be well characterized, the combination of many is ill understood, and therapy-outcome relationships are loose and unpredictable. Clinicians increasingly find themselves facing the uncertainty of patients with multiple diseases and drugs. Care cannot be preplanned and pathways can only be specified in the loosest of terms, if at all. Outcome is not guaranteed by adherence to a particular set of steps. On the contrary, different care strategies may lead to the same outcome. For any one patient, care involves many midcourse reevaluations and corrections and potentially complex trade-offs between risks and benefits. Hence the quality of care is better measured by looking at outcomes than compliance with predetermined process steps.

The complexity introduced by three such different types of care is compounded because diseases or patient health problems may shift from one type to another over time as medical science advances (i.e., the stage of knowledge increases). A disease once so ill understood it required exploratory care can become so well characterized that its management can be described by a linear sequence of steps listed in a protocol.

MATCHING MANAGEMENT APPROACH TO TYPE OF CARE

The importance of differentiating care in this way lies in the impact these distinctions have on a leader's choices of optimal operating system and approach to its day-to-day management. The three types of care are healthcare's equivalent of product types. They are operationally very distinct: what defines high-quality care, which processes achieve it, how those processes are controlled, what it means to be productive, and what is the most appropriate production system are all very different (Table 3.5). Goals differ, and so too do the management tools available. Each type of care demands a different approach to the structure of local operating system, how performance is managed and measured, how risk is addressed, and how success is judged.

In repetitive care, where process predicts outcome, ensuring the process is followed correctly can achieve the desired care outcome. Process is a proxy for outcome. The hallmarks of a well-managed assembly line are high degrees of process standardization, measurement and management of compliance to specification, and minimal unwarranted variation. To fail is to not meet specification. In healthcare the primary management tools are protocols and pathways embedded in the electronic health record system—which intentionally constrain staff discretion in decision-making and task execution—and the key metrics are of resource use and process compliance. Both tasks (e.g., the process by which a chemotherapeutic agent is delivered) and decisions (whether to treat this cancer with that

Table 3.5. Management approach to the three types of care

Repetitive care	Menu-based care	Exploratory care
Clinical care		
Execution of prespecified tests and treatments	Structured search through a well-characterized set of options, choice based on patient's values and preferences	Experimental, emergent, and customized search process
Focus of quality		
How closely the care delivered meets specifications	How closely the care delivered meets the patient's preferences	How effectively the care creates the desired outcome
Key measure		
Process	Satisfaction	Outcome
Managerial goal		
Minimize unwarranted variation	Promote warranted variation	Achieve best possible outcome
System of production		
Assembly line	Job shop	Craft and job shop

chemotherapeutic agent) tend to be standardized in repetitive care. The local culture supports following standard procedures. Lack of variability is a sign of higher-quality care. Unexpected events are typically well known and easily recognized in repetitive care, so much so that they are not really "unexpected." Institutions manage risk by developing contingency plans and subroutines to deal with unexpected problems or complications. These are either integrated into standard pathways or can be easily deployed at a moment's notice.

Process specification and compliance management are necessary but not sufficient in menu-based care. Variation related to individual patient preferences is not just warranted, it is desired. For example, in breast cancer treatment, chemotherapy regimens and the processes by which chemotherapy is delivered should be standardized and tightly controlled. But patient preferences usually determine the overall choice of therapeutic approach, such as mastectomy versus lumpectomy. This aspect of care is necessarily variable. The quality of an individual woman's care is ultimately judged by whether it met her needs and was consistent with her values and preferences. In this context, to fail is to misdiagnose what the patient wants and to provide care incompatible with her preferences.[22]

Hence, although protocols and pathways are still essential process management tools, they must be augmented with shared decision-making tools at key junctures in the patient's journey through the care system. In menu-based care unexpected events can be more complex and less easily predicted, but they are still recognizable, and addressing them will be unlikely to call upon resources or expertise that the institution does not possess. Institutions prepare by ensuring that such resources are available and the routines are practiced, for example, by developing "rapid response teams."

In exploratory care processes and decision rules cannot be prespecified. The stage of knowledge is sufficiently low that we may not even know what we do not know.* Unexpected clinical and operational events are truly unexpected, representing new uncertainty and complexity for which it is difficult to plan. For example, Covid-19, itself unexpected, revealed previously underappreciated supply chain vulnerabilities. It makes little sense to

---

* Donald Rumsfeld, at the time the U.S. Secretary of Defense, famously made such a distinction in 2002 when he differentiated "known knowns," "known unknowns," and "unknown unknowns."

rely on process measures to control or assess the performance of a system delivering exploratory care. Outcomes are less predictable, processes are more variable, decisions are shaped by expert clinicians' own heuristics, and the patient's care has more in common with an experiment than with the creation of a product. In these circumstances management's focus is not on specifying the process but on getting the right team together, ensuring they have the necessary resources, and creating conditions that support teamwork, collaborative problem-solving, and organizational learning. Expert clinical staff need to have maximum flexibility, and the most important performance measure is outcome. Tasks may still be standardized in exploratory care but decisions may not.

It is the local leader's job to ensure a fit between the type of care and the managerial approach: mismatch can reduce the care system's performance. Standardization is not uniformly distributed in a delivery system: some types of care or points in a patient's journey lend themselves to more standardization and some to less. Similarly, different types of metric are suited to different types of care. This means leaders must consider when and how to standardize, what to measure, which targets to set, how to frame success, and how to interpret variation. All are contingent on correctly identifying the type of care being delivered. Imposing inflexible operational measures and targets unsuited to the type of care can alienate clinicians. For instance, a four-hour emergency room target may make more sense for patients needing repetitive care, but less for those requiring exploratory care. Where success in repetitive care is the rapid and reliable execution of process steps, in exploratory care it is the achievement of an optimal outcome with the fewest possible iterations. In neither case is simply measuring the number of visits or therapies per unit time likely to give an accurate picture of system performance.

MATCHING PRODUCTION SYSTEM TO TYPE OF CARE

Not only does the managerial approach to production system control vary by type of care but so too does the choice of production system. Exploratory care, exactly because its details cannot be specified ex ante, is better suited to a craft or job shop model, which provides staff with access to all the resources they might need to plot a course of care for each individual patient. Each patient's pathway through the care system will be unique. In contrast, repetitive care is more amenable to the high degrees of pathway specification and process control usually associated with an assembly-line approach.

In effect, healthcare has its own product-process matrix. Services that have evolved in the last few decades have reflected the design rule implied in the product-process matrix (Table 3.6). Low variation care is often carved off into a unit specifically designed for it, such as an elective surgical center, and regional networks allow centralization of unique and complex cases in academic centers.

Table 3.6. The product-process matrix applied to secondary healthcare

	Repetitive care	Menu-based care	Exploratory care
Focused care center	Elective surgical center		
Condition-specific service/practice unit		Breast center Spine center	
Subspecialist service			Academic medical center

Hayes and Wheelwright argued that, in manufacturing, moving off the diagonal could worsen quality and efficiency.[23] The same has proven true in healthcare. Patients needing repetitive care who are treated in an institution optimized for exploratory care risk inconsistent, delayed, costly, and occasionally unsafe care. Lengths of stay and costs for elective joint replacements are typically higher when they are performed in an academic medical center than when undertaken in an elective orthopedic "focused factory."

But in healthcare the benefits of grouping operationally similar patients and matching care type to production system creates an important dilemma: how many production units should a delivery organization serving a heterogeneous population sustain? How does a delivery organization choose which diseases, conditions, or patient subgroups merit their own disease-specific subunit and uniquely configured production system (especially when care is delivered by a multidisciplinary team drawn from different organizations or departments)? When would a general services production system be more appropriate? Does every disease deserve its own focused unit? How are we to group smaller-scale operating systems into economically efficient institutions? How do we avoid the risk that one set of discipline-based silos (e.g., general medicine, specialty medicine, surgery) will simply be replaced with another set of silos based on care type so that patients are still forced to cross intra- and interorganizational boundaries in an uncoordinated fashion, and on their own?

Other industries deal with heterogeneity in two ways: either by reducing or accommodating it. Heterogeneity can be reduced by limiting the company's service or product offering or by standardizing production processes within a given production system. Accommodation approaches include separating high- and lower-variation customers and processes into different production systems or factoring in additional resources ("slack") to cope with periods of high demand or transient increases in complexity.[24] The models of care in Table 3.6 represent an increasing degree of accommodation. Focused factories, such as elective surgical centers, tend to reject the high-variability cases that would interfere with their high-throughput systems and create backups and queues. Repeatable procedures lend themselves to a less diverse staff and an assembly-line approach to management. In contrast, academic medical centers accommodate variation by deploying additional resources and applying fewer constraints to their use.

Broadly speaking, delivery organizations have taken two approaches to matching care type to production system. One has been to focus on larger populations and create high-level service groupings. For example, they place cardiology and cardiac surgery in a "cardiac institute" or rheumatology, orthopedics, and physical therapy in a "joint center." The other approach has been to focus at a lower level on disease groups and develop disease- or condition-specific subunits such as breast or headache centers (sometimes called "integrated practice units"). Both approaches focus on patients who need multidisciplinary care.* The goal is to group all the necessary resources so that

---

* Singapore's SingHealth defines a disease center as "a patient focused functional structure that integrates professionals from different specialties and institutions to address a specific disease or group of diseases." Similarly, Harvard University's Institute for Strategy and Competitiveness describes an "integrated practice unit" as being "organized around the patient medical condition or group of closely related conditions" and involving "a dedicated, multidisciplinary team devoting a significant portion of their time to the condition." (Institute for Strategy and Competitiveness. Harvard Business School. Accessed Nov 15, 2020. https://www.isc.hbs.edu/health-care/value-based-health-care/key-concepts/Pages/organize-care-around-condition.aspx .)

patients do not need to traverse organizational boundaries to receive their care. Institutes still tend to be internally organized as job shops. Aggregating patients in disease-based integrated practice units gives these units sufficient patient volume to justify the development of standard processes and allow investment in specialized resources—such as staff, equipment, and decision tools—giving these models some of the qualities of an assembly line.

When would a condition or disease group lend itself to an integrated practice unit? Those disease centers that have evolved in recent years, such as headache, breast, and head and neck cancer centers, have tended to share an important characteristic. The care they deliver is integral: its component tasks and decisions are tightly connected and interdependent. But the disease (or disease cluster) is more modular: it is often fairly separate from other diseases. These disease centers co-locate the many professional disciplines needed to provide care, but the nature of the disease is such that the unit as a whole does not need to interact much with the rest of the organization or system that houses it.

LINKING ORGANIZATION DESIGN TO THE TYPE OF CARE: IMPLICATIONS FOR ACTION

Operations research points to the benefits of matching the design of delivery organizations and local operating systems and their approach to day-to-day management with the nature of the care they deliver. Part of the work of transformation involves rebuilding local operating systems to improve that match. The rationale for clinician involvement in operational redesign is that an effective design depends on a deep understanding of the nature of the disease and of its treatments.

Correctly specifying the care is required to ensure such an accurate match. Distinguishing among repetitive, menu-based, and exploratory care and designing an appropriate operating system accordingly require clinical and operational decision-making.

If we are to achieve the benefits of focus and production system matching while serving the needs of a diverse population, our delivery organizations and systems must be able to build in operational diversity, support multiple production systems, and effectively match each production system with the nature of care required by the particular patient subpopulation it serves. So an essential task for clinical leaders is to critically evaluate their local operating system in relation to the patient population it serves. What value is it to deliver? What is the nature of the care required to deliver this value, and thus what operating system is best suited to deliver it? Should the operating system be designed and managed more like an assembly line—with high degrees of standardization and predictability— or more like a job shop or craft model with greater flexibility and more customization? These choices matter to patients: they help define their experience of care and can have an impact on the outcome of that care.

The current move from in-person to virtual care, accelerated in 2020 in response to the Covid-19 pandemic, provides an example of the decisions required. Not all ambulatory appointments are the same, and the goals of care differ from one appointment to the next: initial assessment of a new patient in a first appointment, postprocedure check for complications, or surveillance of a stable patient in remission, for example. Some can be delivered asynchronously via the internet or smartphone app, others by a phone call, others with a video consultation, and still others require an in-person visit. Each is potentially a different operating system that needs matching to the particularities of the care.

Currently, the platform most commonly used to deliver healthcare services is the job shop model: general hospitals and general practitioners. Like all job shops they have the advantage of being able to provide a wide range of services and being very flexible to changes in patient need and preference. Their flexibility and efficient use of expensive human and technical resources have made them well suited as mechanisms for serving a heterogeneous patient population with varying biological needs and personal values and preferences, and allowed them to respond to a novel disease. However, they are not well set up to exploit the quality and efficiency benefits of a more focused production system that has been specifically matched to a subgroup of patients and their particular care needs. In the face of population growth and the advance of medical knowledge the job shop model has struggled to either support integrated care by multidisciplinary teams or efficiently provide standardized care in volume.

In sum, all these design decisions depend first on correctly specifying the nature of care needed for a given health problem or subpopulation of patients. Then modifications can be made to care delivery, production system, and managerial controls:

1. Evaluate each significant patient subpopulation for which care is provided.
2. Determine which type of care is appropriate to meet the health needs of each: repetitive, menu-based, or exploratory (i.e., diagnose the care required).
3. Examine current approaches to care delivery to check that the production approach being used matches patient needs.

4. Redesign the production system and managerial controls to better match the type of care and the care needs of the subpopulation.

Chapter 4 discusses how an individual operating system can be redesigned. Over what elements of a production system do clinicians and local managers have control? And how can that control be best used to improve performance?

Levers of Operational Control

To clinicians, the design considerations discussed in Chapter 3 may sound theoretical. Even when they identify an optimal care delivery model, the many constraints they face—such as resource shortages, scope of practice regulation, payer contracts, internal bureaucratic rules, or the local culture—often lead them to conclude that their operating systems are immutable. How could they possibly be changed to improve patient value and the match between system and care?

Leaders in the middle of care delivery organizations, particularly clinicians, often view the organizational setting of their professional work as a given: something to be coped with and accommodated, not to be influenced or changed. They can feel powerless to improve their system's operational performance and thus retreat into their professional work: doing their best in spite of, not because of, the operating environment in which they practice. Moreover, a common narrative about reform implies that both the motivation and tools for transformation are in the hands of others: agents outside established delivery organizations, such as payers, regulators, and companies. To "transform" healthcare is often taken to mean to respond to external pressure by purchasing innovative communication and digital technologies that facilitate new ways of distributing knowledge and of making clinical and managerial decisions.

FOUR LEVERS OF OPERATIONAL CONTROL

In fact, the power to make positive change to their practice environment and their local system's ability to deliver patient value is within local leaders' grasp. The components of an operating system—the care process, the clinical and managerial workforce, the technical and physical supporting resources, and the mechanisms for exercising operational control—represent points at which operational control can be exercised. These four levers are under local leaders' direct control. By making changes in them, frontline staff can improve their operating system's performance.

Modifying the care process, staffing model, supporting infrastructure, and managerial controls changes the way care is delivered. The levers are easily accessible to frontline staff: they need neither additional resources nor permission to exercise local operational control. Arguably, because operating system performance is an independent determinant of patient outcome, all clinicians should control their local system to ensure the best outcomes for their patients.

Control of these four levers is not only the mechanism of improving local system performance but also an essential part of making the operational changes often needed before a technological innovation can achieve its full potential. Furthermore, organizational transformation requires multiple operating system redesigns. Therefore local staff need to be adept at using the four levers differently in different patient care situations to ensure each operating system is matched to the particular care being delivered.

For each of the four levers there are a number of options from which local leaders can choose: different possible process designs, workforce configurations, therapeutic and information technologies, or metrics. Which they select will depend on their local resources and the needs of the particular patient population.

How they make these design choices will determine the local operating system's capability to deliver the intended patient value efficiently, safely, and reliably. A number of principles that can help guide their choices are discussed in the following sections.

Care Process

The care process is the sequence of decisions and tasks used to diagnose and treat an existing health problem or prevent a future one in an individual or a population: it is the primary mechanism by which science is brought to the patient. It, and the associated flows of information, equipment, and materials, is the way healthcare creates both outcome and experience and ultimately adds value to the patient. In the same way that in a manufacturing setting the production system exists to support a production process, the other three components of the operating system (i.e., the clinical and managerial workforce, the infrastructure, and the mechanisms for exercising operational control) support the care process.

Business processes are intermingled with the core care process. These are, for example, the processes by which information is captured and made available to decision makers, equipment is sterilized and brought to the site of care, procedures and clinic visits are scheduled, routine and on-call staff rosters are created, and patient records and bills are maintained and checked. Experience with Covid-19 revealed just how important such processes can be: for example, the supply chain for personal protective equipment, or the logistics of testing.

All these processes can be designed and managed (although it may seem to practitioners that neither design nor management has played a role in current processes). Process design and control have been the focus of care quality improvement activities for the last two decades since the tools from Japanese improvement methods became widely applied in healthcare. Common visual analytic tools, such as flow diagrams, fishbone and driver diagrams, value stream maps, and statistical process control charts, focus on the process.

Control of care and business processes is achieved first and foremost through good design. The extent to which the process is specified, segmented, and standardized; the number, sequencing, and linearity of steps; the way responsibility for process steps is allocated to the various staff executing the process; and the allocation of responsibility for identifying and addressing process deviation are key design choices. For each choice there is no one right answer: each option has its advantages and disadvantages. For example, organizations, units, or individual clinicians could choose to specify or standardize their processes more or less. The choice will depend on such factors as their evaluation of the strength of the evidence, the availability and capability of local resources such as staff, or the local clinical culture.

Specification and Standardization

The first key design choice is whether to implement a protocol or guideline. "Best practice" protocols define a preferred patient care process for individual diseases, conditions, procedures, or subpopulations. Creating care processes involves two related design choices: With how much detail will each decision or task be specified? and Is the process expected to apply to all patients?

Disease-specific protocols and decision rules define exactly which tests and treatments make up the process, how and when each is to be used, and how patients are to transition from one care site to another.* In the extreme case these protocols can be so specific as to be computerized. By contrast, guidelines are less

---

* Condition nonspecific care processes such as an emergency pathway can be equally and highly specified.

specific than protocols: they leave much more room for discretion in decision-making.

The extent to which a process can be specified depends in part on the designer's evaluation of the stage of medical knowledge relating to each step. As Chapter 3 discussed, the better our understanding is of the science and the relationships between cause and effect, the more we can specify process steps and decision criteria in detail. Tighter links between the process and outcome allow more process specification and tighter process control. Failure to explicitly specify well-understood steps or processes risks inviting unwarranted variation, and possibly, worse outcomes.

Standardization is the application of the specified set of steps to all patients with a particular need, or having a particular procedure as a default. Its goal is to minimize unwarranted variation by ensuring that care conforms to the standard. Despite evidence that specification, standardization, and variance reduction improve patient outcomes, many clinicians still view standardized processes as the antithesis to good care and see in them the potential to reduce the flexibility required to provide care for unique individuals.

Designers face a trade-off here. The more tightly a care process is specified, the more likely it is that it will not adequately describe the care needed by every patient. Intermountain's Brent James put it succinctly: "No protocol fits every patient, and no protocol perfectly fits any patient."[1] He did not mean that processes cannot be specified and standardized, but rather that more highly standardized care processes are more likely to be overridden by clinicians to meet the needs of the particular individual they are treating. More specification and standardization mean more frequent override: the actual care delivered deviates from the standard. Standardization does not prevent warranted variation.

Standardization is therefore a relative term: the extent to which an operating system's care processes are specified and standardized is in part determined by the leader's willingness, and the system's capacity, to accommodate overrides. At Intermountain, protocol overrides are welcomed: they are seen as signs that care is sensitive to patient needs and values. Note that it is possible to specify and standardize a process even though the evidence for a particular process or step is incomplete. In fact, Intermountain has demonstrated that systematic tracking and evaluation of deviations from a standard process are a powerful tool for improving our understanding about both the operating system's processes and the underlying medicine.[2]

Sequencing, Simplicity, and Linearity

Most care processes have evolved over time as medical or societal fashions changed, new insights were gained, and technologies developed. In many organizations, processes have become complex, convoluted, duplicative, and inefficient as more options and activities are added but none removed. Tasks and decisions that could or should be undertaken in parallel occur sequentially, activities that have been shown to add little value to the patient are continued out of habit, and scheduling is driven by a resource's availability rather than an ideal sequence of information-gathering and decision-making activities for a particular patient group or disease type.

In contrast, well-designed processes are simple. They tend to be linear and without unnecessary steps: they are made up only of those activities that create patient value directly or are essential supports for other value-adding steps. Steps are ordered to account for the ideal sequencing of information gathering and decision-making. Well-designed processes use parallel processing when appropriate. Much of the practical work of process redesign and waste reduction is to describe the current process, often in all its frightening detail, to then examine the utility of each and every step, removing those that add nothing or are no

longer relevant.* What to keep, what to add, and what to discard
are key design choices.

Segmentation

Some processes naturally lend themselves to being divided (i.e.,
they are modular). Segmentation can be undertaken in three
ways. First, a more general process may be segmented into several more highly specified ones. For example, Intermountain has
created distinct processes for the management of mild, moderate, and severe depression. A process that may not be specifi-
able or standardizable when applied to a heterogeneous general
population may be when restricted to a well-defined patient
subpopulation.

Second, an individual process may be divisible into component
parts with some steps more highly specified than others. Even if
the decision to order a particular test or therapy may not be spec-
ifiable or standardizable, the execution of that activity may be.
Organizations' goal of zero central line infections is achieved by
standardizing the process for inserting a line, not the decision
of when to insert one. Component decisions and tasks of a longer process can often be treated differently so that standardization is not necessarily uniformly distributed throughout the
entire care process. Deciding when to standardize and when not
to is another important design choice.

Third, processes may be segmented by location. Regional clinical networks sometimes distribute different components of a
care process across multiple locations by determining what
should be done in an inpatient setting, the community, or the
patient's home. These determinations usually vary among re-

---

* This is the purpose of the Toyota Production System's "value stream
mapping" tool.

gions or communities based on local preferences and available resources.

Thus the first way to control an operating system is to design the care process: to deliberately plan what will be specified and standardized, which steps to add or remove, and in what sequence, and where care should be located. But process segmentation, simplification, specification, and standardization are not enough on their own to transform care delivery. Clinical and business processes exist within a supporting operating system. The best processes will fail if the rest of the operating system does not support them: the other three levers must be modified if a process redesign is to be effective and sustained.

Work and Workforce

Health care is as much a human as a technical undertaking, predominantly provided by individual professionals. Although technology is a constant feature and expense in healthcare, caregiving and administrative staff are at the center of any healthcare delivery organization and typically account for the majority of the budget. The care process does not exist in isolation from the workforce responsible for undertaking it: its design and day-to-day management are closely linked to the determination of who will undertake each activity. These staff members are the ones who will put changes in the care process into action, often by changing the way they work. Hence, it is no surprise that ensuring a standardized process is actually executed is often harder than developing it in the first place: writing it down does not make it so.

The term "workforce redesign" means different things at different levels in a healthcare system. At the national level, the focus is typically on such issues as professional staff numbers, funded training programs and residency places, and licensure and scope of practice regulation. Within a delivery organization, workforce design increasingly covers the extent to which the makeup of the workforce reflects that of the patient population. Research shows that black patients are more likely to trust, and to heed the advice of, black physicians.[3] Work design links the care process and the workforce. In a unit-level operating system "workforce redesign" therefore focuses primarily on the distribution of accountabilities for specific activities to individual professionals. This is the way a care process on paper is converted into a routine in practice and the second way a local leader can exercise control over an operating system.

In practice, designing the work and the workforce means defining the roles of medical, nursing, allied health professionals, and support and administrative staff; specifying and allocating tasks and decision rights and responsibilities for each process step to the most appropriately trained and capable member of the team; ensuring that formal role descriptions, accountability mechanisms, and work plans match the distribution of the work; and planning development trajectories and training needs for staff to support ongoing skill enhancement.

Skill Mix and Specialization

At the core of a workforce that can execute a care process with precision, reliability, and flexibility is the matching of staff skill and training with the task and decision requirements. Longstanding notions of which professional training is required for what type of care are changing radically as specialist nurses now deliver anesthetics and run their own clinics, specialist psychologists prescribe psychoactive medication, pharmacists provide some primary care, and midwives practice independently. A notable aspect of many organizations' early response to the 2020 Covid-19 crisis was staff moving out of their established roles: doing what needed to be done regardless of what their role description specified. Carefully defining the nature of the work required to provide care to a particular patient population, and blending a team of professionals accordingly, is an essential step in developing an operating system that implements a care process.

Task and Decision Allocation

Dividing the work among the team and allocating responsibility for each step in a process requires not only deciding who is supposed to do what when but also ensuring that each professional has the requisite skills, authority, and resources needed to undertake their designated tasks and make the associated decisions. Although national "scope of practice" regulations set out which activities and decisions a clinician is allowed to undertake within the terms of his or her professional license, there is often a lot of discretion in the way tasks and decision rights are assigned within the individual delivery organization. Increasingly, clinical tasks and decisions are being shifted to nondoctor clinical professionals in the hope that this will reduce cost, increase reliability, and reduce delay. Nurse-led, criteria-based discharge protocols exemplify such task and decision reallocations.

An example from National Heart Centre in Singapore illustrates the impact of assigning decision authority thoughtfully. The time between a patient's presentation to an emergency department and commencement of definitive intervention (door-to-balloon time) is a common quality measure. Between 2005 and 2007 process improvement projects failed to reduce the mean door-to-balloon time below 109 minutes, well above the internationally recognized target of 60 minutes. Then, in 2007 authority to initiate out-of-hours transfer from the emergency department to the cardiovascular lab was shifted from the on-call consultant cardiologist to the emergency medicine registrar. Door-to-balloon time fell to 82 minutes. In 2010 this authority was transferred once again, this time to the senior emergency department night nurse. The time fell to 60 minutes.[4] Examples such as these show the benefit of decentralizing decision authority to the staff member closest to the care of the patient.

Job Planning and Rostering

The job plan (in the United Kingdom) or job description (in the United States) is the organization's mechanism for translating a work design into individual responsibilities for which staff can be held accountable during regular performance appraisals. Staff can be very sensitive to mismatch between the formal description of their job and the work they are actually called upon to do. It is worth taking the time needed to ensure these are as aligned as possible.

A closely related point of control is the way employed staff of all professions are rostered on duty. Skilled supervisors can use rostering, and the design of on-call rosters, as a highly effective behavioral incentive. Rostering can also have a significant impact on demand and workflow. In England, for example, hospitals struggle to provide acute care to a growing population of elderly medical patients because many medical specialists have opted out of the general medicine on-call roster, leaving only a small group of medical generalists to provide emergency care. This has "increased staffing problems and has increased the pressures on the remaining staff."[5]

Staff Development

The healthcare industry typically relies on agencies outside the delivery organization, such as medical and nursing schools, professional colleges, and boards of professional registration, to prepare staff and equip them with the knowledge and skills required to provide care safely and effectively. Delivery organizations hire from the labor market and make comparatively modest investments in staff development. Organizations approach workforce development differently in other industries. They invest heavily in training their own staff with the goal of developing a workforce that precisely matches the way the organization has chosen to deliver its service or make its product. Although staff training might be considered a long-term approach to operating system control, developing the skill sets of existing staff members may be more effective than hiring new staff. Experience in healthcare suggests "greater benefits may arise from having staff in teams acquire specialist competencies than from having teams acquire specialist staff."[6]

Considerations in Work and Workforce Redesign

Designing the care process and allocating work responsibilities are effective ways frontline leaders can exercise operational control: many of the previously mentioned choices are well within their authority. Some actions, such as task reallocation and rostering, have immediate impact, whereas others, such as training or recruiting new staff, require longer to take effect. Together they improve the match between the difficulty of the task or decision and the skill and training of the staff member.

Making best use of highly skilled and expensive staff has become increasingly important in recent years. If an individual team member has a level of training and skill below that required by a particular task, decision, or process step (underskilling) then care risks being ineffective, or worse, unsafe. On the contrary, assigning a task to a team member who is over trained (over-skilling) wastes a valuable human resource and risks job dissatisfaction and increased staff turnover. Recent Organization for Economic Co-operation and Development (OECD) data point to the urgency of these issues. More than 75 percent of doctors and nurses report being over-skilled for some of the tasks they do, whereas 50 percent of doctors and 40 percent of nurses report being under-skilled for some tasks.

Worse, highly qualified nurses (with a master's degree or equivalent) are more likely to report being over-skilled, suggesting that their capabilities are being underutilized.[7] Ideally, work should be allocated within a unit so that training and skill exactly match task and decision difficulty.

In the short run, under- and over-skilling mismatches can be addressed by reallocating tasks and decisions to staff whose training and skill better match the task needs, assuming such reallocation is within the constraints of national licensure and scope of practice regulation. Under-skilling can be addressed in the longer term by expanding roles and providing additional training. As medical knowledge and technology advance, what was once challenging becomes routine, meaning that skill-task match must be reevaluated constantly.

But as attractive as it is to redesign the workforce to improve quality and efficiency, a number of caveats apply. Although none of these reduce the value of redesigning the staffing model, they do point to the need to carefully plan work and workforce changes to avoid some of the known negative consequences. First, the work and the workforce must be redesigned in tandem. It serves no purpose to reassign tasks and decisions to alternative staff without first evaluating whether those activities are effective in delivering value to patients. As Peter Drucker once observed, "There is surely nothing quite so useless as doing efficiently that which should not be done at all."[8] A similar message emerges from the literature on healthcare workforce redesign: redesign the work first.[9] In practice this means the work of process redesign described previously should come before workforce redesign.

Second, task and role shifting has not been without its difficulties. For example, a key focus of workforce redesign has been on the deployment of alternative, nonspecialist, and nonmedical practitioners to substitute for more expensive specialist physicians. Models include extending primary practitioners' scope of practice into areas of specialist interest,* developing specialist advanced nurse practitioners who can practice independently, hiring physicians' assistants to practice under the supervision of a physician, and creating the role of "health coach." Broadly speaking, such models have not been associated with a decrement in quality as initially feared. In fact, not only are outcomes between role groups such as advanced nurse practitioners and primary care physicians comparable,[10] but some studies have shown an improvement in patient access, experience, and outcomes.[11] However, savings have sometimes not materialized because of unforeseen additional costs beyond the costs of training.[12] Salary savings can be offset by utilization increases as less experienced professionals tend to be more risk averse and order more tests and admissions. Fragmenting the work across a larger team also increases coordination costs.

Furthermore, narrower scope roles can reduce staff flexibility, reducing their ability to cross-cover each other and keeping everyone in tightly defined "swim lanes."[13] Electronic health records (EHRs) can hardwire these constraints by limiting staff's information access and authorization rights. New caregivers can become a complement, not a substitute, when physicians do not relinquish work, thus raising overall staffing costs. Ironically, in pursuit of increased efficiency, organizations risk increasing the size of the workforce and reducing its flexibility.

There is also a risk in defining the tasks to be reallocated simplistically and too narrowly, and in particular, in seeing them in purely mechanistic terms. Lists of tasks that can be reallocated to lower-cost workers can miss the significance of what appear initially to be menial activities. In the hands of an experienced

---

* For instance, the United Kingdom has created a role called "GPs with Special Interest."

nurse what appears as a simple bed bath can in fact be a sophisticated diagnostic evaluation and therapeutic intervention. The nurse can observe how the patient moves and discover previously unreported sources of pain, not to mention reinforce the therapeutic relationship.

Third, work and workforce design has tended to focus on doctors, nurses, and allied health professionals. In reality, these roles are only a fraction of the total workforce. For example, in 2012 the UK's National Health System employed about 100,000 doctors and 300,000 nurses. At the same time there were an estimated 2 million workers in social care, 3 million volunteers, and more than 5 million informal caregivers.[14] Such staff, who are the backbone of residential aged care facilities, have received much less training investment yet are important contributors to the patient's overall care. This imbalance is long-standing. In 1999 the economic value of informal caregiving (unpaid family members and friends) in the United States was estimated to be $196 billion, dwarfing formal spending on home health care ($32 billion) and nursing home care ($83 billion).[15]

Finally, a common response to expected changes in technology and models of care is to plan the training needs of the future workforce. However, the reality is that a large portion of the workforce we are planning for is already employed. Instead of waiting for a new workforce to be trained, the urgent requirement is to address staff's current needs by ensuring that the work of care has been distributed effectively and that existing staff have the skills, support, and training they need to accommodate practice change.

Infrastructure

Technology and physical space are the two main infrastructural components that support the care process and workforce. Staff routinely make use of diagnostic, therapeutic, information, communication, and decision support technologies to implement the care process. Which technology a healthcare delivery organization invests in and makes available to staff has a major impact on which elements of a care process are feasible locally. Two aspects of a delivery organization's technology acquisition policies are important: which individual technologies are purchased and to what extent technologies are standardized within the organization.

Most countries exercise some central control over which technologies are available to care delivery organizations. These are determined either by a national or state regulator (e.g., through a national drug formulary, information technology [IT] strategy, and certificate of need requirements) or through insurance company reimbursement arrangements. Nonetheless, even within restrictive national or payer frameworks, individual organizations have discretion over which individual technologies they purchase and how much technology diversity they accept. An example of using this discretion in practice is that the purchase of only one brand of joint replacement prosthesis allows the negotiation of a lower price for a bulk order and makes it easier for staff to become very familiar with a limited range of instruments. Of course, such an approach implies the need for a tight connection between design of a delivery organization's care process and its technology acquisition or materials management strategy.

Control over technology choices can be exercised in several ways. Organizations can try to influence clinician demand through protocols that define drug or test choices and appropriateness criteria for elective procedures. Alternatively, they can include clinicians in the purchasing process by working to develop departmental agreement on device standardization. They can also establish a specific organizational process for new technology assessment and acquisition. In all of these cases the goal is to ensure that technology strategy and work redesign go hand-in-hand so that the technology deployed directly supports the work of staff implementing the care process.

The second important element of infrastructure is the physical site of care: its location and internal configuration. The care process, workforce, and necessary technology in large part determine where care is delivered and how patients flow through a particular site of care. Like the other control levers, the kinds of locations in which patients receive care are changing rapidly. Telemedicine has made it possible to undertake a consultation remotely. New care models (e.g., retail clinics located in shopping malls and self-testing kiosks in supermarkets) have made care available in locations far away from the conventional doctor's consulting room. Increased availability of smartphone apps and wearable technology are accelerating this trend by connecting patients and their caregivers at a distance and allowing the availability of expert decision-making to be divorced from the location of the expert.

Some organizations deliberately use their physical space strategically. The configuration of a site can be used to reinforce preferred clinician behaviors and attitudes. For instance, Virginia Mason's chemotherapy unit in Seattle famously positions its patient infusion chairs by the windows in rooms that face the outside of the building and places the doctors' offices in windowless cubes in the center of the floor. Giving the prime real estate to patient care rooms, at the expense of doctors' offices, sends both patients and staff a message about the organization's commitment to patient-centered care. Milan's Istituto Clinico Humanitas denies its specialists private offices. They have cubicles in a shared space for the express purpose of promoting informal specialist-to-specialist interaction.

Such examples suggest that there is a close relationship between the care process, workforce, technology, and the physical site. Choices in each frame the choices in the others. Sometimes the first three determine the fourth. Decisions regarding the nature of the care, which caregiver delivers it and how, determine where that care can be delivered: form following function. But sometimes function follows form. A particular physical location may enable or force a particular care process or staffing model. For example, the clinical design of rural services is often defined by constraints imposed by geography.

Managerial Control Policies

Finally, organizations' internal policies directly influence clinician and nonclinician behavior and thus shape the performance of the other three components of the operating system. The contracts, job planning, and appraisals mentioned previously are mechanisms of managerial control. Others include financial and nonfinancial incentives and reward systems, clinician compacts, business planning processes and technology acquisition policies, internally defined process and outcome metrics and their associated targets (usually called "key performance indicators," or KPIs), performance monitoring systems, and formal and informal disciplinary processes for addressing the occasional instance of unprofessional behavior. These tools influence individual behavior directly and contribute to creating the internal organizational culture that is also a mechanism of behavioral influence. Many of these mechanisms allow day-to-day control that complements the longer-term control achieved by redesign of the care process, staffing model, and infrastructure. Two important examples follow.

Measurement

Measurement is a key component of short- and long-term process control (and is discussed in more detail in Chapter 10). Process compliance and resource utilization metrics track the extent to which steps designed into the process are actually undertaken.

Outcome metrics allow the assessment of whether this sequence of tasks and decisions, when delivered in practice, reliably achieves the desired outcome and promised patient value. Detected variations point to where a process must be modified to further improve outcome or uncertainties have to be resolved through further research.

Job Planning and Appraisal

Annual (or more frequent) appraisals that compare individuals' performance with their job plans is a common mechanism in many parts of the world for translating a work specification into practice and exercising control over a process or clinical service. Many organizations fail to use these tools effectively for this purpose, instead making the annual appraisal a perfunctory and pro forma process, or worse, failing to use these as opportunities for mentoring, learning, and staff's personal development.

Some institutions, in contrast, take a very active approach to job planning and appraisal. Cleveland Clinic, for example, appraises its physicians and renews their contracts annually, investing thousands of hours in the process. Physician compacts and codes of conduct (see Chapter 6) are often used to reinforce the behaviors specified and complement the job planning and appraisal process. For instance, the Massachusetts General Hospital's Boundary Statement opens with the commitment to never "knowingly ignore MGH policies and procedures."[16]

The importance of such policies and behavioral influence mechanisms lies in the fact that modern workplaces are truly "sociotechnical systems": their output results from an interaction between people and technology. Nowhere is this more so than in a modern healthcare delivery organization. But only some of the interactions among people, and between people and technologies, can be specified and designed. These tend to be in repetitive care, where processes are more linear and cause-and-effect relationships are well understood, so protocols and explicit decision rules can specify care exactly. They provide a clear blueprint. However, other interactions are nonlinear and cannot be specified in advance. These rely much more on the informal relationships between members of a caregiving team or a wider group, and therefore other mechanisms of behavioral influence such as those listed previously are needed.

In sum, these four levers of operational control can be used to create a well-designed operating system and are tools for its day-to-day management. Changing each or all in concert is the primary mechanism by which an individual delivery organization can improve its operational performance. But, as later sections discuss, optimizing all four jointly is needed if the goal is to create a world-class service, unit, or organization.

USING THE FOUR LEVERS TO EXERCISE OPERATIONAL CONTROL

None of the control levers described previously are particularly esoteric. All are familiar to professional managers; yet, as already noted, clinicians often feel that the system in which they personally practice their professions and deliver their care is under the control of someone else. They come to work and see their patients in an environment that has been created for them. Although they have control over the content of the care they deliver, they feel they have little or no control over the four levers and are unable to shape the context in which they work. Middle-level managers equally feel they cannot make system change, partly because of organizational bureaucracy and partly because they are so busy "fighting fires."

However, many elements of the operating system are in fact directly under the control of clinical staff and local operational managers. Some changes can be made very quickly (see Table 4.1

Table 4.1. Short-term operating system control

Lever of control	Interventions that can be made quickly
Care process **What** care to deliver and **how** to do it • Sequence of tasks and decisions, decision rules, and transfer criteria	• Simplify processes by removing unnecessary and ineffective steps. • Implement standard processes (design steps, structure, and flow) or standard order sets for key tests and medicines. • Specify clinical decision rules/transfer criteria (develop criteria for admission, discharge, transfer, executing common tasks). • Streamline documentation and reduce duplication.
Staffing model **Who** does what • Allocation of task and decision responsibilities and authority, training, oversight, and support	• Reassign tasks or decision rights to alternative staff as appropriate. • Create training to support new role definitions. • Create clear role definition for each staff member. • Merge on-call rosters over multiple care sites.
Infrastructure **What** resources and supports needed • Equipment choice and site configuration	• Provide care in an alternative site (including care moved from hospital to community setting). • Implement technologies and resources to support patients' self-management. • Use standard equipment sets or medication lists.
Behavior influence mechanisms **How** to behave • Metrics and measurement reporting systems	• Identify preferred staff behaviors (including a behavioral compact). • Define patient-focused measurable goals for teams and individuals. • Define standard measures to track care quality and efficiency. • Set unit-level targets and benchmarks. • Institute regular progress reports and feedback sessions.

for some examples). In particular, local leaders have a lot of control over clinical practice. Many of the interventions in Table 4.1 are entirely within a practicing clinician's domain and local leaders' scopes of practice and do not require outside permission. Many can easily be manipulated to achieve meaningful improvement over short periods of time.

Other interventions, which may require more planning and a longer lead time, can also be influenced by local leaders. (Table 4.2 provides some examples.) Although many of these are usually thought of as being solely under corporate control, local clinicians can also exert influence in these areas because corporate leaders look to clinical staff for input and take their lead from them.

OPERATING SYSTEM ALIGNMENT

Each lever of control represents a set of options from which leaders can choose to increase the "product-process" match and the operating system's effectiveness at delivering patient value. Contingent on the type of care being delivered, processes can be more or less highly specified, decision authority can be more centralized or widely distributed, the technology deployed can be more or less supportive of clinical practice, and staff behavior can be more or less highly managed.

However, these choices are not independent. In highly functioning operating systems, each choice reinforces the others so that they are not only individually effective, they also work together as a set. The choices of lever of control must be mutually supporting and collectively focused. Two design characteristics shared by better performing operating systems are internal and external alignment.

Table 4.2. Medium-term operating system control

Lever of control	Interventions with a longer time horizon
Care process **What** care to deliver and **how** to do it • Sequence of tasks and decisions, decision rules, and transfer criteria	• Define referral pathways (work with referrers to define how patients come to the unit and simplify patient entry). • Work with downstream caregivers and organizations to smooth discharge and transfer of care.
Staffing model **Who** does what • Allocation of task and decision responsibilities and authority, training, oversight, and support	• Create team skill mix (professional makeup). • Create new roles for nurse specialist/other alternative providers. • Recruit professionals and personalities to match the new way of working. • Design and deliver internal training programs to support the new way of working.
Infrastructure **What** resources and supports needed • Equipment choice and site configuration	• Reconfigure internal layout of the clinic, ward, office, or unit. • Plan location of the service or unit within the existing plant/buildings. • Develop new services within the region. • Use communication technology to support virtual visits and specialist opinion delivered at a distance.
Behavior influence mechanisms **How** to behave • Metrics and measurement reporting systems	• Collect longer-term outcome measures such as general and disease-specific outcome and experience measures (PROMs[a] and PREMs[b]). • Institute rewards and recognition for preferred behaviors and better performance. • Refine job descriptions and staff assessments to ensure they are well matched to the new way of working.

[a]Patient-reported outcome measure.
[b]Patient-reported experience measure.

Internal Alignment

Internal alignment describes the way the levers interact with one another. In any delivery organization, no matter its purpose or size, the process, staffing, technology, space, and managerial policies act in unison to create the patient's experience and outcome. They are so interdependent that they need to be jointly optimized. Defining what care should be delivered and deciding who should undertake which tasks go hand in hand. The care process and staffing model are intimately linked. The same is true of the staffing model and the ways in which individual clinician performance is influenced by the selected approaches to managerial control. Similarly, the location of care is linked to the technology deployed both at the site and between sites to bring decision makers in remote locations together. It is a hallmark of highly functioning delivery organizations that not only are each of the levers used thoughtfully selected but also they work well together.

The importance of alignment is most obvious when it is absent. Problems arise when the levers are not well aligned; when staff responsible for a task or decision lack the authority, training, or needed information or technology; when incentives or culture do not encourage behaviors in the best interests of patients or other staff; when the layout of the clinic, unit, practice, or institution does not support the smooth flow of patients or staff through the system, and so forth. The symptoms of mismatch between the four levers are familiar to us all. Staff walk huge distances in a working day. Essential information or equipment is missing from the site where patients and staff interact. Tests are repeated and patients complain they are repeatedly asked the same questions. Staff and patients are delayed waiting for the decision maker to arrive or the critical report to be found. And everyone is busy executing their own personal workarounds in an attempt to make the system work for them.

Tests of Internal Alignment

For practical purposes, there are five ways in which alignment is particularly important. Table 4.3 gives examples of the kind of self-assessment questions that can be used to test whether an operating system is internally aligned. Each test looks at key pairs of levers of control. For each individual test it is possible to evaluate the general level of alignment among the levers by asking

Table 4.3. Five tests of internal alignment

Alignment of . . .	Self-assessment questions
Care process to subpopulation	Is the population appropriately subsegmented and cohorted?
	Does the new process deliver appropriate care to each subpopulation?
Staff to task and decision	Are the right people delivering the right components of care?
	Are decisions assigned to staff with appropriate training, skill, and experience?
	Are staff overtrained for the work they are asked to do?
Technology to process	Does the technology provide staff with the data, information, and tools they need to deliver the specified care at the time they need it?
	Does it support patients' and families' participation in their own care?
Physical configuration to process and population	Will care be provided in a location patients value?
	Is the physical site configured to support our staff in the work they do and our patients in their recovery?
Incentives and influences to preferred behaviors	Will the planned financial and nonfinancial incentives, internal culture, values, and boundary conditions reinforce the staff behavior we want?
	Do formal job descriptions accurately reflect the work staff are expected to do?

whether the levers are (1) misaligned and interacting negatively to reduce overall system performance; (2) not well aligned and inconsistent with each other; (3) aligned and consistent with each other but not positively reinforcing each other; or (4) aligned and positively reinforcing each other to improve system performance.

External Alignment

Internal and external alignment each describes a different aspect of the "fit" or "matching" between an operating system and the care. Although internal alignment refers to the relationship between the various individual components of an operating system, external alignment refers to the relationship of the system as a whole to the population it serves and the value it is designed to deliver. Ultimately, an operating system's internal alignment is of little value in isolation of the patient group it is intended to serve. Acting together, all the operating system's components must meet the needs of the patient: they must be externally aligned.

Once again, external alignment is most obvious in its absence or when something changes. For example, early in its history Milan's Istituto Clinico Humanitas (ICH) ran a highly effective system for elective surgery. An important design element of its operating system was a very small emergency department. Having few emergency patients protected ICH's system from unpredictable variability and allowed smooth and rapid throughput of patients with predictable and schedulable care needs. All the levers were optimized to support this type of care, and the operating system was both internally aligned and externally aligned for elective surgical patients. When ICH significantly expanded its emergency department, the system, although still internally aligned, was suddenly no longer externally aligned. Its components still supported each other, but the operating system as a whole was not well matched to the needs of a new population of frail elderly medical patients suffering from diseases such as heart failure, stroke, fractured neck or femur, and chronic airways disease. The impact of increased variability of the emergency patients was to reduce the efficiency of the elective patients' care. To address this problem ICH had to redesign its operating system, creating a new internally aligned system in a separate emergency hospital to meet the needs of this new population.

The U.S. Veterans Health Administration faced a similar challenge. Having developed a very effective system for providing care to aging veterans of the Korean and Vietnam wars suffering long-term conditions, it initially struggled when confronted with large numbers of young soldiers from the two Gulf wars who had survived injuries that would have been fatal in previous generations. Examples of this problem—using an operating system optimized for one patient or customer population to meet the needs of another group for which it has not been optimized—are not hard to find. The key question when assessing external alignment is, "Does the system as a whole meet the needs of its target patient population (i.e., is it fit-for-purpose)?"

SEQUENCING DESIGN AND CONTROL DECISIONS

The many design and control choices described previously can be simplified by approaching them in an orderly sequence: because some are contingent on others, they are best made in the kind of cascade shown in Box 1. The first step is to consider the external environment to which the operating system must be externally aligned. Begin by developing an understanding of what patients value and deciding which dimensions of that overall value will be the focus of this operating system (see Chapter 2). Then describe any impending innovations in technology or professional role that could change the future model of care.

(1) ASSESS THE EXTERNAL ENVIRONMENT

Patient Value

- Develop an understanding of what patients value.
- Determine which dimensions of patient value will be delivered by this part of the service.

Innovation Scan

- Perform an environmental scan to assess current and near future innovations that could enable new models of care. (Review the current state of the medical science and evolving technological capability: what will soon be possible and feasible?)
- Evaluate local applicability of new models of care (e.g., new roles, task distributions, or sites of care).

(2) DESIGN THE CARE PROCESS

- Critically evaluate the current sequence of tasks and decisions and redesign as appropriate.
- Specify the transition criteria that determine patient flow.

(3) DESIGN THE WORK AND DEVELOP THE WORKFORCE

- Allocate tasks and decisions to staff.
- Determine needed future skill mix.

(4) ESTABLISH THE SITE OF CARE

- Determine site of care, distribute components of the care process to the most appropriate site.
- Where possible, configure internal layout to support the ideal patient flow.

(continued)

BOX 1: (*continued*)

(5) DEPLOY TECHNOLOGY

- Assess technology requirements of the future process of care and the technologies needed to support staff in their work.
- Evaluate where technology uniformity will aid staff and promote reliability of process execution.

(6) SELECT METRICS AND TARGETS

- Select overall performance measures, choosing metrics of sufficient granularity to allow tracking of local processes.
- Set targets, develop report format, and allocate responsibility for responding to observed variance.

(7) ESTABLISH BEHAVIORAL INFLUENCES

- Develop collective agreements on preferred behaviors (e.g., credos, compacts).
- Identify financial or nonfinancial rewards for better or improved performance.

With this understanding of the external environment, subsequent design decisions relate to the internal configuration of the operating system. The next set of decisions relates to the design of the care process and supporting business processes. Clarity about the care process allows the work, and then workforce requirements, to be defined. Essential skills can be determined and tasks and decision rights allocated. Finally, choices of the other control levers can be made: what supporting technology to deploy; where to site care and how to configure the physical space; what to measure, how to report variation, and where to set targets; and what other influences on clinician and nonclinician behavior to employ.

Unfortunately, the sequence of operating system design and management choices outlined in Box 1 is contrary to the way many healthcare organizations approach planning for change. More often than not a system's components are developed in isolation from one another. Space is often built before the model of care and the systems that will support it are designed. Few organizations integrate care process design, measurement and reporting development, target selection, work design, recruitment, training, and technology acquisition processes. Corporate functions are often treated as independent from each other and from the clinical divisions.

Finally, in using the levers to design and control their operating system, leaders need to be alert to the wider context in which it is placed. How patients enter the operating system, and where they go after that operating system's work is done, will influence some of the design decisions outlined in Box 1. Clinicians tend to have little insight into the work of those professionals and organizations providing important components of a patient's care upstream and downstream in the longer value chain of which their local operating system is a part. However, the more influence that can be exercised over a system's inputs, and the behavior of the next stage in the longer process, the easier it is to gain control over the local system. Japanese car manufacturers famously work closely with their suppliers to ensure that an assembly plant's inputs arrive in the exact form and sequence needed to fit into its production line. Yet most care delivery organizations treat arriving patients as a random draw from a heterogeneous population of patients and referrers. An exception to this is the evolving approach to population health with its emphasis on proactive case finding, outreach, and community networks. This understanding of an operating system's wider context is sometimes termed "enterprise thinking" and might best be summarized as "know thyself, understand others."

LEVERS OF OPERATIONAL CONTROL: IMPLICATIONS FOR ACTION

Experience has shown that to improve outcomes and ensure patient value it is not enough to create a "best practice protocol." Care pathways and clinical protocols only achieve their full potential in practice when they are supported by well-designed operating systems. Operating systems shape the behavior of the many different types of caregiver and are the mechanism that makes the connection between medical and nursing science and patient outcomes. Effective operating systems are ones that meet the following criteria:

- The elements are well chosen with respect to the clinical condition and the type of care being delivered.
- All the elements "line up" so that they are mutually reinforcing and supportive of each other.
- Collectively the elements provide care that meets patients' needs and values.

In many delivery organizations the operating system or systems have not been explicitly designed, but rather have developed over many decades as staff, technology, and buildings have been recruited, acquired, and funded. Ensuring that future systems more reliably deliver higher quality care of the kind patients want requires the redesign of a multitude of local systems. Operating system change is within the power and capability of leaders in the middle of delivery organizations who are working close to the front line of care. Some of the most effective tools are in their hands, and they can bring about substantial positive change by examining, evaluating, and reforming their local operating systems one at a time.

In sum, the following key actions use the four levers to set the stage for improving patient value and the match between system and care:

1. Examine each of the four levers of operational control to determine whether the option currently employed is best suited for the patient subpopulation and mode of care for which it is intended.
2. Select alternative levers of control as appropriate.
3. Test the internal alignment of the four levers and make any appropriate changes.
4. Check that, as a whole, the operating system is capable of delivering the value and outcomes the patients it serves want and expect.

Of course, most delivery organizations serve many subpopulations. Chapter 5 discusses issues related to designing and managing multiple operating systems at the same time.

CHAPTER 5

Multi-Operating System Models

C ompanies building operating systems to deliver value to their customers have one great advantage denied most healthcare delivery organizations. They can restrict the range of services they provide or products they make. They are at liberty to segment the customer population any way they wish and thus avoid the problem of customer diversity. Should they choose, they can simply not provide services to whole groups of potential customers. For instance, low-cost airlines tend not to cater for business travelers. They largely offer cheap, short, point-to-point flights to second-tier airports—not what the business traveler needs—and optimize their operating systems to this end. Product-process match is easier to achieve when you are free to restrict your range of products. This is, after all, the essence of operational focus. Companies typically select a segment of a larger market and make their business there.

Healthcare has no such luxury. The vast majority of delivery organizations provide care to any patient who needs it and turn no one away. On the contrary, clinicians tend to frown on "cherry picking" by healthcare providers: for example, when for-profit surgical hospitals provide care for low-risk patients (i.e., ASA 1 and 2*) but refer more complex patients elsewhere. Most healthcare delivery organizations provide care for a diverse population.

---

* The American Society of Anesthesiologists physical rating system class 1 (healthy) and class 2 (mild systemic disease only).

The clue is in the names: community medical center, district general hospital, general practitioner. But it is difficult to create one operating system aligned to the needs of a very heterogeneous group of patients. How then may we exploit the benefits of a tighter match between the organization design and the type of care, yet at the same time serve the needs of a heterogeneous population? How can we provide care to whole regions yet not unnecessarily duplicate neighboring services? How can we have focus in the face of patient diversity? Can we have our cake and eat it too?

Multi-operating system models offer a way to address this dilemma: by running more than one operating system in parallel, each optimized separately for a different subset of the overall patient population or for a different dimension of value in a longer patient pathway, but connected and managed as a single system. When applied to a larger geography, this is the model of the new generation of integrated regional networks. Applied within an individual institution this is often called the "hospital-within-a-hospital" or "clinic-within-a-clinic" model. Both at the regional and local levels this design can provide the benefits of focused operations while meeting the needs of population diversity.

REGIONAL MULTI-OPERATING SYSTEM MODELS

For much of the twentieth century the stand-alone multiservices hospital was the central organizing construct of regional or national healthcare systems. Consistent with the late nineteenth-century notion of the hospital as the "doctor's workshop," institutional managers focused on aggregating the radiology, laboratory, and nursing resources the new scientific medicine required and optimizing their capacity utilization: the classic job shop. Each stand-alone hospital was configured and managed independently to achieve its own unique set of goals and serve the particular needs of its patients and doctors.

However, in response to pressure to improve quality and control costs, managers later in the twentieth century shifted their attention from managing the availability of the resources that medical work (and doctors) demanded to managing the care process itself. They defined disease-specific care processes and controlled them through process measurement, targets, and financial incentives. More recently, management focus has shifted yet again: this time to population-based care. In contrast to the intrainstitutional focus of previous eras, population health* demands a cross-organizational perspective. The activities of the multiple organizations providing inpatient, primary, community, and social care must be coordinated and unified so that patients can flow smoothly through a regional system of complementary operating systems capable of providing proactive care for an entire population.

What makes implementing population health so challenging is the fact that organizations that were once fiercely independent must now behave in a completely new way. Stand-alone institutions previously provided all or some key portions of the patient's care often without reference to the referring organization or the organization that subsequently received the patient and provided care at the next stage of the patient's journey. Now organizations delivering population health must find ways to partner and collaborate, sometimes resulting in the transfer of patient volume and revenue from one to another and always needing the transfer of data. Although specific organizational arrangements vary, this usually means creating some form of regional network: a multioperating system model at a regional level.

---

* Population health is commonly defined as "the health outcomes of a group of individuals, including the distribution of such outcomes within the group." (Kindig D, Stoddart G. What is population health? *Am J Pub Health.* 2003;93[3]:380–383.)

PREVIOUS EXPERIENCE WITH NETWORKS

Like other job shop models, national and regional delivery systems based on stand-alone general hospitals have the advantage of being highly flexible: able to address the needs of whole populations and local communities and able to respond to changes in patient preferences, medical technology, and the emergence of novel diseases. But they are also costly. They can result in service and resource duplication, and in some cases they serve such a small population that their subspecialist services are below the critical volumes needed for good outcomes.

Consequently, governments, payers, and delivery organizations have long been interested in networks. In the United States organizations voluntarily joined into integrated delivery networks (IDNs), and in the United Kingdom regional reconfiguration was centrally orchestrated. Governments and payers have seen networks primarily as a mechanism for reducing cost through the reduction of duplication and improving quality through the consolidation of volume at fewer sites. Institutions joining a group see another advantage in consolidation. As a larger group they can pool purchasing and get lower prices for essential goods and services. They can potentially spread the benefits of a particularly advantageous supplier contract from one member to all, fully staff a service localized to one institution when there are staff shortages in the region as a whole, and reduce cost by doing basic tasks—such as financial management, human resources, materials management—once for all.[1] Economies of scale should make each more efficient.

Unfortunately, institutions also saw one other advantage of IDNs: monopoly prices. In the United States organizational mergers and network formation made health care more expensive, not less. Consolidation increased their power in the local market not just to get lower prices for inputs but also to capture more referrals and command higher prices for their services. Especially when the partner organizations are in close proximity, prices tend to be higher after a merger.[2] Overall, the experience on both sides of the Atlantic is that such mergers tend to underperform, typically not living up to expectations.

Beyond the purported economic benefits of consolidation and scale, another reason favors network formation. Dividing the work of care among a group of network members allows each to develop their own centers of expertise, different from those at the other member institutions. A network made up of nonoverlapping, complementary centers of excellence ought to enable each member institution to achieve the benefits of focused operations, while the network as a whole provides full service to the entire population.

However, although the relationship between volume and outcome is well known, it is also imperfect. The quality benefits of aggregation do not increase linearly with increasing volume but attenuate at higher volumes.[3] Beyond some threshold level—which varies by procedure and disease—bigger is not necessarily better. Furthermore, variation in outcome persists among high-volume surgeons, suggesting many other factors are at play including patient selection, differences in preoperative, operative, and postoperative care, and the skill of individuals and teams.[4] Centralizing volume at one site may precipitate deterioration in performance with the increase in workload. Consolidating cases and regionalizing services may not be sufficient to improve clinical performance; something else must be done to realize the benefits of volume.

MAKING A NETWORK WORK

Networks established to support population health typically comprise three related and interacting networks: a network made

Figure 5.1. The structure of a network for population health

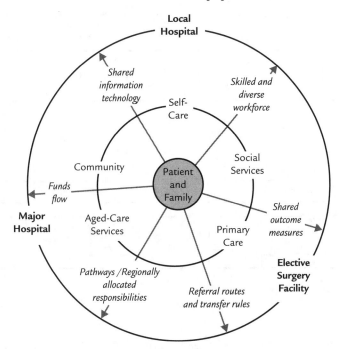

up of the patient and their family and social circle; a network of community and primary services supporting patients in their homes; and a network of hospital services (often represented as concentric circles, as in Figure 5.1). Most of the focus tends to be on the development of the outer ring, the hospital network, doubtless because the hospital is where the expensive resources are concentrated and therefore where most of the gain from reducing duplication might be found. Yet the bulk of care is provided in the inner two rings, and these are particularly important because they have a key role in shaping the demand for hospital services, which are becoming increasingly overburdened as the population ages. In England primary practitioners provide over 300 million consultations compared to 23 million emergency department visits, and a year's worth of primary healthcare costs per patient

Figure 5.2. Joining organizations into a network

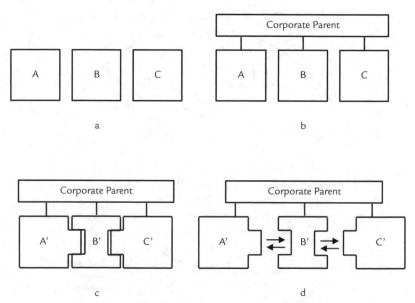

less than two emergency department attendances, yet the country spends less on primary care than on hospital outpatients.[5]

Not surprisingly, when mergers or regional networks are initially being established, senior management tends to concentrate on the upper echelons of the hospital organizations. The conventional approach is to unify member organizations under some form of corporate parent (going from a to b in Figure 5.2). Structures for the corporate parent vary around the world depending on local regulation: for example, a "holding company" with its own board sitting above the institutional boards that are responsible for the local governance of each member organization in the United States, and in the United Kingdom a "committee in common" made up of a board member or two from each institution. These models usually maintain the institutions' operational and clinical independence and leave their clinical services largely unchanged beyond perhaps closing some services that are obviously duplicative. Although unifying corporate functions such as finances, purchasing, and human resources allows some economies of scale for these "back office" operations, it does not necessarily advantage patients or support a population health approach.

Any system is made up of its components and the interactions among them, and the connections between them are as important as the individual components. If these entities are in fact to serve the needs of population health, then the radiating lines of Figure 5.1, representing the connections between the participating organizations and supporting resources, need equal managerial attention. These parts of the network bind its main components together.

Successful system development requires more than placing separate organizations into a group and unifying their corporate functions. Individual, previously independent institutions grouped into a network are not usually set up to collaborate. Each institution in Figure 5.1 has its own mission, revenue source, governance model, and uniquely configured operating system designed to help it execute that mission. Each defines patient value differently and focuses on and optimizes different aspects of performance. Creating a network of complementary centers of excellence that exploits unique institutional strengths and reduces unnecessary duplication requires some internal redesign at each member organization as well as specific design of their new interactions.

Each organization must evolve to be able to contribute to the strategy of the wider network. Some may need to give up entire services, which are transferred to another member of the network. Others may need to create new services or modify old ones so as to provide an element of patients' overall care in a particular location. Thus, institution A becomes A′, B becomes B′, and so on (Figure 5.2c). Building a network is a process of global unification but also local modification.

Finally, a clinical network ultimately creates additional patient value by allowing patients, clinical work, staff, information, and knowledge and expertise to flow smoothly across a set of institutions, each of which is uniquely configured to play its part in a larger whole. It is not sufficient to revise the service structures of each member of the network: the relationships and interactions among members also must also be revised (represented by the arrows in Figure 5.2d). Healthcare institutions do not typically plan the interactions between units and services in any great detail, although this is common practice in manufacturing settings. To do so in healthcare would mean that the clinical rules that govern a patient's journey through a complex system—including the patient pathways, clinical protocols, patient referral and transfer criteria, and repatriation arrangements—all have to be defined or revised. So too do the work rules, such as work allocation, on-call rosters, and clinical support services agreements. Without active management of interinstitutional flow, the network is nothing more than a group of loosely connected care organizations providing the same kind of fragmented care that patients experience currently.

Negotiating these relationships can be controversial, and failure to reach agreement on seemingly simple issues can threaten the success of the network as a whole. For instance, evolving cancer networks often find it challenging to resolve the simple question of who should provide out-of-hours care for patients suffering complications of chemotherapy. If the treatment is planned in one institution in the network, and the chemotherapy delivered by another, then which staff are on call for febrile neutropenia patients? Would staff have to travel to the other site to see a patient?

Making a network work therefore requires four additional bodies of managerial work. The first is to allocate clinical responsibilities among the members of the network. Member institutions need to define which site or service will do what. Which services, parts of a value chain, or care for a subpopulation will be delivered at one site? Which should be delivered at more than one, or at all sites? What core capabilities must each site maintain? These design choices typically must be made service-by-service and subpopulation-by-subpopulation.

The second is to design the connections between the organizations in the network. What are to be the rules governing their interactions? This means developing the transfer rules, clinical protocols, standard procedures, and repatriation agreements that govern how patients, information, and expertise will flow backward and forward across the system. Clinicians need to agree on such issues as the circumstances under which a patient is transferred from one institution to another and from inpatient to community and primary care, when ambulances should or should not bypass a nearby care delivery site, and what criteria define discharge readiness from any particular site of care.

Third, each institution and its local unit-level operating systems must be redesigned to ensure that they are set up to deliver the component of patient value for which they have been allocated network responsibility. Where appropriate, individual units or organizations must take on a larger volume of work and provide some elements of care for the whole regional population on behalf of all the other members of the group.

Finally, access to shared resources has to be negotiated by defining the routines for the management of exceptions or complications, assigning rosters and on-call arrangements, allocating admission rights and accreditation for staff who may work on more than one site (along with the all-important parking rights), agreeing on the distribution of finances, and crafting service agreements that define the use of shared clinical support services such as laboratory and radiology. In effect this requires deciding for which issues decision authority is to remain at the site and for which it will be vested in the group. Each network has to answer these questions about internal structure and function for itself because the answers will depend on the local health needs and the distribution of capabilities, resources, and political power in its region.

Such questions also have to be addressed by each clinical service. Each needs to consider both the clinical issues relevant to the disease groups or subpopulations for which it provides care and the local availability of specialized resources. A network's regional configuration of its stroke service will necessarily differ from its approach to rare cancers, well-child care, or the acute management of fractured neck of femur in frail elderly patients. Thus, although a network's creation, finances, and governance structure are typically the domain of the involved organizations' senior leaders, it is the clinical and administrative leaders in the middle who actually make the care model function. They know the local conditions, staff capabilities, and clinical requirements that any new system configuration must satisfy. The tasks described largely involve these mid-level leaders across the network coming to consensus about the future distribution of clinical work. At its heart, health transformation is a negotiated agreement among respectful colleagues regarding who is going to do what, where, and when.

LOCAL MULTI-OPERATING SYSTEM MODELS

Similar design considerations apply to multi-operating system models at the local level. These models usually take one of two forms: carving out a disease or risk group into a separate operating system or dividing the population within a disease or risk group into two or more subgroups, each cared for within a different operating system. There are many examples of the former: breast centers, back pain centers, or headache centers within a general hospital or health system (sometimes called "integrated practice units") or a separate dedicated elective surgical service or institution. The latter is also common: a separate area for "minors" in an emergency department or separate pathways, protocols, and clinics for patients with mild, moderate, and severe cases of a disease. In some cases the two operating systems occupy the same physical space (as in a clinic-within-a-clinic, or a few beds in a ward reserved for patients receiving a different type of care), and in others they may be set up in separate buildings or campuses.

All such models aim for the same thing: achieve focus in the face of diversity by uniquely matching an operating system to each key subpopulation with meaningfully different care needs. Each component operating system applies the four levers of control differently, and each is both internally and externally aligned to meet the special needs of its target subpopulation. Even though each component operating system is focused on a more narrowly defined subpopulation, the multi-operating system model as a whole is designed and managed as one system to serve the entire population (Figure 5.3).

Many of the design and management issues critical to the functioning of a regional network also apply in the case of local multi-operating system models such as a hospital-within-a-hospital or a clinic-within-a-clinic. In particular, three issues must be addressed to optimize this approach: initially sorting patients into the correct operating system, transferring patients from one operating system to another should the need arise, and managing the demands different operating systems place on the same shared resources.

Figure 5.3. Multi-operating system model

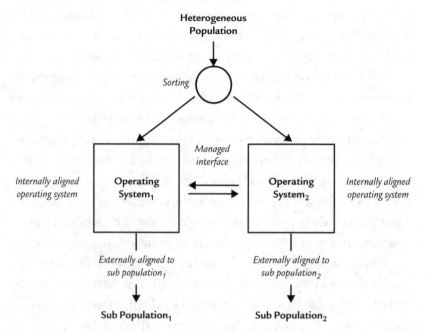

Sorting

Given that the primary purpose of a multi-operating system model is to optimize the match between the patient and the system, sorting patients and directing them to the appropriate operating system or site is critical. This is for two reasons. First and most important, failure to correctly match the patient and operating system has the potential to be, at best, inefficient or, at worst, unsafe. Patients would be receiving care in an operating system wholly unsuited to their needs. Second, the more homogeneous the incoming population, the easier it is to design and manage a smoothly functioning operating system.

Broadly speaking, two approaches are available for sorting patients entering a care delivery organization: sorting before the patient arrives to the site of care or sorting on arrival. In practice, sorting patients before they arrive has always been challenging. Public health and marketing campaigns can encourage patients to access the care system under particular circumstances or in particular ways. Examples include a British campaign to encourage patients with minor illnesses to seek care away from accident and emergency departments, and the FAST campaign (Face, Arm, Speech, Time), which aims to inform patients of the early signs of a stroke and what to do if one is suspected. These are relatively blunt instruments inasmuch as they must target the whole population to find the relevant subpopulation. More specific tactics include referral guidelines and disease-specific patient pathways for acute and elective conditions—now deployable through a smartphone app—that follow the patients from the community to an acute provider and back into the community and include criteria for specialist referral or inpatient admission. Although clinicians at the receiving unit often feel powerless to control patient arrival, they can exercise some, albeit modest, control over how their patients get there, either by working externally with their most frequent referrers and local community agencies, or internally to set up such services as referral hotlines.[6]

For most practitioners, sorting after arrival seems much more practical. The practice of triage in war or mass casualty situations is the most famous historic example. Emergency patients are sorted into three groups: those who are expected to live and those who are expected to die irrespective of the immediate care they receive and those for whom immediate emergency care is most likely to have a positive impact on the outcome.*

In nonemergency situations, sorting is often accomplished in a multidisciplinary team meeting such as a tumor board, paper

---

* In fact the origin of the word "triage" has nothing to do with "three"; it comes from the French "trier" meaning to sort or to separate.

round, or joint nurse-doctor consultation. Duke University Medical Center's heart failure clinic, which streamed less-complicated patients into a nurse practitioner–led clinic and more-complicated patients into their specialist cardiologist service, used an initial joint intake visit with a nurse practitioner and a cardiologist together as its sorting mechanism. An essential output of this meeting was the determination of in which clinic the patient would be treated.[7]

An alternative approach is to use an algorithm to sort patients. The Dartmouth-Hitchcock Center for Pain and Spine is an archetypical integrated practice unit. It is a separate operating system from the general hospital and its orthopedic department. Back pain patients are managed in a multidisciplinary service that brings together "surgeons, medical specialists in functional restoration and pain management, mental health providers, occupational therapists, and physical therapists."[8] Within this center, patients are further streamed using a detailed intake questionnaire and computerized shared decision-making tool into one group likely to benefit from surgery and one not. Once streamed, each patient enters the operating system best matched to his or her disease, needs, and personal preferences: the former focused on surgery and the latter on physiotherapy.

In these examples sorting is with respect to patient pathways and operating systems that have been previously established. The algorithms used by Utah's Intermountain Healthcare sort patient groups into mild, moderate, and severe, each directed to different clinical teams and treatment protocols. Other bases of streaming include by elective versus emergent, with and without complications and comorbidities, and high versus low variability. Typically, delivery organizations sort patients into two or, at most, three tiers.

Transfer

A key underlying assumption of these models is that each patient will be accurately assigned to the optimal operating system. However, patients will always need to move from one operating system to another, either because the initial sorting was incorrect or because something has changed in the patient's condition during the course of care. Patients in acute care settings are constantly being escalated and de-escalated from the ward to the intensive care unit and then back to transitional care and the ward. Although the operating systems are designed to overlap as little as possible, the boundaries between them must be porous. To achieve operational focus while simultaneously meeting the diverse needs of a heterogeneous population, the interface between the component operating systems must be actively managed and the whole system treated as one. Otherwise the model simply increases fragmentation of care.*

If an error has been made or the clinical situation has changed, the patient will be in an operating system that is no longer appropriate. Any multi-operating system model needs a system for re-sorting: to identify patients no longer in the best setting and initiate transfer to an alternative operating system better suited for their health needs. Patients needing to be re-sorted can be identified in a number of ways, some programmed into the formal routines of care and others less formal. Formal methods include sentinel events that trigger transfer, criteria for transfer embedded in care pathways and protocols, and a scheduled patient review for the purpose of assessing whether each patient is still being cared for in the right operating system. If the patient's

---

* Primary and hospital care are, in effect, two operating systems that run in parallel. Typically, however, the interface between them is not actively managed and they are not treated as a single system.

clinical condition changes in a prespecified way, then they are transferred into a new operating system. A unit culture that supports speaking up and leaders who are present and approachable help empower any and all staff members to informally initiate a transfer when, in their clinical judgment, the patient is no longer in the right care setting.

Shared Services

The third important design and management issue relates to the use of shared resources in a system made up of multiple focused operating systems.[9] If a particular operating system provides care for a relatively small volume of patients, it may make little sense to resource it with full-time staff and dedicated technology and space. Instead, these are usually drawn from a shared pool of centralized staff and equipment. However, multiple operating systems can make competing demands on these same resources such that the sum of the demand from all the operating systems is greater than the centralized resource can deliver. Moreover, because each operating system has by design its own structure and processes, the central services may be called upon to deliver very different procedures, resources, and services for each system, thereby increasing the work and strain they feel. Such issues must be negotiated if multiple operating systems are to flourish side by side.

These tensions commonly arise in several predictable areas. One is information systems. Although each operating system may demand a uniquely configured database, IT departments are typically reluctant to support multiple bespoke systems. Another is radiology. Each operating system may design a unique set and sequence of investigations to meet the needs of its subpopulation, but the aggregate demand on radiology from multiple operating systems may be impossible to schedule with its currently available resources. Others are the use of specialist consultations and outpatient appointments, or the use of specialized areas such as operating rooms. In practice, these considerations usually mean each operating system has to make some design compromises to account for the needs of the centralized support departments. And senior institutional leaders and leaders of the centralized services have to set the rules for sharing, adjudicate competing demands, and make some difficult prioritization decisions—usually favoring standardization over local flexibility. For example, in one U.S. institution an orthopedic surgeon established a focused operating system for elective knee replacement capable of doing 10 to 12 procedures per day.[10] His system depended on having two operating rooms side by side, dedicated anesthetic and nursing teams, an anesthetic induction room, and preferential access to central sterile supply staff (who had to give priority to sterilizing his equipment to enable it to be reused multiple times on an operating day). Not surprisingly, his colleagues were resentful, and it fell to the hospital CEO to manage the intradepartmental tensions and restrict the demands he could place on shared resources to two operating days per week.

Hence, although it may be advantageous to create multiple operating systems to better meet the needs of key patient subpopulations, it is not without practical and political challenges. Nonetheless, several situations can justify creating a separate operating system for a particular patient subpopulation.

As already noted, conditions in which the care required is integral but the disease itself is modular lend themselves to an integrated practice unit. Specially configured, condition-focused operating systems are increasingly seen in these diseases. Headache centers, which integrate the work of neurologists, psychiatrists, psychologists, pain specialists, and physical therapists, or spine centers with orthopedic surgeons, physical therapists, mental health professionals, and pain specialists (such as at Dartmouth-Hitchcock) are examples of specific operating systems that target such conditions.* The integrated practice unit structure helps improve patient outcome by facilitating the active management of interdependencies between professionals in a diverse care team. In these examples, the diseases treated or procedures undertaken tend to be relatively isolated inasmuch as patients (at that moment) often need care for the index condition (breast or spine disease, headaches, or an elective procedure) but little else.

High patient volume may justify streaming patients into clinically meaningful subgroups and developing an operating system specifically for each subgroup. Patients are often separated into groups with simple or complex conditions, or into subgroups with mild, moderate, and severe diseases. This is the model used at the Duke heart failure clinic: multiple small-scale operating systems, each falling short of an independent integrated practice unit, managed in the context of the general purposes operating system of the general hospital. When Intermountain applied criteria of volume, health risk, and variability to more than 1,400 clinical "work processes," it found that just 104 processes accounted for 95 percent of care delivery.[11] It divided many of these larger groups into mild, moderate, and severe subgroups and created an operating system for each.

However, every disease should not necessarily have its own specific operating system. Not all conditions lend themselves to an integrated practice unit structure, and for many patients the job shop model of the general hospital or general practice is still the most effective way to deliver care. But there are many circumstances in which consideration should be given to developing a specially configured local operating system to create a better match between the way in which care resources are deployed and the unique needs of the particular patient subpopulation.

---

* Other examples include breast centers and joint replacement centers.

MULTI-OPERATING SYSTEM MODELS: IMPLICATION FOR ACTION

In the same way that design decisions relating to the levers of control can be sequenced when designing a new operating system (see Chapter 4), creating a new network that exploits the different capabilities of the member organizations yet delivers seamless care requires making a set of related design decisions in which each decision builds on the previous ones. Some developing networks have used a deliberate process to work their way through these design issues in an orderly sequence. The following is an example of such a sequence:

1. **Frame the goals.** Begin by framing the case for, and the goals of, a regional service reconfiguration or network development. As discussed previously, clinicians are highly suspicious of cost containment as a rationale for major (and sometimes even minor) system change. They and the affected communities are much more sympathetic to a goal focused on patient benefit. Network configuration is as much a political as a technical issue.

2. **Establish design principles.** Next establish a set of principles and values that will govern the design of the network and be a decision rule that helps make the difficult resource allocation and trade-off decisions that will be needed. These design principles relate to the final form of the system. Examples of such high-level principles include (1) care delivered close to home whenever possible, (2) care only centralized, thus obliging patients to travel, where this delivers higher quality, and (3) same care delivered everywhere no matter where and how a patient enters the network (i.e., standard universal practices).

3. **Identify fixed points.** Identify those services for which relocation to another point in the wider network would be impractical or unsafe. Examples of such services are those with special equipment or those with purpose-built facilities, such as a radiotherapy service or a gamma knife.

4. **Define essential interdependencies.** Identifying the "fixed points" helps determine which services should be co-located with others for clinical reasons: for example, co-locating the burns and the plastic surgery services, or vascular surgery with interventional radiology and cardiac surgery.

5. **Identify essential services.** Identify which services should be available on all sites. Common examples include emergency or urgent care departments, frail elderly and acute medicine services, and emergency surgery. Such an analysis can be completed once for in-hours services and again for out-of-hours services.

6. **Agree on site-specific service reallocation.** Based on the previous assessments consider which services could be centralized and consolidated on one or a few sites because this benefits patients, and therefore which services should move elsewhere.

7. **Define patient pathways.** Design the disease-specific (e.g., stroke) and disease-nonspecific (e.g., emergency pediatrics) patient pathways that govern the flow of patients through the network, define what part of care (which aspect of patient value) is delivered where, and specify the clinical rules that shape cross-service patient flow.

8. **Redesign local operating systems.** Redesign the local site-specific operating systems that deliver the compo-

nent of care at each site such that each is now configured to play its role in the wider network.

9. **Establish ongoing management responsibilities.** Define a clinical governance model that determines how the new system can be managed and improved over the longer term.

As already noted, many of the design decisions outlined here have the potential to be highly controversial, especially if they have significant implications for the local delivery of services to specific communities or the work life of high-profile clinicians. For this reason, establishing a clear decision process and being transparent at all stages, sharing data, and running open public consultations are essential to any network design process.

Condition-specific networks require similar design decisions. Four key areas require substantial leadership and managerial work to create a functioning network. Figure 5.4 shows an example for the development of a regional stroke network:

1. **Mechanisms of unification:** What is the overarching goal that will unify the actions of the component organizations or units in the network? Having a clear goal for the network as a whole serves as the basis for developing a set of metrics that allow tracking of both system and individual institution performance, and potentially as a mechanism of distributing revenue across the system. Possibilities for the latter include a shared bottom line among the members of the system or an agreement about revenue sharing and transfer payments if member organizations are to remain financially independent.

2. **Input control:** This mechanism ensures that patients are directed correctly as they enter the system. Examples

Figure 5.4. Components of a stroke network (numbering relates to the issues discussed below)

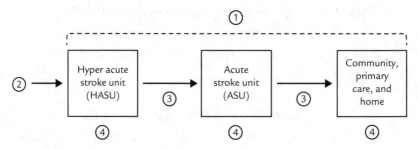

of this are public health campaigns to encourage patients to seek help early, and ambulance protocols to enable appropriate direction of patients.

3. **Transfer rules:** These rules define when patients are transferred and repatriated and establish the standard set of transfer data and information to accompany the patient as he or she moves through the system. Such rules may be formal and programmed or informal. Examples of these include real-time communication between staff at the hyperacute stroke unit (HASU) and the acute stroke unit (ASU), joint staff meetings to ensure that staff at each site are appraised of what each other is doing (how each contributes to the longer value chain), service-level agreements between the units to specify roles and responsibilities, and outreach into the community (community beds, primary care, and home care) to ensure a smooth and supported return home.

4. **Operating system redesign:** The operating system at each site must be specifically configured for the care delivered there. This includes a clear value proposition for each site and the configuration of its resources to deliver this value, protocols for standard care, internal flow rules and transfer criteria, and staffing allocation.

It is particularly important to make sure that the ASU and the community and home services receive adequate investment required to make them two centers of excellence in their own rights (and not just the "poor cousin" of the high-technology HASU).

Implementing a multi-operating system model that targets patient subpopulations and disease subgroups within a local organization requires other actions. As in a network, each focused operating system must be designed to be fit for its particular purpose and the part it is to play in the greater whole. This means, for example, configuring a nurse-led clinic with different resources and clinical routines from those of a doctor-led clinic. Beyond this three other aspects must be planned and managed so that the multiple focused local operating systems act in unison as a single system:

1. **Sorting:** Establishing the mechanisms by which a heterogeneous group will be accurately divided into more homogeneous subgroups
2. **Re-sorting:** Defining formal and informal mechanisms of transferring patients from one focused operating system to another should clinical circumstances change
3. **Interaction management:** Defining rules of engagement and the relationships between individual focused operating systems and between them and the provider of centralized resources

The previous chapters focused on the design decisions required to ensure that an operating system is configured to deliver its intended value. But a good design only achieves its goal if it is effectively implemented. The following section considers the challenges faced by leaders aiming to bring about change.

PART THREE

Implementing New Systems in Existing Organizations

CHAPTER 6

Leading Change in a Clinical Environment

The best-designed systems in the world will fail to effect change if they cannot be implemented. But implementing change in healthcare is no simple undertaking: it is complicated by the need to change clinicians' and patients' behavior. A redesigned operating system usually requires that the individuals doing the work do something differently voluntarily. It is not enough to simply present an improved operating system as a fait accompli to a group of highly trained, independent-minded professionals. A successful change program usually requires involving staff in the redesign process and then leading them through a process of change.

Healthcare delivery organizations responding to cost and quality pressures tend to concentrate their change efforts on the lowest or highest echelons of the institution, with less devoted to the middle. Change is as often done *to* the clinical community as *by* the clinical community. Efforts focused at the lowest level aim to change the behavior of individual professionals, either indirectly through financial incentives for behavior change such as risk sharing and pay-for-quality physician contracts, or directly with rules-based computer order entry systems, often badged as "evidence-based medicine," to constrain professionals' practice choices.

Organizations driving behavior change from above often employ structural mechanisms that change the organizational context in which professionals deliver care. These leverage the operational principles described in the previous chapters: consolidation, focus, and specification to increase volume, limit the range of activities, and reduce variability. Examples of such structural approaches include *vertical integration* (co-locating multiple condition-specific medical, nursing, and therapy specialists in the same integrated practice unit), *horizontal integration* (bringing mental and physical services, or inpatient and community services together into the same organization), and *population segmentation* (in which separate organizations focus on a specific group such as the elderly or vulnerable children).[1]

The final common pathway of many of these approaches is a change in the local operating system. The care delivered to the patient only changes when a new care process is designed, team members work together differently, new technology is deployed, and more accurate metrics are tracked and managed. Leaders in the middle of the organization implementing new operating systems are ultimately trying to bring about change among their colleagues. Those close to the delivery of patient care are pivotal to implementing change: they understand the clinical needs of a given patient population, the implications of new science, the capabilities of specialized technology, and the local organizational dynamics in enough detail to shape the operational arrangements needed to support a new care model. But this is a famously independent group. How do you lead them through change?

TECHNICAL VERSUS ADAPTIVE CHANGE

The first step in any change effort is to understand the fundamental nature of the change you are trying to lead. The literature

Table 6.1. Technical versus adaptive change

	Technical change	**Adaptive change**
Nature of problem	Known, well characterized	Unknown, poorly understood
Nature of solution	Defined, previously used	Ill defined, uncertain
Source of solution	Expert or authority	People doing the work and encountering the problem
Change process	Blueprint-guided implementation	Discovery, learning, experimentation
Key focus of change	Processes and structures Often within the organization	Beliefs, mental models Often across organizational boundaries

on change makes an important distinction between a planned change that can be guided by a blueprint and executed to a schedule, and a change that is emergent and uncertain: technical versus adaptive changes, respectively (Table 6.1).[2] Many approaches to changing clinicians' behavior implicitly treat clinical practice change as a technical change. Technical problems, even when complex, have known solutions that can be implemented with currently available know-how and by applying well-established procedures and routines within the context of existing organizations and industry structures. If clinical behavior change were a technical problem, then once alerted to a change in medical knowledge, or provided with an incentive, the physician would be able to implement a new practice. With technical problems changing behavior is simply a matter of substituting one well-characterized clinical practice for another.

Adaptive changes, by contrast, are those for which a new model is not obvious and the change required is as much to attitudes, beliefs, and ways of working than to a specific operational procedure. They are a step into the unknown, where there is no well-characterized process or model to substitute in. Adaptive change demands learning: new theory and models, new ways of thinking and acting, new relationships, and new roles. Making adaptive changes requires transforming lifelong habits and deeply held beliefs. They can change the way we see ourselves and the purpose of our actions. As such, adaptive changes can engender feelings of loss, anxiety, or betrayal. Hence such changes are, in effect, "adaptive" in two ways: (1) they require an organization to adapt to changes in its operating environment by creating a new model or solution that responds to a problem that has not previously been confronted and (2) they require individuals to adapt to a new role and even sense of professional identity.

The distinction between technical and adaptive change echoes another one made by Harvard Business School's Amy Edmondson. In writing about organizational learning, Professor Edmondson has differentiated *organizing to execute* from *organizing to learn* (Table 6.2).[3] In the former, the leader provides answers and employees follow directions, guided by well-established routines designed in advance. The leader's goal is to ensure conformance to the specified process or routine. In contrast, the leader's role in organizing to learn is to create conditions that enable teams to work effectively together: sharing information, giving feedback, conducting experiments, identifying failure, rapidly planning and executing midcourse corrections, and ultimately creating new knowledge. Execution describes the rollout of a known solution, whereas learning connotes a series of experiments to find an unknown one.

Such distinctions are more than simply theoretical. The importance of distinguishing technical from adaptive change, and therefore organizing to execute or to learn, lies in the potential impact of misspecifying the nature of the behavior

Table 6.2. Organizing to execute versus organizing to learn

	Organizing to execute	Organizing to learn
Goal	Faithful execution of prespecified "best practice"	Figure out what is best for the patient
Nature of quality	Minimal variation and fidelity to original design	Best outcome for the patient
Nature of failure	Deviation from specification	Not meeting the patient's needs and values
Primary measures	Rate of process conformance	Outcome (including clinical and experiential outcomes)
Timing of learning	Before doing	While doing
Key focus of change	Processes	Beliefs, mental models, roles
Clinician's role	Do the specified task well (as an individual)	Work collaboratively to identify and execute the right tasks

change required, or the nature of the learning challenge, and therefore adopting a leadership approach and using a set of tools that are ill-suited for that change.

Misspecification can be costly. Behavior change interventions that assume a change is technical may fail if the change required is, in reality, adaptive. This situation is surprisingly common. Often what looks at first glance to be a simple change in a protocol or medical technology in fact requires redistribution of tasks or decision rights, changes in mental models about cause and effect, changes in the basic goals of care, or changes in working routines, interactions, or status relationships among members of a team. To bring about the behavior change required for the widespread adoption of alternative clinical practices or a new model of care might require more than simply providing staff with information.

Examples of misspecification abound. The case of minimally invasive cardiac surgery (MICS)—in which a heart procedure is undertaken without opening the chest—exemplifies the problem. MICS differs from conventional cardiac surgery in three important ways: the patient is placed on heart-lung bypass via the femoral artery and vein rather than directly from the aorta; the aorta is occluded from the inside using a balloon rather than from the outside with a clamp; and the procedure is conducted through small incisions using long-handled instruments and scopes rather than through a sternotomy. All three of these differences had been previously well described: orthopedic and general surgeons were already very familiar with minimally invasive surgery. What was innovative was putting them together into a truly new cardiac procedure.

However, many teams failed to successfully adopt MICS techniques because they treated them as a technical change and an execution challenge. They focused on the similarities with other recent innovations such as the use of long-handled instruments operated through a small surgical wound, as in the case of knee arthroscopy. They underestimated, or did not even notice, the impact on the operating room team's functioning that resulted from new information flows and the redistribution of roles and decision rights that the new technology necessitated. For example, whereas surgeons could previously visually assess the patient's cardiovascular status directly by feeling the heart and observing the surgical field, they were now dependent on pressure traces displayed on monitors more easily viewed and communicated by other members of the surgical team. In effect, some teams completely missed that the new technology was an adaptive change and a team learning challenge.[4]

New technology often does this: it wraps an adaptive change in a technical disguise. For instance, when CT scanners were first introduced, they precipitated a change in the social order of radiology departments. Relationships between the technicians and doctors were restructured when the radiologists' technical dominance with the old technology was displaced by the technicians' greater facility with the new.[5] When facing an adaptive change, the most successful teams, units, or organizations are those that frame the new technology adoption as a learning challenge and institute a set of routines that facilitate rapid experimentation and learning. The important implication is that leaders planning to help their colleagues through change of technology, clinical practice, or organization structure must therefore first determine the nature of that change and then adopt an appropriate approach to leading the change. Is it technical or adaptive?

This determination is particularly important because many of the changes currently occurring in healthcare delivery have the potential to be adaptive rather than technical in nature. As such, they can be deeply threatening to current clinical and administrative staff because they represent changes to prevailing mental models and ways of thinking, to comfortable social structures, roles, and routines, and to attitudes, beliefs, and lifelong habits. Adapting to new technologies, alternative models of care, and changing disease profiles could do this in the following ways:

- **New kind of teamwork:** Multidisciplinary teams combine not only different professional points of view but also staff, who have different organizational affiliations and responsibilities, and the patient with his or her own unique experience, knowledge, values, and preferences. Teamwork, previously achieved by allocating tasks among co-located staff operating in a clear status hierarchy, now demands sharing work among a group of equals on the basis of a common understanding of each different profession's models of cause and effect, definitions of value, and ways of working together to achieve a greater whole.

- **Enterprise responsibility:** Although individual staff members are typically trained to focus on their local decisions or tasks (and may prefer to do so), the new reality is that few actions are operationally independent. What you do for, with, or to a patient depends more and more on how the patient got to you and where she or he is going next. This demands a deep understanding of the wider care enterprise of which the individual's contribution is only a small part. It can confront individuals with trade-offs between local and global outcomes (e.g., do more now to avoid more later; do less here so more can be done elsewhere). In practice, this means the need to know yourself and understand others. New models of care force staff to develop a clearer understanding of the patient pathway upstream and downstream from their own professional contribution, in effect learning to replace their individualistic purview with a team and system perspective.

- **Data-based decision-making:** Real-time data from wearable monitors and patient registries inform clinical decision-making in exciting new ways, such as allowing earlier intervention or making therapy selections based on the recorded experiences and outcomes of hundreds or thousands of identical patients treated previously. However, increased availability of highly specified data also increases individual clinicians' visibility and accountability for both their own clinical decisions and the performance of the wider system that is the context for their individual professional practices.

Changes such as these are transforming the way professionals work as an individuals, the way they contribute to a team, and the way that team works with a wider system of care. New processes and flows, new decision and task responsibilities, new team members, and new measures and feedback loops are increasingly the norm. Technological advancement is forcing operating system redesign and new managerial roles and responsibilities on clinicians who previously eschewed them.

APPROACHES TO MAKING CHANGE

The way leaders understand the nature of a change will frame the way in which they design and execute the process for making that change. For decades, the prevailing model of the process of change was based on the work of psychologist Kurt Lewin, who described change as having three phases:[6]

1. **Unfreezing:** Overcoming the status quo and related inertia, dismantling existing habitual ways of doing things and their associated mental models
2. **Change:** A somewhat chaotic period during which the change is actually implemented
3. **Refreezing:** Hardwiring new mental models and ways of doing things by embedding them into new organizational routines and norms of behavior

In the mid-1980s McKinsey's influential change management work used a four-stage change model that was rooted in the same concepts: creating a sense of concern, developing a specific commitment to change, pushing for major change, and reinforcing and consolidating the new course.[7] And more recently

Kotter,[8] extending Lewin's model, published a widely used eight-stage change model:

1. Establishing a sense of urgency
2. Forming a powerful guiding coalition
3. Creating a vision
4. Communicating the vision
5. Empowering others to act on the vision
6. Planning for, and creating short-term wins
7. Consolidating improvements and producing still more change
8. Institutionalizing new approaches

All three of these approaches to change share a powerful underlying assumption: that we know what it is we want to change into. They frame change as a journey into the known, the implementation of a model for which we have a plan. They treat change as a one-time event, often one that can be forced through by a re-engineering project, an information system implementation, or by a set of financial incentives. Formal change management approaches, such as Kotter's eight stages or the ADKAR model (awareness, desire, knowledge, ability, and reinforcement), often focus on helping individuals come to terms with the new, and resistance to change is sometimes framed in terms of the classic stages of grief. And, of course, these models represent change as a technical, rather than an adaptive, problem.

Unfortunately, health system change in the current era has been anything but a journey into familiar territory. Too many things are changing at once—disease profiles, patient expectations, national finances, political climates, scientific understanding, and technological capabilities—for this to be the case. Change in healthcare is more likely to be a continuing process as systems constantly evolve in response to new understandings and new technologies, so change itself becomes less of an event and more of an abiding organizational routine. Edmondson, among others, has articulated an alternative perspective—change as a learning journey for teams, comprising a series of experiments, with each building on the results of the former.[9]

When change is a planned implementation, the kinds of leadership behavior that clinicians have often honed on the ward and in the clinic and operating room are highly relevant. Leaders articulate the goal and the necessary work to get there, they model the new preferred behaviors, they distribute roles and responsibilities to subordinates, set targets, and they hold staff accountable for compliance (some call this the "pace-setting" leadership style[10]).

But if change is a team learning journey to a less well-characterized destination, a different style altogether is required. Leading adaptive change—a change in mental models, self-concepts, interactions, and roles—means establishing goals and principles of design and interaction and orchestrating a team of content experts, each of whom is likely to be more skillful in his or her field than the leader will ever be, as they work together to develop a unifying purpose and trial new models likely to achieve it. Leading a process of experimentation means encouraging and modeling relationships, interdisciplinary respect, open communication and self-criticism, and tolerating failure to the point of even welcoming productive failures: not quite issuing instructions in an operating room or punishing noncompliance with the protocol.

Hence clinical change leaders must not only correctly diagnose the nature of any planned change but also correctly match the change process and their leadership approach.

WHAT DO WE MEAN BY LEADERSHIP?

But what do we mean by leadership in this context? The various definitions of leadership share some common features. That widely used in the UK's National Health Service—"the art of motivating a group of people to achieve a common goal"[11]—demonstrates these principles:

- **Achieving a goal requires a group.** Almost axiomatically, leadership exists in relation to collective action. It would not be needed were it not for the fact that achieving a desired outcome depends on others. Put simply, if you could do it all yourself, you would not need to lead.
- **The goal is shared.** Similarly, the members of the group acting interdependently must share a common goal. Should the collective action achieve several goals, not all members of the group need to aspire to the same one, but each must believe that working together increases the likelihood of achieving the goal about which they care.
- **Leaders accept personal accountability.** Leaders share a sense of personal accountability for others' actions and for achieving this shared goal.

These features describe well the leadership of an operating room or cardiac arrest team that executes a familiar and standard procedure. In particular, it takes a leader to help shape a shared goal that can guide the work of the different professionals making up a care team. The different professions represented in a multidisciplinary team—such as nursing, medicine, and social work—each trained its members to optimize different goals. Of course, this is by design. The work to prevent, cure, or ameliorate disease is so complex that it has been subdivided among specialists. But this does mean that clinical teams coming together transiently to address the complex health needs of an individual patient—what Edmonson calls "teaming"[12]—need a person or a process to help the group establish a shared purpose and individual team members to understand their roles in its achievement. This is, after all, one of the key functions that the surgical checklist serves in the operating room.

However, the work for those leading the kind of fundamental transformation being discussed here is also defined by uncertainty. Transformation rarely occurs in circumstances in which either purpose, or the mechanism for achieving it, is necessarily clear at the outset. Ron Heifetz's 1994 definition—"accepting responsibility to create conditions that enable others to achieve shared purpose in the face of uncertainty"[13]—captures this aspect of leadership work particularly well. Heifetz's definition also emphasizes achieving an outcome through the actions of others. But he further implies that assembling the team and assigning roles is not enough. The leader's work is to ensure that others will flourish and be able to do their best work under difficult conditions, something that requires a certain humility. The leader succeeds when others excel.*

In healthcare the "others" referred to in this definition are highly educated and independent professionals with a strong set of values and their own personal aspirations, who are more likely to endorse a shared purpose when it reflects those values and aspirations. Hence, in the setting of healthcare transformation, leadership might equally be considered as the art of helping individuals realize their personal professional ambitions through pursuit of a collective goal. This need for goal alignment is, of course, what is behind the "4 P" model of change in healthcare. An innovation is more likely to be adopted when patients, physicians, provider organizations, and payers all see advantage for themselves in it. This alignment—between the public and the personal—is not just important in the United States, where

---

* Heifetz's definition also implies that the conditions for change may not be ideal. To paraphrase Karl Marx, together we make our own history but rarely under circumstances of our choosing.

many doctors in effect run their own small, for-profit businesses. It applies anywhere where the delivery system must compete for the doctors' attention with academia or private practice.

Finally, all these definitions confirm that leadership is neither power nor authority. Clinicians often mistakenly believe that they must be in a named leadership position before they have the authority to lead change. They confuse leadership position with leadership, and a leader's "power" with power over others. Nothing could be further from clinicians' day-to-day reality of leadership. Clinicians, who have the trust and respect of their colleagues, and the support of their seniors, but none of the formal tools of authority, are often those who are the most effective leaders of change from the middle of a delivery organization.

CHALLENGES OF LEADING
IN A CLINICAL ENVIRONMENT

Unfortunately, correctly diagnosing the fundamental nature of a forthcoming change is only the start. Although in many ways leadership in healthcare is no different from leadership in any other domain, clinicians and managers who choose to lead change among their clinical colleagues face significant challenges, mostly related to the nature of the people being led and the setting in which they practice their professions.

Healthcare delivery organizations are examples of a well-recognized organizational form, the "professional bureaucracy," a term coined by the management theorist Henry Mintzberg.[14] The key workers in a professional bureaucracy are highly trained professionals who provide customized services to their clients. Often working in relative isolation, the professionals enjoy a high degree of autonomy: not only are they the ones doing the work but they also choose what work is to be done, and how. What co-ordination is necessary among professionals is achieved through the standardization of their skills (usually through the professionals' guild). Typically, a large support staff supports the professionals and the managers are usually professionals themselves (often elected by their colleagues, as in a law practice's managing partner).

Such structures have several advantages. They are well suited to complex and uncertain environments, such as the law and medicine, where standard operating procedures are hard to define. Professional bureaucracies deliver value by maximizing client-to-client flexibility and customization. Unfortunately, the strength that stems from autonomy and decentralized authority is also their weakness. These structures are prone to unwarranted variation, and their focus on individual professionals tends to preclude effective management of system interactions and cross boundary coordination. Leading change in these organizations can be painfully slow, made difficult by the need for consensus and the particular power accorded the veto. Peer oversight can be lacking and unprofessional behavior can be tolerated well beyond the point it would in other organizations.

Even as many aspects of care have become less uncertain, and unwarranted variation less acceptable, this organizational form persists: it is the core structure of the hospital and the primary practice and is the setting in which change must be led.

But the challenges of leading change among clinicians come not only from the organizational context. They are compounded by three important characteristics of clinicians themselves:

1. **Clinicians are trained scientists.** Although they may occasionally not appear to act like it, all clinicians have a scientific training and are well versed in the scientific method. They have been trained to be suspicious of unevidenced assertions and critical of the evidence collected by others. Clinicians will want to understand

the model of cause and effect in any proposed change and be given the opportunity to personally assess and publicly debate its plausibility. They are well aware of instances in which seemingly plausible therapeutic interventions were later proven to be ineffective or even harmful as, for example, in the case of autologous bone marrow transplant in metastatic breast cancer.[15] This predilection for evidence is the source of the counsel to "show them the data."[16]

2. **They have a strong pre-existing value set.** Unlike workers in many other industries, clinicians have all sworn an oath of professional dedication as part of their training. The commitment to patient well-being— putting the patient's needs ahead of your own—is a core value of medical, nursing, and therapy practice. As Lee notes, "We were taught to go to the hospital before dawn, stay until our patients were stable, focus on the needs of each patient before us, and not worry about costs."[17] Unlike other settings, in which the organization inducts its employees into its corporate values, healthcare delivery organizations align their values with those of their employees. And clashes occur when clinicians detect a misalignment, as in the case of externally mandated performance targets or a perceived trade-off between quality and revenue.

3. **Each individual has his or her own hopes and aspirations.** Like other science-based businesses, healthcare tends to attract ambitious people. Clinicians, especially doctors, will tend to look at the direction taken by the organization in which they practice in terms of their own professional growth and development. For many, the opportunity for research will be important. And for independent specialists—who are, in effect,

managing a one-employee profit center—such an assessment will be in economic as well as professional terms. Put more crassly, "What's in it for me?" Proposed changes that do not align with physicians' personal agenda are unlikely to gain much traction.

How can changes as profound as the ones described here be made to a visit-based professional expert model that is arguably hundreds (if not thousands) of years old? Who has the skill set to lead such a change among people such as these?

CLINICIANS AS LEADERS OF CHANGE

The characteristics of both the context of care and the individuals delivering it have led some to emphasize the importance of engaging clinicians in leading change. After all, clinicians work where patient needs and preferences intersect with technological feasibility, and they play a central role in manipulating the four levers of control. The ability to influence factors known to improve performance, such as better teamwork[18] and interprofessional communication,[19] standardized care processes,[20] and process compliance,[21] depends on being able to shape individual clinician behavior. And clinician behavior is central to the team-level[22] and organizational[23] culture that has been shown to have a positive impact on outcomes in both surgical and medical settings.

Don Berwick, chairman emeritus of the Institute for Healthcare Improvement, has argued that[24]

it is important to do things properly, according to facts, according to nature, the way nature works . . . that is what we are trained to do, we are trained to understand what the fact base is and we will make very naive decisions as a health service unless it is guided by distinct mastery of science.

He goes on to make the case for clinician engagement in redesign and change leadership on the grounds that

> [redesign] requires deep knowledge of the needs and the condition of the person you are serving. Well who has that? The people serving them, that's where the interface is. If we cut professionals out of the redesign process we lose all the knowledge . . . about what the nature of the proper helping interaction looks like. Pursuing change without the leadership of clinicians is extremely hazardous.

It is the clinicians who understand the nuances of medical science and current technological potential, the motivations and aspirations of their colleagues, and the local availability of resources such as funding, real estate, and staff, and the constraints of local regulation. They are best positioned to translate a constant stream of emerging medical insights and new technologies into revised models of care and redesigned services.

An evolving literature suggests that hospitals with a physician chief executive,[25] or clinically trained senior managers, perform better—either because they are more trusted by clinicians, are better able to communicate to them, or are better positioned to understand the medical aspects of the enterprise.[26] However, Berwick is talking about engaging clinician leadership much deeper in the organization, closer to the clinician-patient interface: the ward, the operating room, the clinic, or the office. Ultimately, it is at this level in the organization that change must be led if it is to have a positive impact on patient care: by leaders in the middle of delivery organizations and not necessarily in named leadership roles.

SPECIAL CHALLENGE FOR DOCTORS LEADING

Despite this case for greater clinician engagement in organizational leadership, doctors who do choose to lead in this environment face a particular hurdle as virtually everything they learned in their medical training works against them when they are called upon to lead change among their colleagues.

Medical training emphasizes personal excellence and individual responsibility. Lee observes that medical training taught doctors that "the only way to ensure quality was to adopt high personal standards for ourselves and then meet them,"[27] not a lesson necessarily consistent with the predominance of teams working in modern healthcare organizations or leadership of such autonomous individuals.

Furthermore, experience gained leading in a clinical environment (e.g., on the ward or in the clinic, consulting room, operating suite, or catheterization lab) often does not prepare clinicians for leading change in a wider and more complex organization. In fact, leadership responsibility in these constrained clinical environments can reinforce habits that are diametrically opposed to those needed for organizational change leadership (Table 6.3). The doctor is typically at the top of a very clear status hierarchy, and those leading in these settings risk getting the impression that leadership is simply a matter of knowing the right answer, issuing instructions to subordinates, and ensuring these are followed, an approach more consistent with technical change than adaptive. Moreover, doctors presume that everyone else in the team shares their goals for care. They do not admit uncertainty about either aim or method and rarely ask for help. For surgeons especially, the OR is often a place where a prespecified plan is executed. Uncertainty is reduced and the plan developed before the procedure.

Organizational and system change is not like this. In fact, change leaders aiming to transform a delivery organization face conditions that are the exact opposite of those mentioned

Table 6.3. Dangerous leadership lessons

Dangerous leadership lessons implied in a medical training	The reality of leading adaptive change among clinicians
• You are the highest-status person in the room.	• Change in complex systems requires teams of equals, each an expert in their field.
• Your job is to have superior experience and knowledge and know the right answer or best process for getting to the right answer.	• Adaptive change is an experimental process to learn how to achieve better results.
• Leadership is giving clear instructions and holding others to account.	• Leaders create an environment and establish a process that allows others to do their best work.
• Do not ask for help beyond the restricted specialist opinion of a physician colleague.	• In a complex system you can never have the right answer, you always need help.
• The problem must be solved now.	• Developing effective approaches/ models requires a set of experiments run over time.
• All our colleagues agree on our goals.	• Diverse teams work to develop shared goals.

previously. Uncertainty abounds, both in the details of the end goal and the best mechanism of achieving it. Almost by definition, the doctor leading cannot have all the answers. The diverse set of skills required for effective system change means a team charged with an operating system or model of care change might not initially share a common knowledge base, set of mental models, or incentives. And, although the general direction may be known (e.g., "We are building a regional network"), solutions to complex organizational and system problems tend to emerge with experience and through trial-and-error as they are rarely fully characterized at the outset. Change occurs less by implementation than experimentation. Thus clinicians choosing to lead local change often have to unlearn the old lessons of their previous experience and learn new ones. In particular, doctors taking a new change leadership role have to learn and adopt a leadership style and set of behaviors very different from those they have been used to in their clinical practices.

To make the situation even more difficult, clinical leaders typically have no access to the traditional formal tools of authority. They cannot write large checks or hire and fire. In practice, organizational transformation or operating system redesign is often a response to urgent short-term financial imperatives or government edicts, not a longer-term strategy to make the organization and system fit for the future or ready to accommodate technological change. This can mean that doctors, so used to dispensing resources unchallenged through the tips of their pens, find themselves charged with leading change while being resource constrained and bound by internal bureaucratic rules regarding operational and capital expenditure. Finally, exactly because clinicians responsible for leading change are often in the middle of delivery organizations, they lack the positional authority that comes with a named leadership position, such as "clinical director," "chief medical officer," or "chief nursing officer."

HOW CLINICIANS LEAD

So how do those without authority bring about delivery system change? Without positional authority or the ability to disburse capital or hire and fire, how do you lead change among highly independent and self-motivated (and self-interested) individuals in a professional bureaucracy? Certainly not by telling them what to do. As far back as 1994, Berwick argued that "if clinical front-line staff decide they do not want to make changes, then no one

Figure 6.1. Leadership in a clinical environment

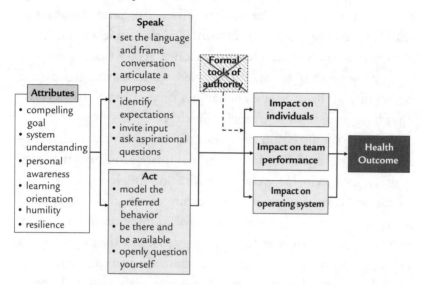

outside the healthcare system can be powerful or clever enough to make them do so."[28] In the more than two decades since, it has become apparent that leading change among clinicians is challenging even for those inside healthcare.

To have an impact on a delivery organization or system's performance, a clinical leader needs to exert influence at three levels (Figure 6.1):[29] individual behavior; team functioning; and operating system performance. After all, patient outcome is driven by the choices and actions of individuals, the way individuals interact in a team, and the way in which the local operating context shapes and supports these behaviors. Absent the tools of authority, clinical change leaders have only two simple tools with which to exercise influence over these factors: what they say and how they act. Yet with these alone they can bring about the transformation of a whole system of care.

Of course, the effectiveness of a leader's speaking and acting is determined by how they speak, what they speak about, and how they act. Ultimately, a change leader's goal is to affect how others think and act and to shape the conversations others are having when they are not there. This means influencing two key aspects of the conversation: its topic and the language used.

Framing the Purpose and Process of Change

At the outset of any clinical change, the leader has to set a team's direction by identifying and articulating the shared purpose that unifies their collective work and motivates their change. This is an essential task and a strategic choice. The terms in which the purpose and goals of the shared enterprise are framed will shape both how engaged individuals will be and how teams and individuals approach the work of system transformation. The fact of clinicians' professional independence demands that the team's purpose be consistent with the individual's own values and goals. Misspecifying these aspects of transformation risks disengaging staff or precipitating design decisions destined to fail. Two potential disconnects between a delivery organization's goals and the values of individual clinicians occur repeatedly: cost versus quality, and implementation of an established model versus experimentation to discover a new one.

Experience suggests that framing the rationale for change in terms of a resource imperative—the need for increased efficiency or revenue—is less likely to be well received by clinicians than framing the change imperative in terms of safety, quality, and patient experience. Terms such as "cost reduction," "productivity," and "value" have become synonymous not only with reduction in physician income (in the United States) and staff reductions and technology underinvestment (in the United Kingdom) but also, in both systems, with the withholding of necessary care and an increase in patient out-of-pocket expenses in addition to staff burnout. At a minimum, such language can impede productive conversations between clinicians and managers about improving system performance.[30]

Clinicians (and patients) frequently view cost and quality as an unavoidable trade-off. To reduce cost is to deny care. This view contrasts with the improvement pioneer Edward Deming's model of improvement, which argues the exact opposite. Cost and quality are one and the same thing: better quality ultimately costs less. This argument—that it is both unsound and unsafe for critically ill patients to wait unnecessarily, be undertreated, or be exposed to the risks of overtreatment or ineffective treatment— is more consistent with clinicians' values than the one that we need to reduce length of stay to meet budget. First, do no harm.

Some organizations—for example, Children's Minnesota Hospital and the aluminum producer Alcoa—have deliberately exploited the positive connection between patient (or worker) safety and productivity in their framing of the goals of change. They reason that the approaches and tools used to improve safety also improve cost and production volume. Safety improvement increases patients' quality of care and staff satisfaction while reducing delays, repetition, and costs. These in turn improve the institution's reputation and market share and, ultimately, its profitability. By choosing to focus improvement efforts on safety, these organizations have selected a framing that meets organizational imperatives of high-quality care within a fixed resource envelope and directly addresses staff values and personal work experience.

The second common point of conflict relates to uncertainty in operating system redesign. Clinicians tend to be suspicious of care models developed and refined elsewhere (even when branded as "best practice"). When doctors find fault with models defined in professional society white papers or regulator reports, their concerns are sometimes dismissed as "not invented here (NIH) syndrome." Yet although doctors certainly have been guilty of using such critiques as a way of avoiding or delaying change, their concerns can also arise from a deep understanding of the particularities of a local operating context, such as the local pattern of disease, community values, or resource availability. Local staff realize that it would be impractical, impossible, or risky to simply "roll out" the centrally determined model. In such circumstances, to downplay the uncertainty by framing change as simply the implementation of a blueprint is to misrepresent the complex interaction between a "best practice" and the local environment in which it is to be applied.

A striking example of the dangers of misalignment between senior leaders' and frontline professionals' understandings of risk comes from the space shuttle *Challenger* disaster. In his "Appendix to the Rogers Commission Report on the Space Shuttle Challenger Accident" Nobel laureate Richard Feynman wrote[31]

> It appears that there are enormous differences of opinion as to the probability of a failure with loss of vehicle and of human life. The estimates range from roughly 1 in 100 to 1 in 100,000. The higher figures come from the working engineers, and the very low figures from management. What are the causes and consequences of this lack of agreement? Since 1 part in 100,000 would imply that one could put a Shuttle up each day for 300 years expecting to lose only one, we could properly ask "What is the cause of management's fantastic faith in the machinery?"

And he concluded his report by pointing out that

> Official management, on the other hand, claims to believe the probability of failure is a thousand times less. One reason for this may be an attempt to assure the government of NASA perfection and success in order to ensure the supply of funds. The other may be that they sincerely believed it to be true, demonstrating an almost incredible

lack of communication between themselves and their
working engineers.

In any event this has had very unfortunate consequences,
the most serious of which is to encourage ordinary citizens
to fly in such a dangerous machine, as if it had attained
the safety of an ordinary airliner.

A mismatch in perspectives between frontline workers and senior
managers is not restricted to space travel. In many industries, those
departments responsible for service delivery and the execution
of corporate plans—IT, operations, human resources, engineers,
clinicians—often rate operational risk higher than those responsible for "vision setting" and strategic planning—finance, marketing,
strategy, and the executive leadership. In healthcare, clinicians
are suspicious of any framing of new services, initiatives, or models of care that appear to make light of clinical risk.

In contrast, choosing a framing that is realistic about risk and
accepts the need for tactics to mitigate it can help to reduce the
potential controversy around a proposed change and to focus action. For example, in 2010 Chile faced the horror of 33 miners
trapped underground. The newly elected president, Sebastián Pi-
ñera, set a clear goal: bring the miners home dead or alive, spar-
ing no expense.[32] This goal recognized the very real possibility
that the miners might not survive, while allowing for hope that
they could be saved. Achieving a balance of aspiration and realism in goal setting is very important. Reflecting on his experience as a prisoner of war in the "Hanoi Hilton," Admiral John
Stockdale famously cautioned against unrealistic expectations,
noting that "you must never confuse faith that you will prevail
in the end—which you can never afford to lose—with the discipline to confront the most brutal facts of your current reality,
whatever they might be."[33] He observed that the unrealistic
optimists were less likely to survive. In *Good to Great,* Jim Collins

identified the ability to "confront the brutal facts" as a key attribute of great organizations.

Clinicians are often concerned that alternative organizational arrangements will be implemented without regard to local conditions. Framing change as a learning process that explores the best way to deploy local resources to achieve the goals inherent in national standards, or set by the board of directors, accepts the need for local testing and adaptation. A learning framing recognizes the uncertainty inherent in new clinical practices and allows for the risk to be reduced through careful experimentation, monitoring, and a commitment to cease anything found to be ineffective, or worse, unsafe. It approaches organizational change with the same scientific mindset as we approach clinical change.

However, such an approach can conflict with current thinking regarding variation and control. In all industries organizations must confront an inherent tension between employee empowerment and discretion, on the one hand, and operational discipline and control on the other. For more than a century companies sought to monitor and control employees to ensure they faithfully executed senior leaders' strategy, an approach that was at the core of Taylor's "scientific management." In the modern era, however, emphasis has pivoted in the opposite direction: to freeing employees' creativity and empowering them to innovate and experiment in the pursuit of corporate goals, all within a framework that guides decision-making by a liberated workforce.[34]

In healthcare the tension is between physician autonomy and unwarranted practice variation. Managers' and policy makers' challenge is to improve outcomes through constraining clinician discretion with appropriate standardization while simultaneously supporting warranted variation. Ironically, the same doctors who insist on freedom from the standard can be loath to vary their practice to deliberately test operating system changes that might improve value, lest these changes increase patient risk.

Framing organizational change as science, in which experiments are planned with the same rigor as would be expected of a clinical change, helps assuage this concern.

Setting the Language

The language used within an organization is both a manifestation and a reinforcement of its culture and the staff's mindset. For example, by the time of the space shuttle *Columbia* disaster in 2003, the experimental mindset of the Apollo program had been replaced with a framing at NASA that near space travel was in some way "routine."[35] President Nixon himself had said of the shuttle program, "This system will center on a space vehicle that can *shuttle* repeatedly from Earth to orbit and back. It will revolutionize *transportation* into near space, by *routinizing* it"[36] (italics added). The agency's focus on the schedule was reinforced with the language of a production industry: terms such as "schedule," "shuttle," "payload," and "operational." In such an environment, it is not surprising that an ambiguous signal of impending disaster (a larger-than-usual piece of foam than those that had been encountered on previous flights had been observed striking the wing on takeoff) was in part evaluated in terms of the potential delay it represented rather than its threat to safety, and it was actively downplayed.[37]

In a similar way, choosing the framing and language of cost containment and deficit reduction can be a risk in healthcare. For example, the 2013 Francis Report into excess mortality at the Mid-Staffordshire NHS Foundation Trust in England concluded that the board's relentless focus on making economies contributed significantly to the degradation of the organization's ability to deliver safe and effective care.[38] In contrast, a framing of the organization's purpose, and the nature of its work, in terms of safety completely changes the board's conversation. An evaluation of the quality and safety program at Boston's Massachusetts General Hospital noted that "as our efforts gained traction, the amount of board meeting time devoted to quality and safety increased to the point at which time spent on quality and safety eclipsed time devoted to finances."[39] Finally, imprecise language can add to risk, as the example of the Dana Farber Cancer Institute's cyclophosphamide overdose illustrates (see Chapter 2).

A leader's language is as much a choice as is the framing of a change. The language a leader uses to describe what we are trying to do, why, and how we might do it reflects and reinforces the framing of the purpose of clinical and operational change. Children's Minnesota Hospital's choice to frame change around safety was risky: it implied that the organization was unsafe, something no clinician likes to hear. Its leaders addressed this problem by changing the language used to discuss patient safety issues, replacing negative and judgmental terms with neutral or positive ones, called "words to work by" (Table 6.4).[40]

Notably, the old terms come from a language of judgment and the law, whereas the alternative choices are from the language of learning and science. In an academic medical center, science—in Children's case, the pursuit of knowledge about how to be safer—is a familiar approach that resonates with clinicians and helps diffuse the cognitive dissonance for clinicians being asked to face up to the possibility that they were participants in causing harm.

Table 6.4. Words to work by

Old term	New term
Error	Accident or failure
Root cause	Multi-causal
Judgment	Learning
Blame	Accountable
Investigation	Examination or study
Isolated event	System

Using the language of science when discussing organizational change in healthcare has several advantages. It supplants the emotive language often used to resist change and reinforces that the adaptive change process is one of learning and experimentation. At the same time, it emphasizes the need for the standardization, measurement, and rigor that are the hallmarks of good experimental practice.

The Intimacy of Leadership

How do leaders communicate a chosen framing and language? Popular representations of inspirational leaders in times of change—Winston Churchill, Martin Luther King, Barack Obama—often highlight their skill in public speaking: soaring rhetoric and pithy quotes. But the reality is far from this. Research shows that CEOs spend the majority of their time communicating and the majority of this is face-to-face (81 percent).[41] Half of their communication is with individuals or small groups: 21 percent of CEO time was spent with someone one-on-one and 29 percent with groups of fewer than 10.[42]

Written corporate communications or speeches to larger audiences reinforce the message and the terminology, but leading change turns out to be an intimate business. Effective leaders spend little time in their offices and concentrate their efforts on the wards, and in the clinics, operating rooms, and practices. Change leadership is surprisingly personal: a leader's communication, both its content and style, is most effective when up close. Moreover, a compelling framing and effective language are not things a leader dreams up alone in her or his office. These typically emerge from conversations with colleagues, developed by inquiring of those who are led. How else are individual personal aspirations, and their connection to the greater enterprise, to be understood and accommodated?

The following summarize some of the key considerations in developing and communicating a clinical change agenda:

- Seek to understand individuals' goals and aspirations by asking them about these.
- Frame a shared purpose in terms that are consistent with patients' and clinicians' core values.
- Acknowledge the risk inherent in change and the pursuit of shared purpose and facilitate a conversation about mitigation.
- Identify and use a language of change that is consistent with the purpose and values (avoid overreliance on the language of economics).
- Clarify the balance between freedom and constraint in the design and management of new approaches to care delivery.
- Focus communication as much on individuals as groups.

These considerations emphasize the importance of personal relationship and individual consultation. They suggest caution with business jargon. For example, although the term "burning platform" may well express the urgency for change felt particularly by policy makers and senior managers, it tends to be unattractive to many clinicians. Long-serving clinicians have seen "burning platforms" come and go. Austerity, managed care, and now value-based care were all expected to take over, yet none did entirely, and the pace of change often seems slower than promised.

The Importance of Action

The previous discussion has focused on the content and style of a clinical leader's communication, but action is equally important.

Observed actions support a leader's communication. If leaders foster change by nurturing a new conversation, they reinforce that change by being seen to behave in ways consistent with the new culture and set of routines. This can be as subtle as the tone of voice or as obvious as deliberate displays of the new, preferred, behaviors.

Some specific actions are particularly important. One of these is transparency. Clinical and operational data are often reported separately, and clinicians can be oblivious to the operational and financial implications of their clinical decisions (as can managers to the clinical impact of operational choices). Although clinicians are increasingly provided with cost data, full disclosure of the organization's financial position is less common. Yet clinicians are trained to demand the data. Of course, they will likely complain about its quality and progress only slowly through the "four stages of data denial" (Stage 1, "The data are wrong"; Stage 2, "The data are right, but there's no problem"; Stage 3, "The data are right; it is a problem; but it's not my problem"; and Stage 4, "I accept responsibility for improvement"),[43] but they will ultimately engage with it. Transparency applies equally to future action. Staff will want to know about planned changes, their rationale, and their proposed mechanism of creating an improvement, in detail.

A second key behavior is the response to failure. By definition, change demands trying new tasks and ways of working together. If only because of unfamiliarity, failure is always a risk. However, especially in healthcare, where the term "failure" usually connotes iatrogenic damage and avoidable patient harm, failure is not an option. So how are we to promote learning, practicing, and experimenting, when failure is viewed so negatively?

Of course, not all failures are the same. An individual professional's negligence is not the same as a well-designed and well-intentioned experiment that did not return the result for which we had hoped. Failure is essential to learning. Moreover, most changes relating to the deployment of new models of care and ways of working are tests of the organizational arrangements that support the delivery of best clinical practice, not changes to the best practices themselves. Organizational failures, although still dangerous, typically pose less immediate risk to patients, especially if, when new organizational arrangements are trialed, measures are put in place to detect and rectify them early.

Leaders' responses to failure of an operational redesign set the tone for learning. A leader whose behavior sends an explicit or tacit message of disapproval will discourage team members from suggesting and trying new, and potentially better, ways of delivering care, or from identifying failures in existing practices and systems. In contrast, being accepting of failures, and even better, admitting to your own fallibility and the failures you have experienced helps create an environment that supports learning and experimentation.

A third important behavior is simply being visible and available.[44] Effective change leaders go out looking for trouble. Working from the office, even with an "open-door policy," is insufficient to keep a leader connected to her or his team, especially important in times of transformation. That the leader's door is open does not guarantee that anyone will walk through it. The following interaction between Linda Ham, mission manager on the ill-fated 2003 space shuttle *Columbia* mission, and an investigator on the accident investigation board—related by William Langewiesche in his 2003 *Atlantic Monthly* article[45]—illustrates the problem:

> INVESTIGATOR: As a manager, how do you seek out dissenting opinions?
>
> MISSION MANAGEMENT TEAM CHAIR: Well, when I hear about them.
>
> INVESTIGATOR: By their very nature, you may not hear about them.

MISSION MANAGEMENT TEAM CHAIR: Well, when somebody
  comes forward and tells me about them.
INVESTIGATOR: But, what techniques do you use to *get*
  them?

The very acts of redesign and transformation intentionally perturb systems, processes, and routines. A change leader needs to
actively seek out problems, dissent, and concerns among team
members. A leader actively seeking input, both positive and negative, creates an environment that legitimizes essential debate
and critical evaluation among a team.

A fourth key behavior, therefore, is inquiry: asking staff about
their experiences, concerns, aspirations, and ideas and interrogating the data for meaningful variation. In the clinical settings
described previously—the ward, clinic, and procedure room—
leaders often "tell." But in the uncertain environment of organizational and system transformation, they need to ask, exactly
because, as already discussed, the right answer may not exist. In
fact, no one member of the team will have the complete right answer. Each will have an important part—a piece of information,
an insight, or an analytic model—but none will have the full data
set or theory that may be needed to inform a major system or
care model redesign. And the only way to uncover these gems is
for the leader to ask. Schein has argued that asking the right
questions is essential to developing the kind of relationships essential for collaborative problem-solving: "what we choose to ask,
when we ask, what our underlying attitude is as we ask—all are
key to relationship building, to communication, and to task
performance."[46]

Unfortunately, telling, with all that it implies about what
others ought to know but do not, is all too often the preferred
communication style in healthcare settings. Interprofessional
and multidisciplinary meetings in healthcare have a habit of de-

scending into a set of dueling assertions in which each expert advocates for his or her point of view, to the exclusion of others and often as loudly as possible. When a new model of care or new system design demands the integration of multiple professional models and points of view, this mode of communication can be destructive. Thus, the leader's role is to ensure that assertions are challenged and the data and reasoning behind them are made transparent, that each contributor's point of view is sought and heard, and that no one is drowned out.

Finally, what a leader says and does is usually closely watched, for better and for worse. Word of the leader's behavior spreads and can easily be misinterpreted: a question may be taken to mean disapproval or casual praise as a sign of executive support.[47] However, a leader can use his or her own behavior for its emblematic value: as a model of what is expected of others. One chief medical officer, for instance, deliberately and publicly walks on the pathway that wraps around the square separating two buildings instead of cutting diagonally across the lawn, as was the usual path. He argues that if he is not seen to be abiding by the guideline implied by the asphalt pathway, then how can he later expect clinicians to attend to clinical guidelines. Skilled change leaders are often on the lookout for opportunistic moments when they can model a preferred behavior.

The importance of these leader behaviors relates to the damage that can be caused when what is said and what is done are in conflict: a mismatch between espoused and observed. A leader cannot assert he or she is "available" and then not be seen on the floor. In an organization that prides itself on "data-based decision making," leaders need to be seen to be looking at the data and interrogating the evidence. The work of operational or role redesign, process innovation, and system transformation typically takes most staff out of their comfort zones. Staff are highly sensitive to inconsistencies between espoused and observed behaviors in their leaders, and any mismatch will contribute to their disengagement from the work and distrust of the motivations for, and processes of, redesign.

Dealing with Difficult Behavior

One final task falls to the clinical change leader. Although unprofessional behavior is certainly not the norm (one estimate suggests that about two-thirds of physicians "never or very rarely generate an unsolicited patient complaint"[48]), times of change raise the risk of unprofessional and destructive behavior, even from the most senior of staff. Hickson and Pichert define disruptive behavior as "any behavior that impairs the medical team's ability to achieve intended outcomes."[49] In the context of healthcare transformation such behavior is that which impairs staff's ability to design and implement improved systems to better deliver excellence in care and benefit to patients.

Such behavior is manifest in myriad ways, some more obvious than others. Obvious examples include open conflict among peers or mistreatment of subordinates, often seen as angry outbursts, bullying or overtly threatening behavior, demeaning comments, or shaming others for negative outcomes. More subtle, and potentially more damaging, are patterns of avoidant or passive-aggressive behavior, or even frank sabotage. As Leape and colleagues describe, "[Passive-aggressive individuals] tend to be unreasonably critical of authority and blame others for their failures."[50] Such behavior includes failing to follow up on or honor agreements, delaying responding to calls, and making negative comments about the institution, unit, or individuals. "The defining characteristics of passive aggression are concealed anger, negativism, and intent to cause psychological harm."[51] Such behavior is all the more disruptive in a professional services organization in which an individual veto carries great weight.

Although such behaviors are hard to quantify, Leape and colleagues argue that they are not so rare they can be ignored. The behaviors are sufficiently likely that a clinical change leader needs to develop a strategy for dealing with them. This strategy has, of course, two parts: dealing with the behaviors if and when they arise and establishing policies, procedures, and a culture that prevents them from arising in the first place. Given that intentional system change is by its nature disruptive, it is wise to think through an approach to prevention in advance of making significant system and process changes.

Prevention of Disruptive Behavior

Most healthcare delivery organizations have well-established values statements and disciplinary procedures, managed by senior leadership and Human Resources, respectively. However, disruptive behavior often fills a leadership vacuum inasmuch as incidents that are not dealt with, by either informal action or the application of corporate policies, are presumed to be acceptable. As Hickson and colleagues point out, "Lack of early intervention . . . allows patterns of behavior to become routine."[52] If bad behavior achieves the desired result of retarding or derailing a program of redesign and transformation, then it is effectively rewarded and even tacitly encouraged.

At their heart, therefore, most prevention approaches rely on explicitness and transparency: of expectations, of acceptable behaviors, of rules, and of consequences. Specific tactics include "credos," "compacts," and lists of acceptable and desired behaviors. By articulating expectations of behavior ex ante organizations hope to prevent some portion of disruptive behaviors in the future. More importantly, a well-established understanding of preferred and expected behaviors serves as a reference point should a leader need to deal with a specific incident at some later time.

A "credo"—a statement of belief—is typically an aspirational expression of an organization's values and beliefs, intended to inspire employees, guide their decisions and actions, and convey to them the way in which senior management wants them to behave to one another and to customers. The Johnson & Johnson credo, written in 1943, is an oft-cited example. This credo sets out the company's responsibilities "to the doctors, nurses and patients, to mothers and fathers and all others who use our products and services"[53] as well as to its customers, suppliers, distributors, employees, communities, and stockholders.

A related corporate tool is a statement of "boundary conditions." Boundary conditions "delineate the acceptable domain of activity for organizational participants."[54] Unlike a credo, which focuses on positive ideals, boundary conditions establish behavioral limits and are often stated in negative terms. The Massachusetts General Hospital sends out a list of "boundary statements" to each attending physician annually[55]:

As a member of the MGH community and in service of our mission, I will never:

- Knowingly ignore MGH policies and procedures.
- Criticize or take action against any member of the MGH community raising or reporting a safety concern.
- Speak or act disrespectfully toward anyone.
- Engage in, tolerate, or fail to address abusive, disruptive, discriminatory, or culturally insensitive behaviors.
- Look up or discuss private information about patients or staff for any purpose outside of my specified job responsibilities.
- Work while impaired by any substance or condition that compromises my ability to function safely and competently.

Some organizations go further than general statements of behavioral injunction. New Zealand's Waitemata District Health Board has developed a detailed list of preferred and unwanted behaviors linked to the organization's corporate values. Each corporate value is associated with four "standards," and for each of these the organization publishes a list of behaviors they "love to see," "expect to see," and "don't want to see." Some examples are shown in Table 6.5.[56]

Finally, the physician compact has gained popularity as a way of clarifying behavioral expectations. Unlike the previous examples, a compact is bilateral. It is a statement of "give and get," in effect, the "deal" physicians are getting when they join a healthcare delivery organization. The rationale for crafting an explicit

Table 6.5. Examples of Waitemata District Health Board preferred and unwanted behaviors

Value	Standard	Behavioral expectations		
		Love to see	Expect to see	Don't want to see
Everyone matters	Listen and understand	Motivates others by making time to listen to their views and feelings	Is interested in what others say	Talks over people, doesn't let them ask questions or express views
With compassion	Compassion for your suffering	Is thoughtful about other people and takes time to "put themselves in other people's shoes"	Checks in to see people are OK Notices pain, and does everything they can to reduce it	Is dismissive of other people's concerns, feelings or pain

compact is to counteract the unstated deal that many U.S. physicians believed governed their relationship with the rest of the delivery organization. This implicit compact has been characterized as autonomy (to practice without interference and to retain control over daily operations), protection (from market forces and change), and entitlement (freedom from involvement in the business side of the delivery organization).[57] It is an extension of the notion of the hospital serving as the "physician's workshop." This deal is, effectively, "I practice my profession and see my patients, and the organization does everything else necessary to provide me with the resources and income I need."

The implicit compact is a significant barrier to change, especially of the variety discussed previously, in which new systems and models of care demand staff take on new roles, responsibilities, and ways of working together. It allows staff to treat redesign for performance improvement as optional, rather than an essential aspect of their job. Moreover, because it is an individual arrangement, it runs counter to the kind of cross-system and cross-silo collaboration and integration needed to create networks and home-to-home patient pathways.

Some institutions, most notably Seattle's Virginia Mason Medical Center, have sought to address this problem by replacing the implicit compact with an explicit, negotiated statement of the expectations the organization may legitimately have of the physician and the physician may have of the organization. Compacts such as these are typically developed bottom-up through consultations with the staff to whom they will apply. They recognize that the organization has a duty to the staff as well as the staff a duty to the organization.

Virginia Mason's compact places emphasis on the individual's participation in the group and engagement in change. For example, physicians' responsibilities include to "include staff, physicians, and management on team," "behave in a manner consistent with group goals," "participate in and support group decisions," "embrace innovation and continuous improvement," and "participate in necessary organizational change." And the organization's responsibilities include to "share information regarding strategic intent, organizational priorities, and business decisions," and "create an environment that supports teams and individuals."[58] More importantly, at Virginia Mason the compact is reflected in the organization's job descriptions, internal metrics and reports, and physician incentives. The behavioral expectations articulated in the compact are reinforced by many other organizational routines.

All these approaches—credos, boundary conditions, and compacts—indicate preferred behaviors in advance, thereby (hopefully) preventing the kind of disruptive and unprofessional behavior described previously. A decentralized model of leadership and control represents some risk for senior managers. If things go wrong, the senior manager can ultimately end up being more accountable than the local leader. Putting these instruments in place provides leaders at the top of the organization with some reassurance that local control and staff independence will be counterbalanced by appropriate constraints. But, although they are typically developed at the organizational level by senior management, they are equally useful for those leading clinical change locally as instruments to reinforce the message that the authority to undertake a redesign of our operating system comes with accountability. Leaders in the middle can use the centrally developed documents as a way to remind staff of the "rules of engagement" as they go about the work of transformation.

Dealing with Incidents

Incidents of unacceptable behavior may nonetheless occur in spite of local leaders' best efforts to prevent them. Hence it is important to have thought through the strategy for dealing with these behaviors in advance. Of course, all organizations have their own sets of internal rules for dealing with such incidents—some more sophisticated than others—that will govern how a local leader should respond to an incident. In many cases the Human Resources department will take the lead.

Nonetheless, Hickson and colleagues have published the approach used at Vanderbilt University Medical Center, which serves as a very helpful model for leaders facing this problem.[59] The Vanderbilt model is based on the observation that the majority of physicians never or rarely exhibit unprofessional behavior, and single unprofessional incidents are more common than patterns of this behavior. Accordingly, Vanderbilt uses the "cup of coffee" as the primary intervention when a physician first generates an unsolicited patient or colleague complaint. This intervention is exactly what it sounds like: an informal private conversation between the professional alleged to have behaved badly and a senior colleague (staff receive training for such conversations). The observed behavior is outlined, the way in which it is not representative of what is expected is noted, and the colleague is allowed to reflect on its causes and respond. Although it is common for individuals to imply that their behavior was justified by the mistake of someone else, many have failed to recognize the wider impact of their bad behavior, are chastened by this realization, and do not reoffend.

A small percentage do reoffend, however, and for these Vanderbilt has developed an "awareness intervention." In contrast to the "cup of coffee," formal records are kept. The awareness intervention centers on keeping data regarding an individual's record of unprofessional behavior and sharing those data with the individual to demonstrate "the appearance of a pattern that sets the professional apart from his/her peers."[60] The majority (58 percent[61]) of physicians presented with these data respond professionally and make appropriate professional and behavioral adjustments; the recidivism rate among this group is almost negligible. "Authority interventions," comprising the development of mandatory, formal, supervised improvement plans, are used for those who do not respond to an awareness intervention. Disciplinary action, including suspension of clinical privileges, is reserved for those who fail to improve after this intervention (with the exception of those behaviors, such as sexual harassment, that warrant a disciplinary intervention on their first occurrence).

The importance of the Vanderbilt approach is that it enables and encourages early intervention, before individual incidents have a chance to become longer-term patterns of behavior. There are many reasons why incidents might not be addressed early: worry that intervention will precipitate the colleague's resignation (especially if the individual is high profile, or brings in a lot of revenue); concern she or he might sue; and concern administrators have the facts wrong about the offenders. However, as already noted, failure to act early may inadvertently reinforce the behavior. Often, if staff have reported a colleague's behavior, the first reported incident is not the first one observed. Failure to act early can damage staff morale and contribute to workplace stress, error, burnout, turnover, and increased risk of staff lawsuit. The individual's behavior affects the whole team.

RISK OF LONELINESS

Finally, it is worth recognizing that leading change among your colleagues and, occasionally, holding them to account, is not without its personal risks. One often unacknowledged risk is loneliness. Managerial work is often less respected than clinical work, and in some places the word "administrator" is even used as an insult. Doctors often refer to those who have given up some clinical time to take on a managerial role as having "gone over to the dark side."

Clinicians' professional identity is rooted in their group. The first time a local leader expresses an opinion or acts in a way that is construed to be the institution's, they risk separating themselves from their colleagues and their group identity: friends and colleagues can become antagonists.[62] The potential for professional isolation can prevent a clinician leader from introducing even those changes that are clearly in the best interests of their patients and their colleagues.

The stresses of leading change among your colleagues can in part be addressed by both attending to your own well-being and by planning your interactions with your colleagues. Any leader needs physical, mental, and emotional stamina and thus needs to ensure not only adequate diet, exercise, and sleep but also enough family time and time to be alone to reflect and think.[63] In addition, leaders, who often mentor others, also benefit from having their own confidant and mentor: preferably someone outside their immediate organization.

Stress can be partially mitigated by predicting difficult situations and conversations in advance and preparing for them. A meeting that is challenging because attendees lack important information is different from one in which a minority or the majority is hostile to a proposed change.[64] The first requires both listening and communicating the detail of the rationale for change. A hostile minority is often made up of a few people who are resisting a new operating system because of its potential impact on them personally. Although their viewpoint may have merit, it can be challenged (and prevented from hijacking a proposed redesign) by explicitly asking if others share this perspective. When the majority is hostile to a proposed change, it is usually a sign that you have something wrong and need to listen and learn.

IMPLICATIONS FOR ACTION: THE WORK OF LEADING CHANGE IN HEALTHCARE

Leading change in healthcare presents a number of challenges related to the independence of individuals, the diversity of teams, and the level of disruption to working relationships and routines that transformation can demand. In the current healthcare delivery environment, issuing instructions or implementing a blueprint is rarely a viable approach. Transformation will occur only when clinicians and managers successfully collaborate to rebuild their local operating systems. The leader's primary job is to help his or her colleagues through a process of adaptive change. In practice this means helping staff take local control over, and accept accountability for, their local operating systems by establishing and supporting a process for change that clinicians find plausible and then letting it do its work.

The first elements of the work of leading clinical change relate to framing a plausible rationale for, and mechanism of, the change and creating a productive conversation among colleagues that will enable them to work together on the details of the new models of care, operating system designs, and technology deployment that a transformed system will require. Use the following checklist to help plan your approach:

- Ensure you have developed a clear understanding of the nature of the change you are leading.
- Take time to think through how you will frame the change and communicate this to your team and colleagues.
- Clarify and articulate the (shared) purpose of the enterprise and the intended transformation.
- Make explicit the mechanisms by which the proposed changes achieve that purpose and will deliver better value to patients and staff.

- Be open and honest about the potential impact the proposed changes will likely have on individuals' working lives.
- Share all the data.
- Be clear about the risks of change and outline contingency plans and mitigation strategies (such as real-time data collection and monitoring as the changes are trialed).

Another body of leadership work relates to creating an environment that allows colleagues to work effectively together to develop and then test alternative models of care and operating systems:

- Meet individually with people in the relevant units and team, including with critics and naysayers (they may really be alert to a risk everyone else has missed), and ask them for their ideas, plans, thoughts, and concerns.
- In group meetings ask people to explain the data, evidence, and rationale behind their assertions (in effect, ask them to teach everyone else how their discipline views and deals with a problem).
- Put some effort into thinking through the language you will use to describe and discuss the change as you go out onto the floor to meet with people (the language they will use when talking to each other).
- Explicitly identify the behaviors we expect to see (and those we do not) as we collaborate on redesign, and deal with the stresses of change.

Yet other work relates to supporting the transformation process as it unfolds:

- Be explicit about the evolving and experimental nature of redesign. Emphasize that we are learning together and that we are unlikely to get it completely right the first time. Articulate the long-term plan: we will keep working at it until we get it working the way we want.

- Should failures occur, treat these instances as data, part of the scientific process we are using to develop improved care models and operating systems, not as evidence of personal failure. Acknowledge your own fallibility publicly.
- Be visible; attend ongoing meetings and continue to meet with individuals as necessary and appropriate.
- Look for opportunities to model through your own behavior the new ways of working together we are designing.

Finally, care for yourself at home and at work:

- Develop your relationships with allies and supporters.
- Ensure you have adequate private time for reflection and planning.

Chapter 7 reviews some of the many other tools for changing clinician, and particularly physician, behavior and discusses some of the considerations in choosing among them and putting them to most effective use.

CHAPTER 7

Tools for Changing Behavior

O f course, the leader is not the only influence on the behavior of clinicians. In spite of a common narrative of physician independence and autonomy, doctors are not free to act as they choose: their discretion has long been constrained, either by harder rules or softer influences. Most constraints on physicians' behavior target their choices of tests, drugs, procedures, or locations of care, quite simply because the majority of healthcare resources are spent on the authority of a doctor. Harder constraints on physician decision-making include the rules embedded in computer drug, radiology, and procedure order entry systems, formulary restrictions imposed by either national bodies or local payers, and the licensure requirements for undertaking particular care decisions or actions. Softer influences include professional socialization, continuing education, best practice guidelines, data feedback and benchmarking, and explicit financial or nonfinancial incentives. Although many of these tools for behavior change operate at the national or organizational level, leaders nearer the front line of care can deploy some locally to support operating system change.

CHANGING DOCTORS' BEHAVIOR

The majority of healthcare resources are expended on the basis of an individual doctor's decision (the pen with which the doctor signs an order being perhaps healthcare's most powerful technology). Hence, as concerns about medical inflation increased in the latter part of the twentieth century, so too did interest in influencing medical decision-making. In the United States the tools for changing physician behavior have largely been used as a counterbalance to fee-for-service reimbursement: a payment model that created a fundamental conflict of interest and an incentive for independent physicians to overprovide tests and therapies. As Arnold Relman, then editor of the *New England Journal of Medicine,* noted so succinctly in 1986, "Fee-for-service physicians are suppliers who are able to determine the demand for their own services."[1]

Today, most American doctors are still not closely affiliated with a delivery organization, although employment is becoming increasingly common and gained in popularity in response to the 2020 Covid-19 pandemic as doctors sought the financial security of a salary. But even when they are salaried employees, as is typically the case in national health systems, doctors do not necessarily behave like corporate employees whose actions can easily be directed. They tend to look outside their organization to their colleagues and licensing and scientific bodies for decision guidance.

For many years, it was assumed that physicians' ethical obligation to place the needs of the patient above their own economic well-being, coupled with social pressure from their colleagues, would serve as a sufficient counterbalance to fee-for-service payment. Indeed, for much of the twentieth century, medicine's professional code was a sufficient restraining influence as it was hard to overprovide when few technologies were available, the majority of practice involved "examining, counseling, and comforting,"[2] and the relative shortage of doctors meant most had more than enough patients and income. However, the explosion of technology, and the increase of hospital beds and specialists—each running their own profit-maximizing small business—created a powerful inflationary force.

Early attempts to constrain costs through changing physician behavior were focused on educating doctors in the use of best practice guidelines. This tactic was based on the key assumption that observed physician practice was a reflection of the individual's underlying knowledge base. It was presumed that the knowledge existed, but the individual doctor did not possess it. Further, when doctors, motivated by their professional code rather than money, learned what the best practice was, they would follow it.

However, knowledge alone proved to be an insufficient practice change tool. That a doctor knows the "right thing to do" does not mean either that he or she will "do the right thing," or "do the right thing right." Although continuing medical education certainly did change physician practice, impact on patient outcomes was less well demonstrated.[3] And the kind of education mattered. Clinical practice guidelines were found to be "remarkably unsuccessful at influencing physicians,"[4] and conferences and unsolicited mailings completely ineffective. More resource-intensive strategies such as physician detailing or the use of local opinion leaders were usually moderately effective (reductions of 20 percent to 50 percent in the incidence of inappropriate performance).[5]

Evidence that doctors were not doing the right thing really began accumulating from the late 1990s when more and more research showed that well-evidenced and no longer controversial practices were slow to be adopted,[6] usage rates of best practices were low, and inappropriate interventions were common. An influential study in 2003 found that the chances of receiving generally agreed best practice on admission to a U.S. hospital were about the same as a coin toss.[7] Average quality of care has remained roughly the same since then.[8]

Even when the medical knowledge base is clear, unequivocal, and applicable to the care of the specific patient under his or her care, the physician may still be neither motivated nor capable of acting accordingly. Research shows that noncompliance with guidelines is driven by much more than simply an individual physician's knowledge deficit. Many other barriers stand in the way, some relating to the nature of the medical knowledge base, but others to the individual physician's attitudes and to the system in which the physician applies the knowledge. One literature review of the impact of guidelines on practice differentiated internal from external barriers to practice guideline adherence.[9] Internal barriers included lack of awareness of, or familiarity with the guideline, disagreement with its recommendations, the doctor's lack of belief that he or she can perform the recommendations, and the inertia of current practice. External barriers relating to the system in which the doctor practices included difficulty of application of the guideline's recommendations, patient resistance, and a lack of time or resources to act in accordance with the guideline.

Thus, to change a physician behavior, one must first understand what enables or impedes the preferred behavior. Many psychological theories and models—taking perspectives ranging from individuals' attitudes and cognitive biases to the operational and social environment in which the behavior occurs—have been developed to explain human behavior. One group of researchers has distilled what can be a confusing array into a simple framework identifying 3 preconditions for a behavior to occur (motivation, capability, and opportunity)[10] and 14 sets of factors that influence the behavior, ranging from "individual knowledge, skills, memory, attention, decision-making, beliefs about capabilities and consequences, goals and emotions to broader physical and social contextual factors, including resource availability and social norms, and professional boundaries/roles."[11] A clearer understanding of these factors allows the behavior change technique to be tailored to the target behavior. Table 7.1[12] gives some examples of behavior change interventions and the influences on behavior that they target.

Two important implications arise from these behavior change models. First, any effective behavior change intervention must be preceded by an accurate diagnosis of the driver of the behavior and the source of any impediment to behavior change. Only with a diagnosis in hand can an appropriate behavior change technique be selected. As Lorencatto and colleagues point out, this is particularly complicated in healthcare delivery because what appears to be one behavior (e.g., prescribing an antibiotic) may in fact be several (e.g., evaluating the applicability of the guideline; assessing the benefits and risks of guideline adherence; choosing drug, dose, route, duration, and reviewing the result; and deciding whether to make further changes).[13] Furthermore, the behavior may involve many individual contributors—such as nurses, pharmacists, doctors, or ward secretaries—each of whom is potentially subject to different behavioral influences.

The second implication is that leaders and organization need to maintain a portfolio of multiple behavior change techniques so as to be able to match the technique to the behavior and barrier. Reflexively reaching for an educational intervention, as is so common, is often insufficient.

Behavior change techniques aimed at increasing physicians' compliance with well-evidenced best practice recommendations assume that the knowledge exists and can be put into the form of an evidence-based guideline. In practice, medical knowledge is often neither clear nor unequivocal. Even in an era of "precision medicine," uncertainty abounds.[14] Understanding of individual

Table 7.1. Behavior change techniques and the behaviors they target

Intervention	Example	Influence on behavior
Capability		
• Having the physical and mental ability to engage in the behavior		
Education		
• Increasing knowledge and understanding	Providing information about a disease or a diagnostic or therapeutic action	Knowledge
Training		
• Developing skills through practice and feedback	Simulation training	Skills
Environmental restructuring		
• Shaping physical or social environment to promote or constrain the behavior	Computerized reminders and default options. Engineered forcing functions such as unique connectors that prevent an oxygen pipe being attached to a nitrous oxide outlet	Memory, attention, and decision-making
Opportunity		
• Being in a physical or social environment that makes possible or supports the behavior		
Modeling		
• Showing examples of the behavior for people to imitate	Local champions demonstrating the behavior	Social influence
Enablement		
• Providing other support to improve people's ability to change	Educating patients what to expect/demand of their caregivers	Memory, attention, decision-making

(continued)

Table 7.1. *(continued)*

Intervention	Example	Influence on behavior
Motivation		
• Being more motivated to undertake the target behavior than other potential behaviors		
Persuasion		
• Changing the way people feel about a behavior (positively or negatively)	Written or visual messaging about a preferred behavior	Emotions
Incentivization		
• Increasing the probability of a behavior by creating an expectation of a reward	Financial incentives, prizes, or public recognition ("worker of the month")	Beliefs about consequences
Coercion		
• Decreasing the probability of a behavior by creating an expectation of punishment or a cost	Charging a "processing" fee for written instead of electronic prescriptions	Beliefs about consequences
Restriction		
• Constraining behavior by setting rules	Limiting the available formulary Defining scope of practice	Behavioral regulation

diseases is evolving, and the increasing numbers of patients with multiple conditions has introduced new uncertainties because the right approach to any individual's care is rarely the sum of the multiple relevant disease-specific guidelines.[15] Uncertainty still underlies daily practice. Not only is the knowledge base incomplete but also doctors in practice often lack the time and resources to implement guideline recommendations and reconcile any potential conflicts between the general guideline and the specific patient, or among multiple applicable guidelines.

All this uncertainty leaves ample room for the decision maker to be influenced by something other than the confluence of the science and the patient's best interests. Often as not, this something is money. The combined effects of physicians' income expectations (no doubt influenced by their residual medical school debts and malpractice insurance fees), deliberate influence by pharmaceutical and device companies, the higher payment of procedures compared to "evaluation and management" visits, and some physicians' ownership stakes in diagnostic and therapeutic service companies provide ample encouragement to conflate financial self-interest and patient well-being.[16]

The money to be made under fee-for-service is now widely accepted as a significant influence on physician behavior, in some cases causing patient harm. Kassirer[17] succinctly asked whether "the fees that physicians charge [have] given them an incentive to bring patients back to their offices too often or to order too many tests that aren't needed. Or have they skimped on tests if ordering too many shrinks their paycheck?" After all, doctors, like everyone else, are economic animals, and they respond to the way they are paid.

For this reason, there has been a growing interest in alternative payment models as a key mechanism for increasing the adoption of "best practice," curbing overuse (and even abuse), moderating the inflationary pressure, and improving quality of care. Financial incentives, long regarded as the root of the problem of overuse and inappropriate use, are now mooted as a potential solution and a mechanism of changing behavior in the absence of a clear guideline.

MOTIVATING CLINICIAN BEHAVIOR

The choice of an approach to influencing behavior will depend in part on the organization's underpinning hypothesis about what actually motivates workers. Education-based approaches to changing physician behavior rest on the assumption that professionalism motivates physicians to bring the most recent medical insight to bear on their patient's health problems: that there is a one-to-one relationship between medical knowledge, professionalism, and practice. For example, one group of authors argued that physicians "who value individual and public health more than other social goods" are motivated to provide high-quality services "whether or not patients are capable of judging their quality."[18]

Other psychological research has focused on alternative, more self-interested, behavioral motivators driving clinician performance including the need for self-esteem and personal fulfillment at work. For example, Frederick Herzberg proposed two factors relating to job satisfaction, which he called hygiene and motivation factors.[19] Hygiene factors are job attributes such as salary, work conditions, and job security that are required to prevent dissatisfaction. Motivation factors are attributes that promote satisfaction and stimulate discretionary activity among workers. These include the opportunity to do something meaningful, inclusion in decision-making, and recognition for one's contribution.*

---

* Maslow's "hierarchy of needs," still referenced in some literature but now discredited partly on the grounds of its individualistic and Western framing, placed the notion of "self-actualization" above "esteem needs": the need for a "high evaluation of themselves, for self-respect, or self-esteem, and for the esteem of others." He wrote, "We may still often (if not always) expect that a new discontent and restlessness will soon develop, unless the individual is doing what he is fitted for. A musician must make music, an artist must paint, a poet must write, if he is to be ultimately happy. What a man can be, he must be. This need we may call self-actualization." (Maslow AH. A theory of human motivation. *Psychol Rev.* 1943;50[4]:370–396.)

Not surprisingly, interest in what motivates people at work and creates job satisfaction is driven by the hypothesis that people who are happy in their work and satisfied with their jobs will be more productive. Unfortunately, such a link is hard to prove. That a worker is motivated does not mean they are able, yet productivity requires both. Motivation is necessary but not sufficient. Moreover, workers are more likely to make discretionary extra effort if the organizational goals that shape their work are consistent with their own personal goals.

Herzberg's model in essence argues that it is the content of the job that is the primary motivator, not the money paid for doing it. Hackman and Oldham extended this thinking with their "Job Characteristics Model," which identified five dimensions of a job that are related to a worker's intrinsic motivation: skill variety, task identity (extent to which the job requires completion of a whole piece of work rather than a component), task significance (degree to which the job impacts the lives of others), autonomy, and feedback (receiving actionable feedback about his or her performance).[20]

The argument that seeking job satisfaction drives a worker's productivity stands in sharp contrast to the view, inherent in pay-for-performance and resource-based relative value scale reimbursement systems, that financial gain is the primary determinant of discretionary activity. The former is an intrinsic motivator: the self-desire for challenge, mastery, or the achievement of a personal goal valued by the individual. The latter is an extrinsic motivator: an externally mediated influence to achieve a specified goal. Extrinsic motivators include both positive rewards and the avoidance of negative punishments. The choice of motivator—extrinsic or intrinsic—has been complicated by experimental evidence that the provision of extrinsic rewards can reduce intrinsic motivation. In healthcare a further concern is that financial rewards for achieving specific quality or efficiency outcomes could damage the sense of professionalism upon which medical practice is based. A 2003 *Wall Street Journal* article describing General Electric's "Bridges to Excellence" program, which paid doctors bonuses for delivering higher-quality care, put the issue succinctly: it ran under the headline "A New Way to Get Doctors to Take Better Care of Patients: Bribe Them."[21]

How are these conflicting points of view—intrinsic motivation by a sense of professionalism, purpose, and value, or external incentives such as money or public recognition—to be reconciled? One way is to consider the nature of the work. Not all work is equal: there are some things we want to do and some we have to do. Put simply, external incentives are less helpful (and may be damaging) as rewards for things people *want* to do, and more helpful with things they *have* to do, such as completing necessary administrative activities or engaging with the electronic medical record. That is, both kinds of motivators have a role in shaping clinician behavior, but they have strengths and weaknesses that demand a well-thought-out behavioral influence strategy.

CHANGING BEHAVIOR BY PAYING FOR PERFORMANCE

If fee-for-service is the villain, then alternative reimbursement models should help realign payment with quality and value and redress the negative impact of fee-for-service. Several have been trialed in recent years, including additional payments for achieving certain goals, payment reduction should certain negative events occur, and various forms of shared financial risk (Table 7.2).[22]

Of course, some of these approaches to incentives are not new. Perhaps the ultimate consequence of a "never event" was in the

Table 7.2. Models of pay-for-performance

Category	Example
Additional payment or nonpayment for specified process or outcome	• Incremental payments for meeting specified targets such as screening rates or intermediate outcomes (e.g., HBA$_1$C level in a population of patients with diabetes) • Nonpayment for "never events" or specified types of readmissions
Additional payment for organizational structure	• Increased fees for practices maintaining patient registries or implementing electronic health records
Financial risk	• Capitation • Global case rates/episode of care payments
Shared saving	• "Gainsharing" (sharing of savings between payer and provider)

Mesopotamian Code of Hammurabi, dating from approximately 1750 BCE. The code included a payment schedule for doctors that varied according to the social status of the patient being treated as follows: Law 215. If a physician make a large incision with an operating knife and cure it, or if he open a tumor (over the eye) with an operating knife, and saves the eye, he shall receive ten shekels in money; Law 216. If the patient be a freed man, he receives five shekels; Law 217. If he be the slave of someone, his owner shall give the physician two shekels. However, this fee-for-service payment model came with downside risk: Law 218. If a physician make a large incision with the operating knife, and kill him, or open a tumor with the operating knife, and cut out the eye, his hands shall be cut off.

Studies of alternative payment models have generally shown a positive impact on quality or cost, although some have found minimal or no impact.[23] James Robinson, an economist at UC

Berkeley's School of Public Health, neatly summarized the challenge of designing a payment method for doctors: "There are many
mechanisms for paying physicians; some are good and some are
bad. The three worst are fee-for-service, capitation, and salary."[24]

Recent eight-year follow-up data from Blue Cross Blue Shield
of Massachusetts' Alternative Quality Contract (AQC)—in which
delivery organizations received shared savings if spending was
below risk-adjusted targets, incurred shared losses if spending exceeded budget, and received incentive payments for meeting
quality targets—showed that healthcare costs grew at a slower
rate under the AQC than in states without the AQC. Furthermore, savings resulted from lower prices and lower utilization
and were greater for populations that had been enrolled longer
in the AQC. In later years, savings exceeded bonus payments. In
addition, most process and outcome measures of quality showed
more improvement than in other comparable regions of the
United States.[25]

In spite of successes such as these, a number of concerns have
dogged financial incentive programs, although some have proven
more theoretical than real. These include the following:

- **Do incentives reward current performance or future
  improvement?** A key question is whether financial
  incentives encourage and support lower-quality providers to improve their performance or whether they simply
  reward those who are already performing well. Rosenthal
  and colleagues found evidence that, although lower
  baseline physicians improved, most of the incentive
  payments went to those with a baseline already above the
  target (and who improved the least).[26] For many doctors,
  achieving the goals required to collect the reward may
  simply be a bridge too far, requiring resources and
  investments to which they do not have access.

- *Are activities not the subject of an incentive neglected?*
  Because, by design, many pay-for-performance schemes
  target specific, measurable care activities such as
  screening or vaccination rates, or focus on specific
  populations such as patients with diabetes, there has
  always been a concern that other, nonincentivized,
  activities or populations would be neglected. Two
  literature reviews of the impact of an incentive scheme
  for general practitioners in the United Kingdom (the
  "Quality-Outcomes Framework") found modest evidence for this effect.[27]
- *Do incentives lead to underprovision?* There has long
  been a concern that risk-sharing models such as capitation or global case rates would create an incentive to
  underprovide, for example, by denying needed services
  such as screening or by encouraging providers to make
  their services hard to access. However, the evidence has
  in fact generally shown that preventive activities have
  tended to be higher under capitated contracts than
  under fee-for-service.[28] More recent capitation-based
  models, such as the AQC, which are supported with
  ever better quality measurement, have emphasized
  specific payments for preventive services to counter
  this risk.
- *Is there potential for gaming?* If a doctor is going to be
  paid more for achieving a given result (measured by
  either a process or outcome measure), would not the
  easiest thing to do to get paid be to game the system by
  misreporting success rate or overclassifying patients? In
  fact there is little evidence to support gaming.[29]
- *What is the impact of financial incentive programs on
  those serving challenging populations?* A final concern
  was that physicians serving deprived populations

would be at a disadvantage relative those serving
higher-socioeconomic-class patients.[30] However, studies
show that a lower baseline level of performance, thus
leaving greater room for improvement, "enables a
higher effect size."[31]

There is no doubt that money shapes behavior. Moving reimbursement away from fee-for-service generally results in more of
the preferred behavior and less of the less preferred. Capitation
has not turned out to be the evil many feared it would be. However, it is also clear that reimbursement systems tend to be blunt
instruments prone to unintended consequences. More recent insights suggest ways incentives can be used to encourage positive
behavior while avoiding their downsides. Two basic options exist to address problems with financial incentives: design better
incentives and develop behavior change mechanisms centered on
something other than money.

DESIGNING BETTER FINANCIAL INCENTIVES

Research into the effectiveness of pay-for-performance programs
suggests a number of design features of better performing financial incentive programs (Table 7.3).[32]

But the most important feature of any incentive program is
the way individual doctors are actually paid. A contract held at
the level of a delivery organization has to be translated into an
effective reimbursement model to influence a doctor's care decisions. This requires understanding the subtle relationship between the individual, the incentive, and the way the incentive is
delivered.[33] The science of behavioral economics has provided
insight into how to use incentives to their maximum effect.

It has long been assumed that bigger rewards (or punishments)
exert greater influence over behavior than smaller. According to

Table 7.3. Characteristics of successful pay-for-performance programs

Category	Program characteristic
Focus	• Incentives aimed at chronic diseases performed better than acute. • Programs with incentives focused on individual or team level performed better than those focused at the organizational level.
Measures	• Process and intermediate outcome measures are associated with higher improvement rates than outcome measures. • Programs with clinical outcomes (rather than patient experience) are associated with positive results.
Rewards	• Programs are more successful when all participants can achieve a gain rather than when structured as a zero sum game with winners and losers. • Programs do better when there are new funds made available than when existing funds are reallocated.

classical economic theory, rational humans should make choices that maximize their personal profit. However, behavioral economics, the study of how people respond to incentives in practice, reveals that the way in which the reward is structured and delivered can be even more influential than the size of the reward. People do not always behave "rationally." For example, behavioral research has shown that people tend to exhibit the following traits:

- React more to the risk of a loss than to the promise of a gain (even when their value is the same)
- Highly value their social ranking (how they compare to their known peers)
- Respond more to immediate than delayed consequences
- Favor the status quo
- Try harder when they are close to achieving a goal than when it is distant

The design features of more successful pay-for-performance programs, summarized in Table 7.3, reflect these research insights into human behavior. Other design features that can improve the performance of pay-for-performance programs include reward timing, target structure, loss aversion, and simplicity.[34,35]

Reward timing is influential in two ways. First, the lag between the desired behavior and the reward affects the incentive's impact: more frequent smaller rewards are more effective than less frequent larger rewards. Second, the point during the year that the reward is distributed affects its salience. A reward that is separate from usual reimbursement (e.g., a check in the mail rather than an addition to the usual electronic deposit) and arrives just before taxes are due or before a holiday shopping season is likely to be more important to the recipient than one that arrives at other times of the year.

Structuring the target so that it supports a trajectory of performance improvement is also important. The more likely it is that the rewarded level of performance can be achieved, the more motivating it is. If the targeted level of performance seems unachievable, the reward will not be motivating. Effort is greater if the gap between current level of performance and the target level is smaller (termed the "goal gradient"). Hence it is better to divide a lump sum reward into a series of smaller incentive payments set at levels that are achievable (e.g., tiered absolute thresholds such as 25, 50, 75, and 90 percent of an ultimate goal, each with an interim reward). This design feature in part addresses the concern that incentives tend to preferentially reward the already good rather than those we are encouraging to improve.[36]

Another important design consideration is loss aversion. A basic tenet of behavioral economics is that people base decisions on the expected, rather than the real, loss or gain. They view equivalent losses and gains very differently, tending to prefer avoiding a loss to making a gain, even when that gain could be greater than the loss. In the words of Kahneman and Tversky's seminal paper on prospect theory, "people underweight outcomes that are merely probable in comparison with outcomes that are obtained with certainty."[37]

This principle underpins the design of "return of withhold" incentives: a potential loss of income for not achieving the target. However, this design comes with a caveat. Although such incentive structures can be more powerful than outright rewards, they risk a backlash because they may be perceived as unfair.[38] Nonetheless, there can be little doubt about the power of small negative financial incentives after the use of single-use plastic supermarket carrier bags dropped 85 percent (6.5 billion bags fewer) within the first 6 months after a 5-pence charge was introduced in England.[39]

A final design feature involves complexity. Does the system seem too complicated? Some pay-for-performance systems are sufficiently complex, and the trade-offs in time and effort so difficult, that doctors may not be sure what they must do to meet the goal and be rewarded. Simplicity, with as direct a line as possible between action and reward, makes the preferred behavior clearer. Complexity and uncertainty reduce an incentive's impact: for example, when multiple dimensions of quality and efficiency are bundled or when the level of required performance or the size of the reward can only be known at year end after the books are balanced.

The dilemma, of course, is that the simplest incentive is fee-for-service, in which there is a very direct line between the behavior and the reward, which is exactly what modern pay-for-performance systems are trying to avoid. Hence the connection between an individual clinical decision and a financial reward cannot be too tight, lest it encourage undue focus on only that activity to the exclusion of other preferred behaviors.

In summary, although financial incentives are highly effective in shaping physician behavior and clinical decision-making, the details of the incentive design have a strong impact on the ultimate outcome of any pay-for-performance program. Subtle changes in incentive design can be very influential and errors in design risk inadvertently encouraging decision-making and behavior that is not desired.

NONFINANCIAL INCENTIVES

One need only watch a skilled charge nurse as she or he allocates shifts to see that incentives that reward high-quality care do not have to be financial. In a similar vein, a physician friend hosts his residents at the end of their rotation and explains at the beginning that he will either be serving beer or champagne at the event. Which they are served depends entirely on their performance in delivering excellent patient care. He reports that this low-cost and simple "incentive" is remarkably effective, in part because it spurs an implicit competition with previous generations of residents.

Nonfinancial incentives are as important as financial mechanisms for influencing clinician behavior and bringing about changes in how teams and systems perform. They have several distinct advantages. Nonfinancial incentives avoid the risk of "deprofessionalizing" clinical care and making it "all about the money." Although most financial incentives require a substantial institutional infrastructure (e.g., contract negotiation with payers, internal accounting to track performance), nonfinancial incentives do not require a complex organizational support system.

In theory, nonfinancial incentives can be more easily applied to teams. A distinct disadvantage of financial incentives is that they tend to be focused on individual (usually doctor) behavior, whereas many, if not most, patient outcomes are a function of interdependent behavior and team performance. Unfortunately, other clinical professions are rarely included in financial incentive programs, and, in practice, most nonfinancial incentives continue to focus on individual behavior.

One of the most common nonfinancial incentives is reporting, either externally to the delivery organization as a public "report card," or internally as peer-to-peer comparison and private individual feedback. Historically, public comparison (or "ranking") has focused on hospitals and individual doctors. This approach is based on the idea that institutions or individuals will be motivated to improve their performance—by implementing quality improvement schemes and improving their practices, respectively—to avoid the loss of market share, reputation, or referral stream that might follow publication of a bad grade.

Despite the intuitive appeal of public transparency, evidence of report cards' effectiveness in motivating positive change has been mixed, and they risk unintended consequences. The canonical example of public reporting is the New York State Cardiac Surgery Reporting System, which began reporting risk-adjusted coronary bypass graft mortality rates for hospitals and surgeons in the early 1990s. Although the mortality rate in New York State was reported to have dropped 41 percent (from 4.17 percent to 2.45 percent), other states without a public reporting system reported a similar reduction.[40] More controversially, some studies reported that higher-risk patients were being referred out of New York State. And "the decrease in risk-adjusted mortality was not due to shifts from low-volume to high-volume surgeons" but by the low-volume surgeons stopping practicing.[41] In other words, observed performance improvement associated with publishing performance data may just as likely come from selection—of hospitals and doctors—than change in the organizational and individual routines and practices that are the ultimate determinants of patient outcome.

One problem with public report cards is distance between the intervention and the preferred action. Public reporting aims to provide consumers with choice and doctors and hospitals with an incentive to improve their practices and processes. New York's Cardiac Surgery report card, for example, assumes that the public report will change patient and referring cardiologist decision-making, this will divert volume away from poorer-performing institutions, and the risk of income and reputation loss will motivate internal process improvements that will, in turn, improve outcomes. There are many opportunities for failure in such a long causal chain. Patients may not attend to the data, relying instead on the decisions of people they know like them (a phenomenon termed "social proof").[42] Even if they attend to the data, research has shown that the way data are presented influences their effectiveness. Recent experiments in reporting value by displaying quality and cost data side by side show that a significant patient minority still treats cost as a proxy for quality.[43] Even if they are motivated to make an alternative choice of provider, their insurance plan may not allow them. Most studies showed no or minimal impact on cardiac surgery market share in New York.[44]

An alternative use of comparative performance data to influence behavior, given the unreliable connection between public reporting and internal process improvement, is to share data directly with clinical staff within the delivery organization. This is usually termed "audit and feedback." This approach, in effect, gives individual clinicians a private report card: data about their personal performance, usually as utilization rates of key tests or therapies, or as comparisons to standard practice (i.e., variation data). The connection between the report and the intended behavior is tighter than in public reporting. Numerous studies have shown that such feedback increases compliance with evidence-based guidelines.[45,46] Well-designed delivery systems associate every meaningful action with a measure fed back to the person who undertook the action.

Peer comparison (also called profiling) exploits the fact that relative social ranking is especially important for professionals. Individual reputation among one's colleagues is much more important in shaping behavior than the reputation in the marketplace of the institution in which that individual practices. Change is more likely promoted by the private sharing of comparative data among a group of clinicians who practice together,[47] and sharing unblinded comparisons among a group of peers is more likely to precipitate behavior change than anonymous rankings. Doctors' natural competitiveness when confronted with their deviation from the norm has the power to motivate change where money cannot.

Feeding data back to patients can also motivate their behavior change. Not only can public information campaigns reduce patient demand for unwarranted procedures[48] but also sharing internal data with patients can have a similar effect. Intermountain Healthcare addressed an inappropriately high early elective cesarean section rate in part by sharing the institution's own performance results with patients. These demonstrated a U-shaped relationship between week of delivery and probability of the baby's admission to the neonatal ICU with the bottom of the U at 40 weeks.[49] Patients elected to delay their deliveries.

Although not strictly an "incentive," one more important technique for bringing about change—based on the well-recognized human preference for the status quo—deserves mention. When the preferred action is the "default," baked into organizational routines, cultural norms, information system defaults, standardized protocols and care processes, and standing order sets, it is much more likely to be followed. Organ donation rates are lower when people must actively sign up than when they are the default from which people may opt out. Similarly, when computerized drug order entry systems default to the generic drug, physicians order generic drugs at higher rates.[50] As Intermountain's Brent James said so succinctly, "Make it easy to do it right."[51]

One final advantage of nonfinancial incentives such as feedback and peer comparison is that they may be more easily applied at the unit level as a lever of local control. Most financial incentive programs are organized centrally, either by the payer or the delivery organization. Physician pay is usually set at the institutional level or, as in many countries, nationally. However, when change is driven locally, financial and nonfinancial incentives, much like local operating system design, have a powerful influence on the way patients experience care. Data measuring operating system performance that are collected and managed locally, even without the support of centrally managed information systems, can be used as part of a nonfinancial incentive for change and improved performance.

Where do these considerations of incentive design and impact leave leaders in the middle of organizations trying to change operating systems and their colleagues' behavior? The reality is that all doctors are subject to incentives that shape their behavior, some financial, and some not. Not only do these incentives potentially conflict (such as when a protocol recommends clinical parsimony but fee-for-service reimbursement encourages overprovision) but also different individuals may be more motivated by different incentives. Those aiming to lead clinical change therefore need to understand what motivates those whom they are leading and to what external incentives they are subject. Leaders then consider what incentive design changes they could make to complement and reinforce their other change leadership efforts.

PRACTICAL APPLICATION: USING INCENTIVES TO MOTIVATE CHANGE AT MASSACHUSETTS GENERAL HOSPITAL

All too often institutions deploy incentives as a mechanism of operational control. Report cards based on complication rates, protocol compliance rates, or service volumes are used as substitutes for the kind of local change leadership described in Chapter 6. Moreover, as already noted, using incentives to increase compliance with an "evidence-based best practice" presupposes that what is "best" is known and that change is therefore technical. But rewarding compliance with narrowly defined processes, or punishing process noncompliance, as governments often seek to do through externally set targets, does not promote the kind of learning and improvement needed when an institution or unit is undergoing adaptive change. Although management by target setting has certainly improved performance in some areas, it has also risked retarding innovation, learning, and improvement, and worsening clinicians' sense of disenfranchisement.[52] One academic dubbed the approach of setting targets, inspecting, and sanctioning poor performers as "targets and terror."[53]

Incentives, both financial and nonfinancial, can be used in a different way when change is adaptive: to complement the process of innovation adoption and to evolve clinician behavior over time. Employing incentives to support learning and to effect a change is different from using them to exercise operational control.* Boston's Massachusetts General Hospital has used a program of multiple incentives that evolve over time to help shift its culture and support significant changes in the way the work of care is done.

---

* The former promotes and exploits deviation whereas the latter aims to prevent deviation and limit change.

Faced with a new generation of payer contracts that included substantial payments for the achievement of quality goals, the Massachusetts General Physicians Organization (MGPO) started paying salaried physicians a quality incentive, beginning in 2006.[54] The MGPO's goal was to translate the external incentive, at the level of the organization, into internal incentives that applied to the individual behavior of those working within the institution.

Under the MGPO quality incentive program the maximum potential annual bonus payment for the most clinically active physicians was $5000, or about 2 percent of the average physician salary. Less-active physicians, as measured by annual relative value units, could receive $2500 per annum, and the least active, $1000.

Physicians were set performance targets for three quality measures every six months—predominantly process measures—and bonus payments were made twice a year. The program leadership selected two of the measures and the associated target performance levels, and the clinical departments or divisions selected the third. Measures were matched to the physicians' work—for instance, specialties that tend not to prescribe, such as pathologists, were not given medication-related targets. Measures were in place for one or more six-month periods and then replaced; 130 measures had been applied over the thirteen successive six-month terms reported.[55] For those measures used in multiple terms, the performance targets were raised over time.

The incentive program has been highly successful and has been credited with improving the ease of implementation of the EHR, compliance with hand hygiene, increased efficiency of radiology, and reduced emergency department utilization.[56] This success is in no small part attributable to the thoughtful use of many of the principles of incentive design described previously,[57] such as the following:

- **Short cycles:** Setting the behavior to be rewarded and the target level of performance required, measuring that behavior, and delivering the reward all occurred within six months, thereby reducing the time lag between evidencing the preferred behavior and receiving the reward.
- **Reward timing:** Rewards were deliberately delivered twice a year, at times in the annual calendar that were important to recipients—before the summer and winter holiday seasons—thereby increasing their saliency.
- **Rotating measures:** The focus of the incentive changed every six months (new metrics and performance targets were chosen twice a year), thus reducing the risk of complacency or undue focus on a very limited set of behaviors to the neglect of other important activities.
- **Clinician input into measure selection:** Although the majority of the metrics in the incentive program were chosen centrally, clinicians did have input into the selection of some metrics set at the department or specialty level, in effect "judging us for what we think is important." Of 130 measures applied over thirteen successive six-month cycles, only fifteen applied to all physicians.
- **Separation from usual reimbursement:** In the early phases, rewards were paid as separate checks mailed to the participating physician's home—again as a way of increasing saliency—and were accompanied with a letter specifying the level of performance required in the next cycle to gain the reward.
- **Specified value:** The total maximum reward was very clear, and physicians received a reward early in the program, to frame the incentive as a risk of a loss rather

than a possible gain (thus exploiting the lessons of prospect theory).

- **Staged (rising) targets:** Target levels of performance were set low initially and rose over successive six-month cycles so that increasing target levels of performance over time were set as an achievable goal gradient.
- **Balanced set of metrics:** The metrics chosen in any time period were a blend of measures relating to organizational and clinical imperatives, processes and outcomes, and infrastructural and clinical change.
- **Focus on the "work" of clinical practice:** The majority of metrics focused on adoption of new technologies or ways of working that might be considered "work" by clinicians—going to training sessions or learning to use new information technologies—thus avoiding interference with the important intrinsic motivations of the professional commitment to patient well-being, and the membership of a society of peers. The program focused more on repetitive tasks than the knowledge work of clinical practice. Nonetheless, all the chosen metrics related to activities physicians would agree were in patients' best interest.

Several other aspects of this incentive program are notable. First, the incentive system focused primarily on encouraging the adoption of new processes essential to accomplishing the work of care, not on the specific clinical care of a particular disease or patient risk group. Second, the conventional wisdom is that rewards have to be high enough to attract physicians' attention, and of course bonus sizes on Wall Street are legendary. Yet, in keeping with experience elsewhere (e.g., Intermountain Healthcare), the MGPO achieved its goals with relatively small amounts.

The incentive was conceived of less as a "payment" and more as a "financial recognition of the effort made."[58]

Third, the program's primary focus was the increased use of infrastructure known to be associated with increased quality and safety, such as electronic order entry and EHR use, and of well-accepted clinical practices such as hand washing and perioperative antibiotic use.

Fourth, the program was associated with other collateral benefits beyond changed physician practices, such as improved data quality and reporting capability. Its built-in flexibility—changing metrics or targets over time and with experience—doubtless contributed to this.

But the most important aspect of the MGPO's program is its intention. This is a program designed less for behavioral control and more to support the management of change and transition. Its goal was to "move behavior along a path at a tolerable pace."[59] This stands in contrast to conceiving of incentives as a mechanism of achieving performance control over their workers and process control in their operations, or worse, as a convenient substitute for the hard work of day-to-day leadership. The MGPO deployed a sequence of short-term incentives to guide long-term change.

Experience such as the MGPO's suggests an alternative framing for incentives—as a mechanism of helping staff through change. Habits are hard to break, and even when new technologies or practices are clearly in patients' best interests, those needing to learn new roles or new ways of working sometimes need encouragement, especially if productivity or the experience of work is worsened on the early part of the learning curve. In the MGPO model, the evolving nature of the metrics and targets chosen served to move a population of clinicians through adaptive change by treating clinical practice change as the adoption of an innovation. The institution played the long game and used the

incentive system to move the physician population along the innovation adoption curve.

LEADING CHANGE OVER TIME: THE INNOVATION
ADOPTION CURVE

In his seminal work *The Diffusion of Innovations*,[60] Everett Rogers
proposed a model of the spread of innovations through a population as a social phenomenon that is influenced by the nature
of the innovation and the social system through which it spread.*
He proposed five classes of adopter—innovators, early adopters,
early majority, late majority, and laggards—ranging from most
to least likely to adopt a new idea (Table 7.4).[61] Each group has a
different approach to the innovation adoption decision, each
adopts for a different reason, and if the innovation is to be promoted, each needs to be engaged in a different way.

Innovators and early adopters are actively interested in new
products, services, or practices and tend to be well connected to
innovation developers, sometimes working as "beta testers" of
a new product. They have sufficient social standing and resources to allow them to test an innovation that may fail and
tend to adopt for instrumental reasons: both the status con-
ferred by being seen to be at the leading edge and because the
specific innovation is of practical use to them.** Later adopters,
in contrast, typically need something else to initiate and sustain
the effort required to change their routines.

---

* Rogers based his model on a synthesis of sociological studies of the
uptake of hybrid corn seed by farmers in Iowa.
** Opinion leaders, who tend to be more exposed to new innovations
and are influential in communicating information about the innovation
to those who may adopt later, come from this group.

Table 7.4. Categories of innovation adopters, and the size of each subpopulation based on a normal distribution

Category	Percentage	Description
Innovators	2.5	Sufficient tolerance for risk that they are willing to adopt a technology or new practice that may ultimately fail and have sufficient resources to be able to withstand a loss
Early adopters	13.5	Have social status as "opinion leaders" and adopt innovations that will contribute to their success in their chosen field
Early majority	34	Adopt an innovation once it is proven
Late majority	34	Risk averse and tend to be skeptical about an innovation, adopt in response to peer pressure and emerging norms of practice
Laggards	16	Tend to be "traditional" and may only adopt if forced

Figure 7.1 represents the normal distribution of these subpopulations of adopters and the application of different incentives to each category.[62] Early adopters tend to be influenced by the nature of the innovation itself: the way it contributes to achieving their goal. They adopt the innovation because it meets their needs. Other incentives, financial or nonfinancial, positive or negative, help encourage later adopters to try the innovation and make the effort to learn new practices and to change their routines (Figure 7.1). By design, the MGPO's use of positive incentives (albeit framed as a risk of loss to exploit prospect theory) focused on the early majority, relying in part

Figure 7.1. Innovation adoption curve, and proposed incentive structure

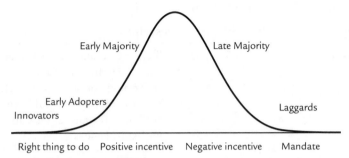

on peer pressure to encourage the later adopters to change their practices.

Other delivery organizations have used nonfinancial incentives in a similar way as the MGPO. Seattle's Virginia Mason Medical Center, for instance, has used the promise of a ward refit as the staff benefit for undertaking the work of a pathway and model of care redesign. Intermountain Healthcare structured in a "personal return on investment" (ROI) for physicians at each stage of its EHR implementation. These ROIs included automated discharge letter writing, or transcription, so that at each stage physicians experienced the reward of some noticeable improvement in the ease of their work. Mass General Brigham's Gregg Meyer, MD, cites charging doctors for paper prescriptions (to cover the costs of prescription processing) as an example of a negative incentive to help change the behavior of later adopters at the right-hand side of the curve.

Such institutions are not using an incentive as a substitute for operational control and performance management but are using a carefully selected set of related incentives deployed over a period of time as a component of their overall approach to managing change in a longer-term transition process.

SUMMARY: IMPLICATIONS FOR ACTION

To transform healthcare means to change clinician—particularly physician—behavior. Although new technologies may force a new way of working and the redesign of the operating system to support them, individual clinicians who are called upon to think and behave differently may need additional encouragement to change their clinical practices and work routines. Thinking through the use of personal incentives—financial and nonfinancial—and other behavior change techniques is an important part of implementing change. To use incentives thoughtfully does not necessarily make it "all about the money." Rather, it recognizes a pragmatic reality: rewards shape behavior, even among healthcare professionals dedicated to higher ideals. Thus the question is not whether to employ incentives to help the wider transformation process or the adoption of a more focused operating system change, it is how to create incentives that are consistent with the broader organizational or national culture and how to use those incentives well. This analysis is as applicable in countries with national health systems, in which most doctors and nurses are salaried state employees, as it is in situations where staff are independent practitioners. There is no such thing as an incentive-free environment. Other behavior change techniques also need thoughtful consideration and a careful evaluation of the possible enablers of or barriers to the desired behavior.

In sum, the following are steps for implementing incentives to support clinician behavior change:

1. Evaluate the nature of the planned change.
   a. Characterize the proposed change accurately. (Is it a new process or a new way of working? Is it a new technology or a new mindset? Is this a technical or adaptive change?)

b. Clarify exactly what behavior change you are asking people to make.

c. Consider the barriers staff face in behaving in the desired way, their current motivations, and the incentives to which they are already subject.

2. Consider what incentives would be appropriate. (How should they change over time? What capabilities will people need to be able to respond to these incentives? How can the principles of behavior change and behavioral economics be used to make the incentives more effective?) Keep your answers to these questions in mind as you follow the remaining steps.

3. Plan the use of incentives not as a manager of performance but as a support for longer-term change by

a. Engaging staff in the identification and selection of metrics and targets

b. Focusing on key infrastructure and well-evidenced behaviors

c. Rotating metrics over time

d. Evolving targets over time

e. Clearly identifying (and naming) the preferred behaviors

4. Create incentives consistent with professional culture and clinician values.

5. Exploit the power of nonfinancial incentives, particularly peer-to-peer comparison.

6. Reward at the group or team level wherever possible and at the individual level only in specific circumstances when an individual behavior is the primary determinant of outcome.

7. Ensure that staff have the skills and resources necessary to respond appropriately to the incentives (capability).

8. Develop the necessary pre-existing infrastructure such as the measurement system and data quality improvement processes.
9. Ensure that the incentives chosen are consistent with the culture you are trying to create.
10. Support a portfolio of behavior change methods, incentives, and metrics, such as
    a. Financial incentives to encourage compliance with repetitive tasks or engagement with new infrastructure (leaving intrinsic motivations for knowledge work)
    b. Process measures when the "stage of knowledge" is high (see Chapter 3), outcome measures for low "stage of knowledge" environments
    c. Other behavior change techniques to encourage compliance with a guideline when appropriate

Unfortunately, the sad reality is that implementations of new operating systems and care models rarely go as smoothly as intended, even with the best-planned approaches to change. Multiple midcourse corrections and constant refinement of the design and the approach to execution are a more common experience. Thus, Chapter 8 discusses the structured approaches to supporting ongoing improvement.

CHAPTER 8

Structured Approaches to Improvement and Innovation

Constant change is a fact of life for healthcare delivery organizations. Technologies advance, understanding of disease evolves, and patients' and regulators' expectations rise. New technologies force organizational change, for example, as the development of thrombolysis did by precipitating the reconfiguration of local services into stroke networks with specialist stroke units and physicians. Operating systems only last as long as their design fits with the current technology and the value patients expect it to deliver.

Organizations therefore need to be flexible and nimble and be able to respond to changing external conditions such as improved understanding in biology and engineering, new technological capability, changed regulatory constraints, and new financing and reimbursement models by constantly changing their operational approaches. The ability to adopt technological advances, develop new models of care, and manage small-scale changes incrementally is an essential characteristic of all successful delivery organizations and systems.

It is unfortunately rare that a new operating system or care model works perfectly the first time. New operating systems rarely survive first contact with a real patient or customer. Developing new internal systems to accommodate external changes is a necessarily imprecise activity, for which there is often no right answer and no single model or blueprint that can be implemented without adjustment or midcourse correction. Delivery organizations developing and deploying new operating systems need the ability to detect and correct small- and large-scale operational failures. They need a systematic and orchestrated approach to ongoing performance improvement.

All this means that improvement and innovation must be approached less as events and more as long-term organizational capabilities. Redesign is not an exception but a routine. Transformation is best viewed as an ongoing process: the ability to redesign the redesign. How do we embed the capability for constant change into routine operations in a coherent and structured way? Improvement and innovation have been the subjects of much hype, an abundant literature, and a confusing terminology. What are their key underlying general principles that can be applied in any setting?

PERSPECTIVES ON IMPROVEMENT

The idea that improvement methods developed in the Japanese manufacturing sector could be used as the basis for reform of U.S. healthcare's approach to quality of care was first proposed in the late 1980s.[1,2] Since then, the philosophy and improvement methods of total quality management (TQM) and the TPS have become the bedrock of healthcare efficiency and quality programs.

Previously, quality improvement had been approached as "quality assurance." Surveillance systems (either within institutions or at a regional or federal level) predominantly focused on physicians. They monitored for and sanctioned instances of individual physician failure in a process often characterized as "quality by inspection." The well-known disadvantages of this approach included that it focused on individuals not systems, assessed lapses in quality after the fact, was punitive and thus incentivized underreporting and hiding errors, required a substantial management infrastructure to administer, forced a division between managers and clinicians, and was prone to gaming. More important, quality assurance externalized quality to a "risk management" function, separate from other operations.

The roots of this approach to quality lie in "scientific management," a management philosophy attributed to Frederick Taylor's work at the turn of the twentieth century. Taylor argued that, in pursuit of efficiency and profit, production processes should be broken down into their component tasks and studied scientifically to identify the best way of doing each. Taylor made a clear distinction between the work of management—to design the work (mental labor)—and workers—to execute the tasks according to specification (manual labor). In 1911 he wrote

> It is only through *enforced* standardization of methods, *enforced* adoption of the best implements and working conditions, and *enforced* cooperation that this faster work can be assured. And the duty of enforcing the adoption of standards and enforcing this cooperation rests with *management* alone.
>
> > Taylor FW. Principles of Scientific Management.
> > Harper and Brothers; 1911:83 (italics in original)

Taylor also believed that workers should equally be subject to scientific scrutiny and the best worker chosen for the job: "In the past the man has been first; in the future the system must be first" (p. 7). He was not popular among the unions.

By contrast, the Japanese improvement models offered a distinctly different approach. Although there are many differences among the various approaches, which include TQM, TPS, continuous quality improvement (CQI), and Six-Sigma (an approach to improvement developed by General Electric), all share some important common philosophies of design and practical approaches:

- **Role of quality within the corporation:** The methodologies combine a set of quality improvement tools with a management philosophy. These place quality at the heart of the corporate enterprise, not as something "nice to have" but as a central requirement for competitiveness. The first of Deming's famous list of 14 key principles was "create constancy of purpose toward improvement of product and service, with the aim to become competitive."[3] Moreover, quality and efficiency are not seen to be in conflict with each other. On the contrary, quality is viewed as costing less in the long run. The primary motivation for quality, therefore, is to improve competitiveness: the economic and quality imperatives are conjoined.

- **Integration of quality and quality improvement:** In contrast to post hoc inspection of the outcome, quality improvement is treated as integral to daily production. Deming suggested to "eliminate the need for massive inspection by building quality into the product in the first place" (principle 3). This means that quality improvement philosophies and tools are integrated into production routines rather than managed as a separate activity with responsibility given to a separate department. The implications of this are, first, that quality improvement becomes a continuous activity rather than a periodic one and, second, that improvement is part of everybody's "day job," not an add-on for after the day's "real" work has been done.

- **Worker motivation for improvement:** If quality is to be managed in concert with routine operations, then frontline workers need to be engaged, not controlled. The Japanese quality philosophies all make the assumption that workers (including blue-collar workers) want to do a good job and that they derive satisfaction and meaning from being able to do so. This stands in sharp contrast to the outdated classist Taylorist notion that blue-collar workers are only there for the income and need to be controlled.

This assumption leads the Japanese models to conceptualize the role of management differently. Management's task is to support workers (who are treated as intellectually capable) to do a better job. This means not only providing training and resources, but also addressing those system issues driving low quality and productivity that are largely out of the control of frontline workers.

- **Democratization of science:** Further, if frontline workers are to be engaged in the work of improving quality and productivity and are to take more control over production quality, then they need the tools to do so. The Japanese models all incorporate tools that make the analytic methods of statistics and operations research easily accessible by those without formal training in these disciplines. These include the run charts and control charts of statistical process control, process evaluation tools such as flowcharts, value-stream maps, and fishbone diagrams, and the routine of the experimental method through the P-D-S-A (plan, do, study, act) cycle. In effect, these tools are intended to bring the methods of science to routine production.

- **Process focus:** The Japanese methodologies replace inspection's outcome focus with a process orientation.

This allows the prospective design of quality into future activities and focuses quality attention away from the individual person to the system. Frontline workers can most easily exercise their control rights through surveillance and modification of the production process.

The process orientation has other advantages. It provides a framework for variation reduction, not just by analysis of aggregated data, but through the early identification and correction of individual process deviations as they occur. And it facilitates connections along longer patient pathways, facilitating collaboration among the different specialist individuals and organizations contributing to the patient's overall care. In effect, it supports an enterprise perspective.

- **Incrementalism:** Solving many smaller production problems early and often is core to the Japanese methodologies. Daily improvements over long periods of time—the aggregation of marginal gains—add up to significant improvements in the limit. An equation describing the approach could be written as

$$\sum_{i=1}^{i=\infty} Small\ improvement_i = Big\ improvement$$

Statistical process control in TQM, and the "andon" cord* in the TPS, are mechanisms of identifying deviations from expected performance early so that they may be acted on immediately.

---

* When workers on the Toyota assembly line encounter a quality or process problem, they sound the alert by pulling a cord at their workstation, called an "andon" cord.

Since the 1990s, these models of improvement have become an integral part of healthcare management. However, as influential as these ideas have been, they have not been without their controversy. Much of this relates not to the principles themselves but to the way they have been applied, in particular to the use of standardization in healthcare. Inflexible clinical or operational standards expressed, for example, as mandated clinical decision rules or maximum visit durations or emergency room waits, typically elicit complaints of "cookbook medicine," or "medical Taylorism," or that "people are not cars."[4] Physicians fear the loss of professional autonomy and the personal touch, and most importantly they fear that the complexity of medical problems and the sophistication of clinical decision-making will be lost in standardized processes.[5]

Standardization is core to the Japanese improvement methodologies. It brings reliability to production and makes deviation (both warranted and unwarranted variation) easier to observe. The same is true in healthcare. We no longer doubt that standardization generally improves outcomes. However, it is also clear that, as Swensen and colleagues note, "Undiscerning enforcement of even excellent guidelines can be dangerous."[6] So the important question is, how do we realize the benefits of these approaches to improvement while avoiding any potential harms? And how do we bake quality improvement into daily practices and routines so that it is indistinguishable from routine care?

STRUCTURED APPROACHES TO IMPROVEMENT

One of the Japanese improvement methods' keys to success is that they are highly structured. Improvement processes are specifically defined, rigorously implemented, and closely integrated into the activities of day-to-day work. The various approaches to improvement all have two related features in common. First, they focus on process specification and analysis of deviation. A clinical or operational process is mapped out and specified in detail, using any one of several tools such as flow diagramming and value-stream mapping. The purpose of this is to make the opaque transparent. It is hard to improve what you cannot see.

In many delivery organizations, critical processes—including disease-specific protocols, patient pathways, and clinical and operational tasks—are not well defined. This lack of specificity can lead to essential treatments not being delivered, ineffective therapies being overused, avoidable complications and costs, and lapses in safety. And it leads to inconsistent practice and unwarranted variation from which it is impossible to learn. Standardization's benefit is that it makes the nonstandard all that more obvious and easier to analyze. Clinical and operational performance is improved when deviations associated with a better outcome are repeated for all future eligible patients, and those associated with a worse outcome, or no impact, are ceased. A process cannot be improved without specification of what should happen, monitoring of what does happen, and measurement of its impact.

The second feature common to improvement methodologies is their integration of design and execution: designs are executed into practice and experience from practice informs future designs (Figure 8.1). Formal improvement methodologies all incorporate redesign and updating of the previously specified process. The routine of specification, observation, analysis, and correction of deviation ensures that over time the intended process is faithfully executed. Execution failures are corrected and their underlying causes removed so that the process's *yield*—its actual performance under current conditions—is improved.

Figure 8.1. Interplay between design and execution

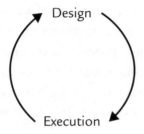

However, the observation of deviation can also reveal places where the process as designed is not up to its task. The process's *potential*—its maximum possible performance in ideal conditions— is inadequate. Even if executed perfectly, it would not achieve its intended goal, and it would have to be substantially redesigned to do so.

In clinical care the equivalent of the "design" in car manufacture is the protocol, which specifies the sequence of tasks and decisions that defines the patient's care. The operating system is the mechanism of that design's execution: it supports all the clinical and administrative tasks that typically follow a decision, such as scheduling and completing a diagnostic test, placing the central line, or undertaking an invasive procedure.

All structured approaches to improvement make extensive use of process standardization, something doctors often eschew. In the Japanese approaches "standards" are temporary, in place only until a better one comes along. Production systems get better through constant revision, over the short term to improve their yield and over the long term to improve their potential. At Toyota learning occurs at two levels: learning related to the core design of the car and learning related to the process of producing it.

KEY COMPONENTS OF A STRUCTURED APPROACH TO IMPROVEMENT

Structured approaches to improvement combine philosophies, processes, and tools to form a complete system. Advocates of the Japanese approaches argue that the individual tools are less effective on their own, and experience suggests that the same is true when models developed in production industries are applied in healthcare. An improvement system's key components, described next, all need to be in place and interacting together for the system to be most effective. Some elements support the execution of an existing design and others the process of longer-term improvement in the design. The key components of any structured approach to improvement include the following.

Specification of a Standard

Specifying a process defines what should happen.* Although standard processes do guide staff behavior, their more important role is to act as the benchmark against which future performance can be judged and to serve as a reference that makes instances of a nonstandard process more evident. Standard processes improve the signal-to-noise ratio. Standard pathways and protocols are often thought of, and used as, mechanisms of operational and behavioral control, but their real potential is as mechanisms of learning.

Standards also improve predictability for staff. In describing the essence of the Toyota system, Spear and Bowen summarized one of the Toyota "rules in use" as "all work shall be highly specified as to content, sequence, timing, and outcome."[7] Linkages between tasks or steps in the assembly of components into a part

---

* In TPS this is called "standard work."

are similarly highly specified so that handoffs—a known point of safety risk in healthcare—are direct and between named individuals, and communication of request and response is clear and unambiguous.*

Such practices stand in sharp contrast to much of healthcare, where guidelines are typically written specifically to allow room for discretion. The usual rationale for less specification is biological uncertainty and patient variability. Specifications are often intentionally loose to allow room for flexibility in the face of the uncertainty—in diagnosis, likely response to therapy, or patient preference—that attends most patients' care. Unfortunately, the result is often that patient pathways are jumbled and communication can be delayed or ambiguous. Intermountain Healthcare takes an alternative approach. It maintains flexibility not by avoiding specification but by combining high degrees of specification with processes that make it easy to override the specified care. Standardized does not mean invariant. Notably, Intermountain specifies and standardizes both clinical decisions and practical tasks: whether to initiate an intervention and how to do it. More often, as previously noted, delivery organizations that willingly specify and standardize the routine for the placement of a central line do not specify the (potentially more controversial) decision of when to place one.

Detection of Deviation

Accordingly, all the improvement models incorporate tools and routines for the early detection of deviation from the specification. These tools, for example process flow diagrams and control charts, are typically agnostic to the nature of the deviation: whether it is positive (causally related to a positive outcome), neg-

---

* This is the essence of the SBAR communication model used by the military (Situation, Background, Assessment, Recommendation).

ative (related to a poor outcome), or unrelated to the ultimate outcome. They tend not to apportion blame to an individual. Although specification makes detection of deviation easier (i.e., you cannot detect the "unexpected" if you do not know what to expect), differentiating meaningful deviation from the random variation inherent in all processes remains challenging. Not only does the deviation have to be observed but it must also be easy for the observer to bring it to others' attention. Hence, many of the tools not only aid in the detection of a deviation but also amplify the signal of abnormality so that it is noticed and brings a response. Amplification remains a problem in healthcare. One study, for example, found that only 7 percent of problems encountered by nurses in their daily work were elevated within the organization to a point where a generalized solution could be designed and implemented.[8]

Methods of facilitating detection include the tools of statistical process control—run charts, control charts, and the run rules—and what Toyota calls "visual controls." These are simple visual cues that make it easy to see if something is out of place: for example, shadow boards, kanban cards,* colorful labeling, and lines on the floor indicating where equipment should be placed. The "andon" cord is less a mechanism to aid in detection of a deviation than one to amplify a signal of abnormality. It primarily alerts others to the presence of a problem. These tools all aim to ensure that the feedback loop between deviation, detection, and action is as quick as possible.

---

* The kanban card is part of Toyota's "pull" system of parts management and product flow control. It is a signal that parts are depleted and triggers ordering of more. Because parts are only ordered when needed less inventory is kept on hand, supporting Toyota's "lean" approach to manufacturing.

Analysis: Making Meaning of Deviation

Not all deviation from a specified process is meaningful: random variation is a fact of life in any complex process. Reacting to a random deviation as if it were nonrandom can worsen, not improve, operational control. Hence all the methodologies incorporate mechanisms to aid in making meaning of an observed deviation, in effect differentiating meaningful variation from random noise. Some rely on statistical methods, others on qualitative techniques, and still others on human interpretation and team-based routines. All analyze deviation in a structured way.

The tools of statistical process control use the statistical principles underlying the "run rules"—a set of tests that identify nonrandom variation in real time—to achieve this. The run rules are mathematical tests that are satisfied when an observed deviation is statistically significant (i.e., occurs with a probability ≤ 0.05). Other tools, such as Pareto analysis, allow analysis of aggregated observations to help pinpoint the causes of the deviation. Qualitative and team tools include fishbone or driver diagrams, and the process of "5-whys" to help staff attribute cause to observed deviations. All these tools tend to focus on system, rather than individual worker, causes of deviation.

Implementation of Countermeasures

Finding deviations and understanding their underlying causes serves no purpose if these causes are not corrected. The improvement methodologies aim to simplify frontline intervention to correct process errors. In effect, they push problem-solving capability and authority as close to the front line as possible. In the manufacturing setting this means giving control to blue-collar workers, in keeping with the notion of "democratization" discussed previously. Hence in TPS, the purpose of pulling the andon cord is not so much to "stop the line" as it is popularly represented: it is to call for help. When the andon cord is pulled, a supervisor goes to that point in the production line to help the worker there solve the problem. The signal escalates the observed problem up a chain of problem-solving capability.

The andon cord interrupts routine work to allow a problem to be fixed. Applied in healthcare this principle translates to the ability to override the standard clinical recommendation and pursue an alternative course when, in the physician's clinical judgment, standard care does not meet the current patient's needs. This principle is central to Intermountain Healthcare's approach to clinical protocols. Intermountain expects, and intends, that its standard protocols will be overridden. The countermeasure is a justified instance of nonstandard care, or, in other words, warranted variation.

Taken together, these four components are nothing more than the application of the scientific method to routine operations. The cycle of "specify, detect, evaluate, correct" (and the process of "plan, do, study act") is no different than the experimental routine of establishing a hypothesis (or differential diagnosis), collecting data, analyzing, and drawing a conclusion. And, like the scientific and clinical methods, these components are only effective if they are linked together in a closed-loop system. There is no point detecting an abnormality if it is not easy to respond and similarly no point being good at responding if you cannot detect.

Longer-Term Redesign

Other elements in the improvement methodologies more specifically support the process of long-term redesign. They approach fundamental redesign in two ways. First, although correcting deviations as they occur ensures that the current design is well executed—and better executed over time—it also reveals needs or opportunities for fundamental redesign in the future. At Intermountain Healthcare the reasons for physician override of standard clinical protocols are fed back to the teams responsible for designing the protocol. Protocols are completely redesigned every two years, and interim changes are made more frequently as necessary.

Second, in addition to responding to problems that have already happened, the principle of "kaizen"—continuous improvement—in the TPS focuses on addressing problems before they have occurred by harnessing frontline worker ideas for improvement. Toyota is reputed to receive over a million employee suggestions for improvement each year, the vast majority of which are acted upon.

Summary of an Improvement System's Key Components

The various improvement methodologies use a range of tools to implement the features described (Table 8.1). CQI/TQM and TPS each use their own preferred set of tools, but there are many others available that achieve the same ends (the right-hand column in Table 8.1). The TPS embeds best practice for undertaking a task or assembling a component in "standard work"—comprising the precise definition of a sequence of actions, the time the sequence should take ("takt time"), and the standard inventory required. Evidence-based protocols and pathways do something similar by specifying a standard protocol and then reinforcing its adoption using pay-for-performance reimbursement systems, standing order sets, electronic order entry, and quality metrics.

In sum, the essence of these structured approaches to improvement is the development of a frontline workforce that is supported to focus on systematic problem-solving and that can both identify and correct deviations in real time during routine operations and incorporate improvements into future practice. These approaches to improvement not only provide tools that empower the front line but also emphasize creating a cultural context in

Table 8.1. Examples of improvement system tools to support the execution of a design

Component	CQI[a]/TQM[b]	TPS[c]	Other
Specify a standard	Flow diagram	Value-stream map Standard work	Evidence-based medicine Protocols and pathways Clinical decision criteria
Detect (and amplify) deviation from the standard	Statistical process control (run chart, control chart, and run rules)	Kanban card Visual controls Andon cord	Sentinel event reporting Variance reports (outcomes, PREMs[d], PROMs[e]) Targets Culture of speaking up/blame-free reporting SBAR[f]
Analyze/make meaning of the deviation	Pareto chart Fishbone diagram Driver diagram	5-whys	Morbidity and mortality meetings/critical incident review Root cause analysis
Take corrective steps/implement countermeasures	"Future state" process design	Supervisor support of local problem-solving	Protocol override Rapid response/ medical emergency team PDSA[g]/rapid cycle testing

[a]Continuous quality improvement.
[b]Total quality management.
[c]Toyota Production System.
[d]Patient-reported experience measure.
[e]Patient-reported outcome measure.
[f]Situation, background, assessment, recommendation.
[g]Plan, do, study, act.

which those tools are used that encourages speaking up about current problems and a relentless search for better ways of doing things in the future: setting the tool use in a supportive learning environment with leadership that reinforces learning behavior. The key point is that these five features of improvement systems are more important than the particular tool any given delivery organization chooses for the purpose of implementing that feature. In the words of Deng Xiaoping, "It does not matter if it is a yellow cat or a black cat as long as it catches mice."[9]

THE TOYOTA PRODUCTION SYSTEM

The TPS is one of several structured approaches to improvement applied to healthcare in recent years. At its heart TPS is a management philosophy that embodies many of the principles described previously. As with the other approaches to improvement, TPS combines key concepts and principles with specific tools for putting them into action. And, as with others, although the tools are more obvious, the principles are more important. Some of the key concepts are muda (eliminate waste), jidoka (solve problems in real time), kaizen (continuous improvement), and heijunka (level flow).

Muda (Eliminate Waste)

Toyota systematically strips waste ("muda," strictly wastefulness, uselessness, and futility) from its production processes: hence the common term "lean" for the TPS. Much is written about what constitutes waste, and TPS itself identifies seven kinds (overproduction, inventory, waiting, transport, defects, motion, and overprocessing).* The unifying common thread is that waste in TPS is regarded as any activity that is "non-value adding."

---

* An eighth waste, unutilized or underutilized employee talent, is sometimes added to this list.

Toyota's very wide definition of waste has the effect of forcing an important discipline. In defining waste as non-value-adding activity, Toyota must first define value, and equally important, identify *for whom* the value is added. Of course, like any complex system, the Toyota production line has internal and intermediate customers, but ultimately by "value" TPS means the value received by the end customer, the car buyer. Healthcare has not always been so clear. Although the patient is usually identified as the key customer, in practice healthcare delivery systems often act as if others—physicians, referrers, staff, students, teachers, insurers, regulators, and researchers—are equally, or even more important, customers. TPS is not so confused.

Second, connecting waste to value forces Toyota to understand its own processes in sufficient detail to be able to identify which of its activities indeed do add value and which do not: this is the primary purpose of the "value-stream map." Toyota's definition of waste, and the internal discipline it forces, echoes the production system's origins in postwar Japan, when materials and capital were in such short supply that industry could simply not afford the seven types of waste.

Jidoka (Solve Problems in Real Time)

Jidoka, literally "intelligent automation" or "automation with a human touch," represents a principle of solving problems in real time. In its original expression "jidoka" meant that an automated machine stopped when it detected a deviation. The operator then identified and removed the cause and integrated any improvement into the standard workflow and future automated functioning (thus embedding human insight into inanimate equipment and processes). Because equipment stopped only when it detected problems, a single operator could oversee many machines, a significant increase in productivity.

Jidoka incorporates detection and amplification of an abnormality and immediate response. It could be argued that such an approach to problem-solving is expensive. Surely interrupting production to immediately deal with individual defective items and maintaining sufficient spare staff to aid in problem-solving all adds cost. In fact, TPS presumes the exact opposite. It is easier to correct defects as they occur than to disassemble and repair a completed, but defective, product later. And it is also less expensive than discarding a defective product entirely. Errors' long cost tail is avoided by early intervention. The same is true in healthcare.

Moreover, TPS treats defects as a source of short-term and long-term learning for staff and for the production system as a whole. Data about the problem are maximal in the moments after the problem is discovered. Data decay after that, particularly being lost at shift change when the workers present at the time the problem occurred leave the building, taking with them whatever insights they may have into the problem's cause. Furthermore, the data available immediately when a problem is detected are both sociological (i.e., human) and technological. Subtleties relating to lighting, or worker fatigue, or environmental conditions, might be missed when incidents are reported in aggregate later.

The andon cord is central to the implementation of the principle of jidoka. Contrary to common belief, the production line does not stop every time the cord is pulled (the ratio of cord pulls to line stoppages is about 12:1). The andon cord is first and foremost a signal to call a more experienced problem solver to the workstation. If the problem cannot be solved immediately, more senior workers come to help to conduct what is in effect a real-time root cause analysis. Hence the andon cord is a mechanism for escalating a problem up a chain of ever more experienced problem solvers. Other tools supporting the principle of jidoka include standard work, 5S (a workplace organization tool—sort, set in order, shine, standardize, and sustain), and visual controls, all of which make it easier to detect non-standard events and thus identify when the andon cord should be pulled.

This approach to problem-solving differs markedly from the way some problems, including some related to patient safety, are dealt with in healthcare. Morbidity and mortality rounds, for example, review groups of cases often weeks after incidents have occurred. These can be far from safe environments for junior staff to engage in frank discussions about the sources of a failure.

Kaizen (Continuous Improvement)

Although jidoka solves problems as they arise, kaizen solves them before they happen. The forward-looking principle of continuous improvement engages workers in searching for better ways to do things. In the Toyota system, improvement is not something developed by experts in a distant lab. It is just as much under the control of blue-collar workers on the production line. Toyota's system implicitly assumes that workers want to do a better job and draw meaning and satisfaction from being able to do so: an assumption reflected in the number of employee suggestions for improvement and the proportion ultimately implemented into practice. The classic description is that everybody at Toyota has two jobs: doing the job and making the job better. Implementing the majority of a huge number of employee suggestions for improvement not only improves the quality, efficacy, and cost of the production process but also makes the job easier to do and more pleasant. Workers benefit as much as Toyota: implementing many improvements rapidly ensures that workers receive a personal return on investment for contributing to the work of improving processes.

Heijunka (Level Flow)

Fluctuation is the Achilles heel of a production system. It can waste time, effort, or cash, and Toyota strives to avoid it. In TPS reducing unevenness reduces waste. Fluctuation can arise from variation in demand and the production process itself, and demand variation can be external (deriving from customers' orders) or internal: what TPS terms "failure demand," the additional work required to correct avoidable errors. Jidoka and kaizen together act to prevent failure demand. Customer demand can be foretold by predictive modeling in the sales cycle and accommodated in the production process. TPS production lines deliberately make multiple models at once (in contrast to making batches of uniform products) so that the specific car for each customer can be made to order. The practice of "just-in-time" means that intermediate parts are produced only when needed, and where possible at a constant rate and in a known sequence. For example, car seats, produced by an external supplier, are delivered in the same sequence as the cars to which they will be fitted are being produced. The net result is predictability at every point in the production process all the way to predictability of delivery for the customer.

The Toyota Production System as a System for Learning

Taken together, these interacting principles in Toyota constitute a system for learning: encode best practice in standard work, identify and correct problems in its execution in real time, and use these insights to drive the next generation of design. Jidoka and kaizen can be seen as simply two different approaches to problem-solving: the former reactive (rapid response to a problem as soon as possible after it has occurred) and the latter proactive (identify a problem that has not happened yet or a system that has not failed, and improve it). And, as already noted, the principles are more important than the tools used to implement them into practice.

In their study of the TPS, Spear and Bowen observed that these principles find expression in four implicit "rules in use":[10]

Rule 1: All work shall be highly specified as to content, sequence, timing, and outcome.

Rule 2: Every customer-supplier connection must be direct, **and** there must be an unambiguous yes-or-no way to send requests and receive responses.

Rule 3: The pathway for every product and service must be simple and direct.

Rule 4: Any improvement must be made in accordance with the scientific method, under the guidance of a teacher, at the lowest possible level in the organization.

These rules are the mechanism by which the low waste of "lean manufacturing" is actually achieved, and the tools such as standard work, the andon cord, and visual controls are simply methods of implementing the principles and putting the rules into practice.

DEFINING AN APPROACH TO IMPROVEMENT

The structured models of improvement all create, and then manage, a tension between imposed temporary standardization and observed variance in a way that allows them to learn. The more tightly specified the standard, the more likely it is to be overridden in practice; therefore the more episodes of

Figure 8.2. The "double-loop" learning model of improvement

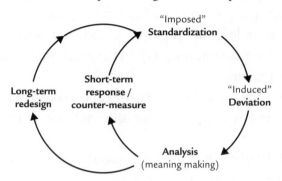

deviation there are to analyze and from which to potentially learn. Learning occurs in the short term through the development and deployment of countermeasures to address an immediate problem, and in the long term through larger-scale product and process redesign: a "double-loop"[11] learning model (Figure 8.2).

Intermountain Healthcare is a well-known proponent of using clinical standardization in this way. Teams develop well-designed protocols covering a large proportion of the common conditions treated by the organization (called "clinical process models" at Intermountain).[12] These protocols are embedded into its information system so that they are available at the point of care. When the treating clinician concludes that the protocol does not meet the needs of the individual patient being treated, he or she overrides the protocol recommendations and provides a reason for doing so. These reasons for override are collated and analyzed by a central group at Intermountain's Healthcare Delivery Institute, and the lessons learned are used to update the next generation of protocols, either routinely on a two-year cycle, or more frequently if necessary. By closing the feedback loop in this way, Intermountain ensures that its standard protocols are always temporary.

Intermountain, like Toyota, takes a particular approach to learning and knowledge management. It treats knowledge as an organizational, not individual, property and uses its standardized routines for production and clinical care as vehicles for knowledge maintenance and transfer. Intermountain actively curates that knowledge by constantly updating its processes and protocols in response to insights gained not only from others' published research but also from its own practice. The improvement system puts the tools and authority for managing the learning potential inherent in routine practice in the hands of the frontline workforce in a way that maximizes process transparency and local control.

Most healthcare delivery organizations use improvement tools, although not all organize them into a complete system. Some have stayed close to a particular improvement model such as TPS or CQI. Others have been more catholic in their approach, combining tools drawn from multiple improvement philosophies. For some it has been important to avoid a Japanese lexicon or philosophy. Intermountain has created a clinical improvement and knowledge management system using the same principles but its own set of tools. For any local leader the most important thing is to carefully choose, from the many available, a portfolio of tools that is sensitive to the local culture and conditions and that implements the principles described previously in an integrated way to create a learning system (see Chapter 9).

PERSPECTIVES ON INNOVATION

Where improvement systems exploit the tension between the standard and a variance, innovation systems focus on a creative tension between current reality and aspiration about the future. Innovation concentrates less on refining what is already there than on creating something new.

For generations, innovativeness was regarded as an individual characteristic. Great thinkers had flashes of brilliance: for example, Archimedes' eureka moment in the bath or Newton's falling apple. Organizations were innovative to the extent they were able to attract and support such individuals—the "out-of-the-box" thinkers—often housing them with their essential resources in an experimental laboratory or "skunkworks" that were not only far away from routine operations but also apart from the main research division. In this model, innovations found their way into daily use through the separate processes of innovation diffusion and technology adoption by which potential users were first attracted to an innovation and then integrated it into their contexts and work routines. Those in routine practice did not innovate; they adopted.

Recent years have seen the development of a more nuanced model of innovation, in which organizations are thought of as creating cultures of innovation and innovative capacity is more widely spread among staff at all levels. This approach treats innovation as a learnable skill and blurs the line between innovator and user. This change in perspective—from individual characteristic to organizational capability—challenges previous notions of the nature of innovations and the process by which they are created.

Writing in 1990, Henderson and Clark characterized what they called "architectural" innovations: those in which the products' basic components do not change, but the relationship among them does.[13] They observed that seemingly minor changes in technology could have "disastrous effects on industry incumbents." Organizations were prone to underestimating the extent of the change because relationships among a product's components were baked into the firm's structure: although the product had changed, the firm had not.

We usually think of basic laboratory research, drug development and clinical trials, and medical device invention as the primary sources of innovation in healthcare. However, not all innovation requires de novo drug or device invention. Some healthcare innovations are architectural: based on the reconfigurations of old components into new processes or models of care, or the application of an existing idea or technology to a new context. A new process can be an innovation as much as a new product, and a practitioner can innovate as much as a researcher or developer. Breakthroughs can be developed in everyday settings.

MICS provides a case in point. As described in Chapter 6, none of the three key components of the innovative MICS procedure were that new: occluding the aorta internally with a balloon rather than externally with a clamp, establishing arterovenous access for heart-lung bypass through the femoral artery and vein rather than directly into the central vessels through a sternotomy, and small incision "port" access to the surgical site with long-shafted instruments and flexible scopes had all been described previously. And minimally invasive surgery was already well established in orthopedics and general surgery. What was new was recombining these three components into a genuinely new cardiac procedure.

Not only can innovations be developed in routine settings, but the process by which innovative designs are created can also be routine. Art and business schools and product design companies such as IDEO have "industrialized" innovation by codifying the design process into a set of reproducible sequential steps demonstrating that it is possible to approach innovation in a very structured way. Although several models of the innovation process have been described, they all share some common themes. They all manage variance for the purposes of creating learning and insight: variance is at the heart of all creative learning.

KEY COMPONENTS OF A STRUCTURED APPROACH TO INNOVATION

As with improvement methodologies, the observable tactics of the structured approaches to innovation reflect some deeper underlying principles for creating a new product or service. Each phase of the design process is associated with multiple tools. The key phases are developing a deep understanding of need, creating a large pool of potential options (divergent thinking), winnowing options (convergent thinking), and rapid testing.

Developing a Deep Understanding of Need

An innovation is often thought of as an "invention implemented." At the heart of any innovation is an understanding of the adopter's need that it is to satisfy. Without understanding what motivates a user to adopt, an innovator cannot address the gap between the current reality and the future aspiration the innovation must address. All structured approaches to innovation emphasize this phase, in part because adequate problem definition is so central to successful solution development (or to quote the American philosopher John Dewey, "A problem well put is half solved").[14]

Customer problems are commonly misspecified. For example, in trying to address long waiting lines, Hertz realized that what customers really wanted was not to spend less time in line but to get on their way as fast as possible. Instead of adding agents and simplifying paperwork, it created "Hertz Gold" with no line at all.[15] Christensen and colleagues argue that a fundamental misunderstanding of customer need is behind the failure of many potential innovations.[16] In part because of an overreliance on aggregated customer survey data and in part because customers find it challenging to describe an unimagined future, companies risk innovating to solve the wrong problem.

To some extent, skilled innovators do not listen to their customers. Henry Ford is often reported to have said, "If I'd asked my customers what they wanted, they'd have said a faster horse."* In a similar vein, David Lewis, for many years Bang & Olufsen's lead product designer, commented, "I don't care what customers want, I give them what they need."[17] This does not mean that designers are uninterested in what their customers have to say. It is simply that in addition to asking customers what they want, designers tend to watch what they do. This phase of the design process emphasizes field research and direct observation of customers in their own environment, using the techniques from ethnography. Only by direct observation can an innovator understand what triggers a product or service's use, how customers make their own adjustments and customize the product, how the product interacts with the customer's environment, or what other intangible attributes are important.[18] Zenios and colleagues point out that, in healthcare, certain circumstances are likely to have a higher yield of problems that can lead to the identification of needs. For patients these include pain, stress, or the risk of procedure-related premature death; for clinicians, heightened clinical risk, device malfunction, uncertainty, and dogma ("It's always been done this way"); and for systems, inefficiency and excess cost.[19]

It might be assumed that clinicians, who are so close to each patient, would be perfectly positioned to understand what pa-

---

* In fact, there is no evidence that he actually said this. However, his freezing of the design of the Model T did allow him to refine his assembly process and thus compete on price. In the longer term, however, his lack of sensitivity to customer preferences ultimately saw him lose out to Alfred Sloan and General Motors. See Vlaskovits P. Henry Ford, innovation, and that "Faster Horse" quote. *Harv Bus Rev* August 11, 2011. Accessed Nov 19, 2020. https://hbr.org/2011/08/henry-ford-never-said-the-fast.

tients need and want from a healthcare system. But, as noted in Chapter 2, this is not necessarily so. Physicians are trained to think diseases are the problem, when for patients the problem is typically the impact of the disease on their lives. Because they tend to focus on the treatment that solves the immediate health problem, doctors may miss other needs that are only revealed by deeper inquiry and observation. Physicians can be blind to the myriad other factors influencing patients' priorities and compliance, from the cost of medications or transport, to the distance to the bathroom, or the difficulty interpreting food labels.

Creating a Large Pool of Potential Options (Divergent Thinking)

Innovation processes also emphasize developing an expanded set of solutions to the customer's problem, and they use team-based techniques, such as brainstorming or IDEO's version, the "Deep Dive," to achieve this. The goal is to encourage divergent thinking: the development of a wide range of options that will be evaluated and narrowed later. IDEO has established seven brainstorming rules for the "Deep Dive" that help its staff ensure a rich flow of ideas:[20]

1. Defer judgment
2. Encourage wild ideas
3. Build on the ideas of others
4. Go for quantity
5. Have one conversation at a time
6. Stay focused on the topic
7. Be visual

This is idea volume over idea quality. IDEO argues that even ideas that may initially seem offbeat and irrelevant can provide the germ of another idea or precipitate a suggestion that will ultimately prove vital (hence their mantra "encourage wild ideas"). Other design houses, for instance the Helen Hamlyn Centre for Design at London's Royal College of Art, frame this "ideating" as a deliberate focus on thinking in the abstract, unconstrained by the materiality of the real world.[21]

A process that forces conceptual thinking partly serves to prevent teams going straight from an articulation of a problem to the design of a concrete solution without first giving deeper consideration to both the nature of the problem and the range of possible solutions. This of course is a particular risk in healthcare, where clinicians habitually solve problems under time pressure. They have been specifically trained in rapid diagnosis and solution selection, an approach that works well when problems have previously been well described and solutions tested over years of experience. However, this way of working is less helpful when clinical staff confront organizational and system design problems with which they have little experience and for which there are few precompiled responses available.

A consistent feature of organized approaches to innovation is the diversity of the team. Innovations often originate from a happy collision among seemingly unrelated disciplines—exactly what the divergent thinking phase is intended to encourage. Hence, for innovators a "diverse" team is not one that comprises an orthopedic surgeon and a neurosurgeon, nor a doctor and a nurse, but one with a doctor, nurse, social worker, informatician, anthropologist, ambulance driver, process engineer, poet, and a patient. It is exactly because some members of the team are not immersed in a lifetime's details of care delivery that they are well positioned to frame a problem differently and propose alternative models and potential solutions. Insiders can be less "able to imagine alternatives."[22]

As another way of expanding the pool of available ideas and options, the innovation literature also emphasizes looking in unconventional places. The term "reverse innovation" describes the practice of sourcing innovative ideas and products from the developing world on the grounds that resource constraint spurs innovation (so "reversing" the more usual flow of goods and service ideas from the developed to the developing world).

Winnowing Options (Convergent Thinking)

The ultimate purpose of the divergent thinking phase is to create a wide range of design options. However, at some point these must be narrowed. Although delaying "design freeze" as late as possible is usually associated with developing more effective designs—a practice common in software development, for instance—eventually choices must be made. Otherwise, the risk is paralytic analysis.

Once again, this process is team-based on the grounds that a single master designer often cannot know enough about all the aspects of a technology or model of care to make a choice (at IDEO it is argued that "enlightened trial-and-error succeeds over the planning of a lone genius"[23]). Several specific tools can be used to help with the task of consolidating ideas into a smaller set of high potential options, including a clustering (of like or related ideas), mapping (creating "mind maps" that show the relationships between clusters), and multivoting in which team members have to use multiple votes to rank the ideas.

This phase is closely connected to the next, rapid prototyping. Ultimately, complete certainty can never exist. Questions about the utility and practicality of an innovation can never be fully resolved through theoretical exercises: they must be tested in practice. This is the "enlightened trial-and-error" referenced earlier.

Rapid Testing

Rapid prototyping and testing of still incomplete designs is a way of generating information that cannot be collected in other ways.

This is learning "by doing," rather than learning "before doing."[24] Clinicians are often uncomfortable with this approach. They see it as high risk and are used to being able to collect more data through diagnostic testing, or running controlled trials. However, there are few "diagnostic tests" available for an organizational or operational rearrangement or the deployment of a new model of care. A randomized trial of organizational arrangements is difficult to execute and the medical literature can provide little guidance. Even observational studies of alternative operating system designs can fail to account for many unobservable local contextual factors and thus mean that their results are difficult to interpret or generalize. For example, studies of the use of the surgical checklist have failed to confirm early promising results, in part because successfully rearranging an organization around a new technology so often requires local cultural change as well.[25] Only so much uncertainty can be reduced ahead of time.

So for innovators, rapid prototyping and testing is essential. Prototyping means more than building a model. It also means responding rapidly to the information a test or model generates, making multiple midcourse corrections, and testing a series of models. The keys to reducing uncertainty are flexibility, adjustment, and iteration. In one sense the purpose of a prototype is to fail, and the more failures the better. Only thus are remediable flaws revealed. IDEO's motto is "fail often to succeed sooner."

Prototypes take many forms: physical models, a test ward, or a new care process (in one sense a "future state" value-stream map is a prototype). None of them are meant to be the final form of the new product or clinical service. They are all meant to generate information: about the challenges of building the product or service, of customers' or patients' likely responses, and of the likely impact of a new work environment or routine on staff. Prototypes are repeated as the design process moves along, with later prototypes being more detailed than earlier.

In effect, a prototype is a tentative answer to a question, and the prototype will be more useful if the question is clarified first. "What are we trying to find out by testing the new care process or service design in this way?" As understanding improves, the prototypes tend to get more focused and realistic. Each successive prototype attempts to answer a different question. Physical models of products in development could test what the finished device could look like, feel like, or work like. "Prototype" new processes of care can test such issues as the best sequence of activities, when and how to make transitions, or which professional is best suited for a given task or decision.

Creating multiple prototypes to test different elements of a product or service is simpler if the product or service can be broken down into smaller, independent parts (i.e., is modular). Modern digital equipment often has this property. Research and development in chip technology can be undertaken independently from research into screens. Unfortunately, healthcare processes are often integral: their components are so interdependent that it is hard to innovate in each separately. The patient's operating room care defines the care needed in the postoperative unit, for instance. Hence, those testing a new model of care in one part of a larger system need to take a wide view and be alert to potential influences upstream from, and effects downstream of their immediate changes. This is another rationale for the multidisciplinary makeup of innovation teams. As with the approaches to improvement, there are many tools available to implement the four phases of a structured approach to innovation. Table 8.2 summarizes the phases of the process and some of the tools.

EXPERIMENTATION, LEARNING, AND FAILURE

On the surface, a process made up of needs analysis, options generation, and rapid testing does not seem so different from that

Table 8.2. The phases and tools of a structured approach to innovation design

Design process phase	Description	Examples of tools
Understanding needs	Data collection to identify unmet needs, what customers really value, or gaps in the performance of current systems or technologies	Interview / focus groups Empathic interviewing Empathic design / field observation Patient-centered co-design Customer shadowing Mystery shopper
Creating options	Group processes and team characteristics that encourage divergent thinking to create a wide range of options (volume over quality)	Deep dive at IDEO Brainstorming Team diversity Encouraging "wild" ideas
Selecting options	Group process for convergent thinking to develop a narrow range of high-quality options	Multivoting Clustering and mapping
Testing	Decreasing uncertainty through rapid testing of multiple prototypes and learning from failures	Rapid cycle prototyping In silica testing Simulation

used to address individual patients' health needs every day. But a successful innovation process typically takes place in a cultural context that encourages experimentation, tolerates and even welcomes failure, flattens status hierarchies, nurtures speaking up, and welcomes dissenting opinions. This is often a far cry from the routine healthcare environment. Professional disciplinary processes, perceived medicolegal risk, and bureaucratic business approval and capital allocation processes can prevent clinicians and managers from feeling empowered to experiment with new models of care or use failures as learning opportunities. The innovator's aphorism "fail early and often" is somewhat countercultural in the healthcare setting.

Furthermore, whichever way it is cast—as learning, the scientific method, Plan-Do-Study-Act, prototyping, or rapid cycle innovation—experimentation is at the heart of all approaches to improvement and innovation. But experimentation can be a challenging subject in healthcare, in part because of the specter of the Tuskegee syphilis experiment and Nazi human experimentation.*

Thus, to create an environment that supports innovation, leaders need to frame experimentation in a way clinicians will find acceptable and to address their concerns about failure. In common use, the word "experiment" usually means a formal trial of a new therapy, and the word "failure" connotes a missed or incorrect diagnosis, or an avoidable complication of treatment. But in the context of healthcare transformation, experiments usually test alternative organizational arrangements for delivering a best practice, not the best practice itself. They are trials of new work routines and operating systems for safely and reliably delivering well-established clinical best practices, not unsanctioned medical experiments or tests of new therapies outside of the framework of research ethics or the oversight of an institutional review board.

---

* In the infamous Tuskegee Study of Untreated Syphilis patients had treatment withheld for over 40 years without their knowledge and consent despite the fact that penicillin had become standard treatment. It gave rise to regulations requiring institutional review boards and protections for human subjects in research studies.

Table 8.3. Possible types of failure in healthcare delivery

Failure	Characteristics
Negligence	Individual professionals operate outside their training and competence or knowingly disregard accepted practice.
Mistake	Individual professional makes an error in the context of a system that fails to provide adequate resources and support.
Failure to meet specification	Process varies outside defined parameters.
Complex system failure	Unpredictable interactions in an interactively complex system result in unexpected outcomes.
Experimental failure	Well-intentioned, well-designed experiment testing a defined hypothesis does not deliver the hoped-for outcome.

In addition, not all failures are the same. The failure of an individual professional through negligence is not the same as a well-intentioned, well-designed experiment that proves the null hypothesis and does not deliver the hoped-for outcome. Table 8.3 lists different types of failure in the context of healthcare delivery and transformation.

These different types of failure demand different responses.[26] Negligence has medicolegal consequences, but we no longer punish well-trained and well-meaning individuals whose capacity to perform to the best of their abilities has been impaired by poorly designed systems. Quite the contrary, the mainstay of modern thinking about safety improvement and safety culture has been openness about errors and problems and a recognition that they are expected in complex operations and therefore must be reported and evaluated early. A process not meeting specification results in increased process control, often using the tools of the TPS. And a failed experiment usually gives rise to another, better, one.

However, there is an important caveat here. Rigor is not suspended just because the experiments that test new operating system designs are organizational, not clinical. The same rules of good experimental practice still apply. Prototypes of new models of care are tests of a hypothesis, and if such tests are to yield maximum information, the hypothesis should be well defined, appropriate metrics identified (especially including metrics focused on safety and reliability), adequate data collected, and appropriate comparison made to a control arm—the current process or system. In sum, in any redesign, perturbation of a system should be deliberate and analysis of observed deviance rigorous.

Leaders have a crucial role in creating an environment that supports innovation and effective experimentation. They do so by modeling key behaviors such as expecting analytical and experimental rigor ("Show me the data"), admitting to their own fallibility and failures ("That has happened to me too"), openly and publicly welcoming constructive dissent, admitting to the limitations of current models, and relentlessly searching for improvements over the status quo.

However, innovation leaders cannot be exclusively welcoming of dissent and deviance. Occasionally they are called upon to be decisive and directive. It is the leader who usually marks the transition between divergent and convergent thinking in each innovation cycle by shutting down unproductive lines of inquiry and redirecting the team's focus and resources to more promising areas. Occasional autocracy is required.

INNOVATION ADOPTION

One of the great challenges in healthcare is not innovation but innovation adoption. In their paper titled, "Health Care Needs

Less Innovation and More Imitation," Roth and Lee argue that "when organizations overemphasize innovation, they can miss out on the power of imitation—copying existing approaches that actually work. Providers need to actively seek out good ideas that have been tried and refined, bring those ideas home, and adapt them for local use."[27]

Unfortunately, healthcare has a long history of failed or slow innovation adoptions. Organizations often underestimate an architectural innovation's potential to disrupt systems, processes, and relationships. They fail to plan for the extent of cultural and organizational change required to implement, and then extract value from, a given technological innovation or new model of care. They fail to differentiate technical from adaptive changes.

In healthcare, component innovations often require only an individual to learn something new: replace an old drug with a new one in an otherwise unchanged treatment plan or learn a new software application. But architectural innovations, which create new models of care by reconfiguring existing delivery system components, are characterized by changed relationships among provider organizations and professionals. The new relationships are expressed in new referral pathways, task and decision rights allocations, reporting and status relationships, communication patterns, information flows, or in alternative access points and sites for care. Team members may need to learn not only how to use a new technology but also a whole new way of working together. This can be a significant barrier to its adoption into routine care. The innovation changes the adopter.

But the adopter can also change the innovation. As adopting care teams and delivery organizations test new technologies or care models, they may adapt them to the local conditions. Rogers's innovation diffusion model (see Chapter 7) initially proposed five characteristics of an innovation that might influence

Table 8.4. Rogers's characteristics of innovations

Characteristic of innovation	Description
Relative advantage	Degree to which an innovation is perceived to be better than the idea it supersedes (measured in economic, social prestige, or convenience terms)
Compatibility	Degree to which an innovation is perceived to be consistent with existing values, past experiences, and needs of potential adopters
Complexity	Degree to which an innovation is perceived to be difficult to understand or use
Trialability	Degree to which the innovation can be experimented with on a limited basis
Observability	Degree to which the results of an innovation are visible to others
Potential for reinvention	Degree to which an innovation can be modified by a user and even used for alternative, initially unintended, purposes

its adoption (Table 8.4).[28] It largely treated the innovation as static and focused on adoption by an individual. But a sixth characteristic, "potential for reinvention," was added to the original list in recognition of the dynamic relationship between an innovation and the adopter and the potential of the adoption process to contribute to changes in the innovation: in effect, the ongoing interaction between design and execution.

Even component innovations have the potential to drive extensive change in the adopting organization. As noted earlier, the invention of a new drug treatment for stroke, thrombolysis, to a large degree forced the creation of stroke networks and specialist centers because the nature of this therapy required rapid imaging, specialist assessment, and immediate intervention. Innovations such as these may become the norm as more and more technologies require changed delivery system relationships to realize their full potential. In the future, most advances in patient outcome may come from combinations of innovative therapeutics and services.[29]

Thus, in many situations, adopting new technology into routine care is both an individual and a team learning challenge. Innovation does not just require a structured approach to learning by the innovator. Adoption is more likely to succeed if it is framed as a learning process, rather than treating it as the onboarding of a passive piece of technology by a group of individuals.[30] Successful organizations actively treat innovation adoption as a learning problem[31] and use the same kinds of learning activities and leadership styles as those deployed by the structured approaches to improvement and innovation.

For example, as neonatal intensive care units brought on new technologies and new practices, the use of deliberate learning activities was associated with an improvement in long-term outcomes such as infant mortality.[32] These activities included solicitation of staff ideas, opportunities for staff to provide feedback before full implementation, education sessions with staff, pilot runs, dry runs, project team meetings, and problem-solving cycles (i.e., Plan-Do-Study-Act).

In practice this means that leaders in the middle must explicitly describe to the adopting team that the innovation will require them to learn together, set up separate opportunities to practice, and measure and track progress over a series of iterations, each in effect a prototype. Teams that were successful in adopting MICS techniques, for example, set the equipment up in a fully operational operating room, lacking only a patient, and practiced the procedure together. They planned the sequence of steps and the words team members would use to communicate with each other, brainstormed the things that could go wrong, and planned their responses in advance. They met together after each of the early cases to review what went well and what did not and what changes they would make for the very next case (a technique called an "after action review"). Adoption success was determined as much by the team members' interactions with each other as it was by the individuals' interactions with the technology.

The learning required of individuals and teams to successfully adopt an innovative technology or practice is local. The exact nature of the relationships between organizations, units, and professionals differs for each organization and each part of the country. Each organization adopting a new technology or model of care needs to manage the learning process for itself. Innovations are not so much "rolled out" to a community of users as they are adopted locally, one user at a time, each managing its own adoption process and making whatever modifications to the innovation and its use that they see fit. This may go partway in explaining why so many "pilots" successful at one location fail to be widely adopted, widespread innovation adoption can be so slow, and so few service innovations turn out to have as large an impact as initially hoped.

PUTTING IT TOGETHER: THE RELATIONSHIP BETWEEN INNOVATION AND IMPROVEMENT

Improvement, innovation, and innovation adoption are all variants of the same challenge: the management of individual, team, and organizational learning. The structured approaches to innovation and improvement have much in common. They share

Figure 8.3. Relationship between improvement and innovation in new models of care

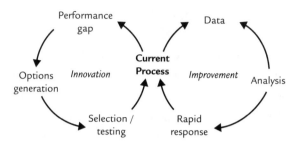

many of the same or similar tools, and they all deal with variance in one way or another. However, they differ in that they address subtly different problems. Figure 8.3 represents both their differences and the way in which innovation and improvement processes are related and interact as a larger system for improving performance.

The goal of improvement (right-hand cycle in Figure 8.3) is to reduce the variance between the process or technology's performance as specified by its design and that realized in practice: in effect, to increase the system's yield, the extent to which a practice, process, or technology performs as initially designed. In this cycle a deviance is an execution failure: a failure to meet specification.

However, if a process or technology is not generating positive outcomes, there are two possible explanations: either the process has not been faithfully executed according to its specification or even when perfectly executed, the process as designed is simply not capable of delivering the desired outcome. An "aspiration gap" exists between system, process, or technology, even when performing perfectly, and what we want for our patients. Improvement methodologies focused on the identification and removal of process deviance ensure that the standardized process is executed with high fidelity. In so doing, they reveal places in which the process is not capable: a design failure. Innovation (the left-hand cycle in Figure 8.3) addresses this gap. Hence Figure 8.3 represents a way of thinking about the relationship between improvement and innovation activities. Although they are separate tools for different purposes, both are intended to reduce gaps, the former between observed and specified performance, and the latter between perfect performance of the current system and the performance to which we aspire. Note that because of their different purposes the two cycles have different frequencies: usually many iterations of the improvement cycle have occurred before an innovation cycle is initiated.

In an environment in which technologies and models of care are continually changing as both science and public expectations evolve, delivery organization transformation is a pressing need. Organizations have to be able to both improve and innovate because our aspirations are a moving target. Otherwise they will be left behind.

For individual delivery organizations the key challenge is how to do this in a systematic way. Those organizations that are frequently studied and lauded—such as Toyota, Virginia Mason Medical Center, or Intermountain Healthcare—are notable for having successfully integrated innovation, improvement, and implementation. Some have created separate venues—skunkworks—for their innovation activities as a way of taking people out of their routine environment to innovate and redesign. For instance, Kaiser Permanente has created the Garfield Innovation Center and the Mayo Clinic its Center for Innovation for this purpose. However, an essential strength of the TPS model is that it ensures the free flow of ideas from the innovation side to the execution side of the enterprise and back again. Innovation is connected to the shop floor.

IMPLICATIONS FOR ACTION: IMPLEMENTING STRUCTURED APPROACHES TO IMPROVEMENT, INNOVATION, AND TECHNOLOGY ADOPTION

Structured approaches to improvement, innovation, and technology adoption are made up of a small group of core principles and a set of tools for implementing them into practice. They all center on deliberately using the identification of and response to short- and long-term variation as a mechanism of institutional learning. And they all make the use of their learning tools part of the day-to-day routine so that the organization as a whole has the capability for constant change.

Different healthcare delivery organizations have chosen different tools for putting these principles into action in their local environments: selecting tools that are consistent with their local culture and resources. Some have adhered closely to a well-described management approach such as the TPS, and others have chosen to create their own approach.

Consider, therefore, what will be the best method and set of tools that you can apply locally in your organization, unit, service, or practice in order to accomplish the following:

- Define a standard, including deciding what to standardize, and what not to
- Identify and amplify a deviation from what is expected
- Override the standard procedure where appropriate
- Evaluate the reason for the deviation and the effectiveness of the override
- React to the deviation or override in the shortterm with immediate adjustments
- Redesign over the longer term

In addition to learning in the short term, consider also what will be your preferred methods for long-term redesign, including how you and your unit will invite and act on staff and patient suggestions for improvement and recognize things that might go wrong, before they have gone wrong.

Finally, recognize that the behaviors the structured approaches rely upon and that were developed in the context of other industries are often countercultural in healthcare, including the following:

- The use of standardization as a tool for learning in improvement processes, rather than as a tool for process control
- The deliberate induction of variance in innovation processes
- Experimenting in less than perfectly controlled circumstances
- Distributing problem-solving authority to the most junior and lowest status staff
- Making clinicians accountable for system redesign and improvement in addition to their professional duties

Consider how you can introduce these behaviors to clinical staff and help them understand their rationale and applicability, and how you will provide a context for learning these different behaviors and develop experience with them.

Previous chapters have focused on the redesign of local operating systems and leading staff through the change. The next section considers the challenges of doing this at an organizational scale.

PART FOUR

Transforming Organizations

CHAPTER 9

Learning Systems and Leading Learning

The Covid-19 pandemic laid bare many long-standing flaws in our healthcare systems, such as the fragility of our supply lines, critical staff shortages, the parlous state of hospital finances, the physical and psychological vulnerability of our staff, and the racial and ethnic inequalities in access to and outcome of care. What the pandemic has also made obvious is the extent of medical and operational uncertainty under which healthcare delivery organizations operate. At its outset, not only was the nature of the novel disease unclear, but so too was its treatment and the optimal way to organize acute and public health services in response.

Organizations can address uncertainty by trying to accommodate or reduce it. Tactics to accommodate uncertainty include deploying a flexible operating system, such as a job shop model, and resourcing built-in redundancy. NASA's "tiger teams" and healthcare's "rapid response teams"—teams explicitly trained in problem-solving under time pressure—are an example of one such redundancy. Another is Walter Reed Army Medical Center, which in the past kept fully equipped floors spare.[1] Organizations can reduce uncertainty in the short term by creating clear pathways and protocols and by cohorting like patients, for example, in a multi-operating system model. But in the longer term, uncertainty can be reduced only by learning.

Children learn naturally, organizations do not. Most health-care organizations are structured for delivery, not discovery. They are judged, and increasingly are paid, according to how well they put evidence-based medicine into practice. The knowledge for care is presumed to flow one way: created through basic and clinical research, communicated to practitioners through under-graduate and continuing education, and applied at the bedside by individuals whose accreditation depends on demonstrating mastery of the knowledge base. Organizations support individ-ual clinicians by reminding them of, or mandating, evidence-based choices, frequently via the EHR. This approach works best when the evidence guiding practice is clear and unequivo-cal, but less well when our understanding is incomplete and when care is exploratory.

But a model of knowledge as a one-way flow ignores the way in which routine practice can be a fertile source of new knowl-edge and insight, both medical and operational.[2] Unfortunately, organizations often fail to capture such insights and use them systematically to advantage future patients. They have to be de-liberately designed to learn. The Covid-19 pandemic only served to highlight the importance of learning from practice. Some in-stitutions reported responding to the uncertainty during the pandemic by making multiple clinical and operational changes every day in response to what was being learned at the bedside.[3] What systems did they use to achieve this?

ANATOMY AND PHYSIOLOGY
OF A LEARNING SYSTEM

The term *learning system* has been used in two healthcare contexts over recent years. At the system level, it describes an approach to capturing, pooling, and analyzing aggregate patient data from multiple delivery organizations and looking for opportunities for improvement.[4] At the organizational level, it connotes a *"learning organization"*:[5] the term used to describe that set of organizational structures, processes, and culture that promote internal learning. The structured approaches to improvement and innovation discussed in Chapter 8 are examples of learning systems. All these approaches are based on systematically detecting, capturing, and analyzing data from routine operations and then implementing operational and practice changes based on what is learned.

What is learned is both what to do and how to do it: design and execution (see Chapter 8). In industry this translates to learning both how to implement the existing production process more efficiently and effectively and how to design better future products that are also easier to manufacture. In healthcare it is how to deliver care and what care to deliver.

Organizational learning systems are based on the idea that the knowledge for clinical care comes not only from research conducted outside the organization but also from experience accrued within it. Organizations learn predominantly by detecting gaps between what is observed and expected, making meaning of these discrepancies by comparing them to other internal and external data, conducting tests, and then designing and implementing effective changes in response. These gaps may be operational or clinical. Learning systems have been designed and implemented in delivery organizations as diverse as short-lived field hospitals, such as the NHS Nightingale, the emergency hospital built in London to respond to the early phase of the Covid-19 pandemic,[6] and established multi-institution systems, such as Intermountain Healthcare, a 24-hospital system spanning Utah and Idaho.[7]

To learn from its own experience an organization must sense, interpret, and respond: learning systems have the same basic structure as a nervous system with an afferent arm, a central

Figure 9.1. Anatomy of a learning system

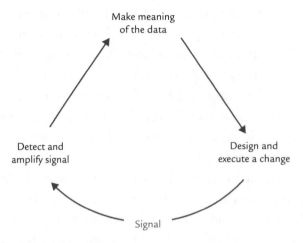

cognitive function, and an efferent arm (Figure 9.1).[8] Actions are converted into data, data are converted into knowledge, and knowledge then informs future action. This process has five steps: (1) collect data, (2) collate, integrate, and analyze them, (3) design and validate a response, (4) implement it, and then (5) close the loop by checking the implementation and impact of the response and using these data as an input into the next cycle of learning. None of these steps are in and of themselves unusual: most delivery organizations do them all. But what many fail to do is link these steps in a closed loop and manage them collectively.

In healthcare three issues complicate the learning process outlined previously. First, routine care creates multiple data streams that need to be integrated: some quantitative, some structured qualitative, and some unstructured qualitative data. Internal data sources include patient surveys, clinical audits, mortality reports, patient complaints, incident reports, outcomes surveys, and cost and revenue analyses. Additional external data sources include published research and expert opinion, population data, and benchmarking comparisons with other delivery organizations. All these data are potentially signals that point to two key gaps: between what was intended and what was achieved, and between what was achieved and what is aspired to.

Unlike data from the electronic record or periodic outbound surveys, some internal data such as staff observations and suggestions for improvement are not easily accessed without deliberate organizational effort. Organizations need not only a culture that supports speaking up but also mechanisms for actively seeking staff input. This input can occur through structured means such as interviews and focus groups and less structured mechanisms such as phone apps or anonymous reporting to capture spontaneous staff observations. In short, the data from which an organization can learn must be actively created.

Furthermore, some signals can be weak, and meaningful patterns only emerge when time trends are analyzed or several data sources are combined. Integrating these diverse data sources and searching for patterns within and across them typically require dedicated resources. In many delivery organizations not only are long-term patterns within a data set not evaluated but also these multiple data sources are not linked together. For instance, organizations may not track long-term patterns of patient complaints, in spite of a known association between complaints and both the risk of lawsuit[9] and the rate of postoperative surgical complication.[10] Incident reports usually flow to a dedicated clinical governance group that makes intermittent quality assurance reports to the board of directors but may not triangulate them with patient survey and complaints data and informal staff suggestions for improvement. Finally, some signals are only detected when clinicians meet and talk. For example, the toxicity of the fenfluramine-phentermine diet drug combination was detected when a group of cardiologists compared notes.[11]

A second issue relates to the validation of potential insights. Not all observations are signals of an important underlying phenomenon. Early in the Covid-19 pandemic, social media were alive with rumor, unconfirmed hypotheses, misinformation, and anecdotes. But the consequences of getting it wrong are so great that changing practice on the basis of informal observations and small sample sizes is regarded as riskier in healthcare than in other settings. It is not sufficient for a learning system to aggregate and compare observations and look for trends. It needs a structured process for evaluating the safety and effectiveness of proposed changes that incorporates formal research methods, practice-based testing, and simulation into a rigorous method for separating out the noise. Patterns observed, and any actions they imply, must also be tested against the results of external research. And subsequent changes made must be tracked to ensure that they are properly implemented and are having the desired effect so that if not, an appropriate corrective action can be taken. In practice this means that a learning system needs individuals or a group dedicated to analysis and internal research: for example, the Healthcare Delivery Institute at Intermountain. Such groups are usually made up of staff with a wide range of expertise including in financial analysis, statistics, improvement science, project management, and simulation, for example.

Third, not all lessons learned from practice imply the same type of actions. Learning systems must maintain a capability for responding to insights in many different ways. Broadly, this falls into three groups: actions to resolve problems in reliably executing a process, usually by making operational changes ("fix"); finding better ways of delivering current care, often through the process of improvement ("improve"); and substantially changing clinical practice or redesigning an operating system ("change").[12] Many signals relate to problems in the execution of current processes: reliably doing what we said we would do. Fixing these often simple operational problems improves the fidelity with which the process as designed is executed in practice (in effect, improving its yield). Other signals ultimately point to the need of finding an improved way of doing what we already do, but more effectively and efficiently. This usually means making process changes. Finally, some insights require the wholesale redesign of an operating system—fundamentally changing the process, staff allocation, technology, and so on—to achieve a better outcome by doing something we have never done before.

The need to fix operational problems, improve processes, and change operating systems do not all occur with the same frequency. In London's NHS Nightingale, a new hospital built in a convention center in 9 days, we found that for every major clinical practice or operating system change there were 14 improvements and 18 operational fixes.[13] In more stable settings, introducing a major operating system redesign will generate the need for a host of subsequent improvements and operational fixes. A learning system must maintain a diverse portfolio of tools with which it can implement a simple fix immediately, improve a process, and completely redesign an operating system.

EXAMPLES OF A LEARNING SYSTEM

To create a learning system leaders must focus on structure and behavior. Two delivery organizations provide practical examples of organizational structures that bring data flows and actions together into a closed-loop learning system. The first of these, the NHS Nightingale London, was specifically designed to address the complicating issues discussed previously, albeit in a highly

Figure 9.2. The NHS Nightingale London learning system: structures, data flows, and actions

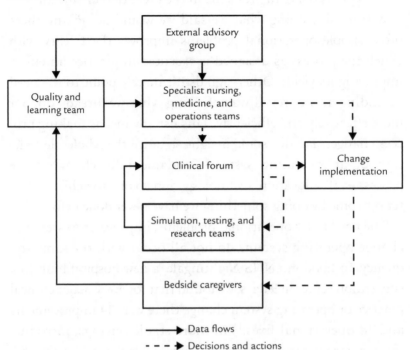

constrained and controlled environment (Figure 9.2).[14] Covid-19 created urgency for learning.

Data were captured from nurses, allied health professionals, doctors, and assistants working at the bedside through several mechanisms: interview, self-report on a phone app, and surveying. These internal data were complemented with incident reports, process measures, and mortality and other outcome reports. An internal group, the Quality and Learning Team, reviewed all incoming data looking for consistent themes and passed ideas to one of several specialist teams (medical, nursing, and operational) for further review, analysis, and action. These teams (and the clinical forum) also reviewed input from an external advisory group that synthesized international reports and external research and made practice change recommendations based on review of the current evidence.

Some internal observations were acted on immediately (operational fixes). Recommendations for other, more significant changes were sent to the clinical forum—a body made up of research, clinical, and operational staff—which reviewed them and either recommended implementation or sent them for further evaluation or development, either through formal research or simulation. Changes were implemented through a number of mechanisms: changes to the clinical protocols and standard operating procedures at the bedside, staff in-service training, new staff orientation and simulation training, and reminders sent via text and email and placed on signs in the patient care areas. A new role, the "bedside learning coordinator," interviewed staff at the bedside to gather data, educated staff in practice and operating procedure changes, and conducted audits of new practices and procedures to check on their implementation progress.

An organization at the other end of the spectrum of size and complexity, Intermountain Healthcare, has created a learning system with the same basic structure. The centerpiece of its learning system is the clinical process model (CPM), which incorporates the patient pathway, the associated clinical decision rules, and a set of tracking metrics: in effect the "standard work" for each condition (see Chapter 8). The CPMs are the responsibility of a set of standing committees—the clinical guidance councils, made up of clinical and operational representatives—which are in effect a service-line management structure. These bodies oversee the development and updating of the CPM: reviewing performance data and making protocol changes.

The protocols are implemented into practice through default options in the electronic record and continuing professional education. However, clinicians are both free to override protocol-recommended care and encouraged to do so when the protocol does not in their judgment meet the patient's needs. And when they do, they log the reason for doing so, thus creating data about the fidelity of implementation of the CPM and its outcomes.

Data are analyzed by staff at the Healthcare Delivery Institute and fed back to the guidance councils: one of the key data elements relates to those instances in which a clinician chose to override the protocol, and the reasons why. These data are collected, integrated with other process variance and outcome data, and compared to external research to identify places in which the protocol could be improved. Protocols are updated routinely, and these changes are disseminated both through updates to the EHR system and ongoing clinician education. Like the previous example, Intermountain systematically turns action into data, data into insight, and insight into action.

But both these examples are exceptional in one way or another: the NHS Nightingale's learning system was created in a small, single-specialty hospital purpose-built de novo in a greenfield site and Intermountain Healthcare built the structures and refined the processes of its learning system over decades. Established institutions wanting to create a learning system must deal with the existing structures and routines they already have in place. For them, creating a learning system is often a matter of organizing these into a closed loop, either at the level of a unit or the whole organization: to ensure that internal and external data are integrated, design and oversight responsibility is vested with a single authority, and implementation is managed and audited. This may require redirecting existing data flows, revising the terms of reference of existing committees, and investing in enhanced analytic resources.

ENVIRONMENT FOR LEARNING

The structures and processes described previously depend on a set of staff behaviors. The tools and activities for learning are more effective if they are used in a context that specifically promotes team and organizational learning: what is usually called a learning organization. Garvin and colleagues point out that a learning organization is based on three foundational pillars: a supportive learning environment, concrete learning processes, and leadership that reinforces learning.[15] Table 9.1[16] outlines some of the core components of each of these pillars. Together they provide the essential organizational substrate for the approaches to improvement, innovation, and learning discussed previously.

These three pillars are not independent of each other. They act together as part of a larger system of learning (Figure 9.3). The leader helps a team identify shared goals and a guiding value proposition for patients and staff and select metrics by which to gauge the success of their joint enterprise. The leader's behavior helps create a culture that supports speaking up, transparency, experimentation, self-criticism, and reflection. And leaders institute specific routines that support learning, such as surveillance, feedback, analysis, and readjustment.

What Garvin and colleagues also make clear is that a learning organization can be created. Just as the principles of the structured approaches to innovation and improvement can be applied to any organization—adapted to local conditions and deployed using local systems—local leaders can purposefully create an environment in their units that underpins learning.

LEADING LEARNING

Leaders are an essential component of any learning system. Not only do they provide essential resources, such as the structures, routines, and time needed for learning activities, but their behavior

Table 9.1. Three pillars of a learning organization

Supportive learning environment	Concrete learning processes and practices	Leadership that reinforces learning
A culture that supports speaking up ("psychological safety")	Experimentation and short cycle tests of change	Inviting input and encouraging different points of view
Time allowed for reflection, analysis, and redesign	Horizon scanning and external visits to understand what other services are doing	Asking questions that challenge the prevailing orthodoxy
Tolerance (and encouragement of) different points of view	Frequent comparison to others and to best in class	Active listening
Openness to new ideas and to trying new ways of working	Feedback loops and data sharing	Leaders openly acknowledge their own limitations
Tolerance of experimental failure	Deliberate seeking of dissenting views	Leaders create time and resources for identifying problems, reflection, and improvement
	Forums for sharing information with each other	
	Use of pilot projects and simulations to try out new ideas	
	Education and training	

also sets the tone needed for group learning. They must model fallibility, self-criticism, tolerance for intelligent failure, curiosity, interest for diverse perspectives, an outward-looking perspective, and a relentless thirst for better outcomes for our patients. The work of leading learning falls into three broad categories: establishing the need for learning by framing the problem as a learning challenge, building the structures and routines for learning,

Figure 9.3. A causal model of organizational learning

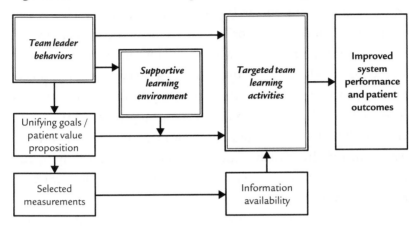

and nurturing the environment and ongoing activities that support learning.

First, it goes without saying that a unit or institution does not establish a learning system, and individuals do not study unless they think they have something to learn. For example, the teams that were successful in adopting MICS from the outset approached the new technology adoption as a learning process and put in place the learning practices described in Chapter 8.[17] It is typically up to leaders to frame the current situation as a learning challenge, first and foremost by publicly admitting to their own uncertainty. Of course, anyone leading a learning system has to be comfortable admitting uncertainty. It will be harder if leaders continue to believe and act like they have all the answers: staff are usually fully aware of the situation's uncertainty, and false certainty only risks losing them. In fact, when leaders admit their own uncertainty they do not diminish their status. They enable members of their team to also admit to the uncertainty and then initiate a learning process.[18]

But acknowledging uncertainty is not enough. The leader has to focus the search on the key areas of uncertainty, clarify the goals, and establish the priorities. By focusing the search, a leader is also helping staff identify what is less important and can wait. In the case of MICS, for example, there were two primary uncertainties, both directly related to the value the new procedure was intended to deliver: how to undertake the procedure in a time close to that of a conventional procedure, and for which patients was a minimally invasive approach most suited. Many of the other aspects of the surgery were well understood. Ignorance is rarely uniformly distributed.

Second, leaders must establish the structures and processes for learning by delegating authority and by building a team to address the uncertainty and solve the problem. The leader needs to ensure that the right people are on the team given the learning challenge: identify and convene content experts with clinical and operational skill sets suitable to the problem and learning need. And those individuals need the authority to make decisions and to access resources. Importantly, this means ensuring adequate diversity, even staffing a team with people from disciplines not typically represented in healthcare improvement and innovation teams and deliberately seeking their alternative points of view. Transformative insight often arises from the interaction of seemingly unrelated disciplines.

When the right person for the job occupies a lower position in the established hierarchy, decision rights must be formally and publicly confirmed. For example, during the Chilean mine rescue, its leader, Andre Sougarret, received a suggestion from a 24-year-old field engineer, Igor Proestakis, who had come to the rescue site on his own. Despite Proestakis's youth and relative inexperience Sougarret listened, evaluated the idea, and then backed Proestakis. Proestakis's drilling team was the first to reach the miners.[19]

The primary mechanisms by which the team generates learning are experimentation, observation, and the evaluation of variation. A natural tendency to conservatism in healthcare delivery often derives from clinicians' reluctance to act without solid research-based evidence. Almost by definition, such evidence is lacking in situations requiring learning, especially when the uncertainty relates to the organizational arrangements for undertaking the evidence-based practice, not the practice itself. Nonetheless, clinicians' preference for more data, more debate, and more evaluation can disincline them to experiment. So teams sometimes have to be actively encouraged to deliberately create variation and to "try it and see," either in simulation or through a series of carefully monitored tests. Creating a local, working example by running small-scale trials—focused tests of parts of an operating system change—help demonstrate the method and give team members an opportunity to practice it.

At the same time as encouraging initiative, the leader also must demand discipline. The authority to experiment must be accompanied by accountability for results. Actions must be associated with metrics to track progress and warn of risk, especially to safety, and monitoring and reporting must be on a schedule so as to create the data flow that is central to a learning system. Experiments that are not yielding results must be shut down quickly so that the team can move on.

The third set of leaders' tasks support the ongoing work of learning. The rapid turnover of data and decisions is the oil that keeps a smooth learning process going. Slow senior decision-making can hamstring innovation. A quick "no" may be better than a long delayed "yes." Rapid leader decision-making not only ensures that precious time, energy, and resources are allocated to the most promising lines of enquiry but it also legitimizes reversal. It sends the message that it is acceptable to try something, find it does not work, and move on to try something else.

The ability to rapidly reverse course can reassure clinicians being asked to try something new. A well-designed experiment that does not yield the hoped-for outcome is not a failure, it is data. If experiments are well planned, a midcourse reversal is not a sign of failure, or worse, a source of shame, but rather a signal that the learning system is working.

Decision velocity depends on the leader being there: present in the clinics, on the wards, in the operating rooms, and in the multidisciplinary meetings where the work of learning is being done. Improvement and innovation are much less easily led from afar. Leaders in the middle of the organization juggle lots of competing demands on their time: they are simultaneously dealing with ill patients; potentially critical shortages of staff, equipment, and space; and contractual and regulatory demands. But they need to go looking for trouble: problems that need their attention, teams that need their input, difficult decisions that must be made. It is not sufficient to wait for problems to come to you.

However, it is not enough to simply make a quick decision. Clinical teams usually need transparency including of the rationale for a decision, of the data, and of the progress and possibly the failure of current trials of potential solutions, and of the plans for the future. You cannot engage bright and well-trained people in an experimental learning process without being completely open about all its details.

DIFFICULT WORK OF LEADING LEARNING

The image of an empowering and inclusive leader is a popular management trope. Innovative businesses are often viewed as freewheeling idea factories. But the usual counsel to seek contrary views, get every opinion in the room, expand the set of options, and encourage and allow staff to run lots of parallel experiments risks missing an important subtlety. Both in crises, when teams must make decisions under conditions of uncertainty and time pressure, and during more stable times, the best leaders are occasionally very autocratic. Sure, they empower and enable a wide-ranging search of diverse solution spaces and multiple rapid cycle experiments, but they are also quick to shut down unproductive experiments, choose among competing alternative proposals, dismiss unproductive individuals, or reallocate staff to more pressing problems. In managing the *Apollo 13* rescue, Flight Director Gene Kranz famously deployed multiple "tiger teams" to address multiple problems. He listened to all their outputs, but then he unashamedly picked winners. Successful pharmaceutical companies are notable for their willingness to kill failing research quickly. Divergent experimentation is not helpful unless it ultimately converges to a conclusion.

And although tolerance of failure, willingness to experiment, and empowered teams form a popular narrative about innovation and learning, it is not all smooth sailing. Some important caveats apply. Harvard Business School's Gary Pisano has pointed out that although management books expound these broadly accepted principles, many organizations still do not behave this way. He argues that several uncomfortable tensions have to be addressed if leaders want to create an environment that supports innovation.[20]

First, although we need to tolerate, and even welcome, intelligent failure, we cannot accept poor experimental practice or incompetence. Innovation is not a free-for-all: as noted in Chapter 8, it requires methodological rigor. We cannot tolerate shoddy science for the simple reason that a negative result from a poorly designed experiment yields no useful information. A failure makes no contribution if it is not, and cannot be, learned from.

Second, leaders aiming to create a psychologically safe environment by encouraging staff to speak up must themselves be prepared to accept blunt criticism of their own ideas. The senior who is seen to be willing to learn from the junior's critique is more likely to promote learning among his or her team than one not.

Finally, although we extol the virtue of systems and cross-boundary collaboration in multidisciplinary teams, individuals still need to be held accountable for their performance and professionalism. Although we now predominantly focus on system causes of patient harm, we must still expect individual professionalism. Pisano argues that failure to manage these three tensions is behind many organizations' inability to create effective learning and innovation cultures.

The practical implications of Pisano's caveats make leading learning in a delivery organization hard work. Individual team members who are not performing well should be replaced. After deciding on a preferred drilling technology at the Chilean mine head, Andre Sougarret asked all the other drilling engineers to leave. And the same experimental rigor we expect in clinical trials should be demanded when we are testing new operating system designs and alternative organizational arrangements for delivering care. This includes not just good trial design (e.g., a clearly stated goal and hypothesis for the mechanism of action by which a new operating system would improve performance) but also well-defined process metrics and end points, a comparison group or process, and the establishment of the routines of good experimental science such as regular review meetings and data feedback.

PERSONAL CHALLENGES OF COLLECTIVE LEARNING

The approach to learning and leading learning described previously is not only difficult because it involves making tough choices. It can also be personally challenging. Clinicians are often

Table 9.2. Clashing norms of clinical practice and innovation

Norms of routine clinical care	Norms of innovation and improvement
Reduce variance	Seek deviance
Maintain options	Standardize
Implement best practice	Research routine care
Manage the patient	Manage the system
Avoid risk	Experiment
Individual accountability	Team interdependence

ill prepared for many of the behaviors that characterize learning and innovation processes, such as rapid testing and failure, or decision-making in multidisciplinary teams with flat hierarchies. Improvement models that creatively manage the tension between standardization and variance run counter to the usual narrative that variance reduction is a route to cost control and quality improvement. Why would an organization deliberately increase the risk of variation—through clinician override of a protocol—by increasing the level of standardization? And clinicians tend to view new technology adoption as requiring them to learn as an individual, rather than seeing it as a learning challenge for the team.

Moreover, innovation practice clashes with the common norms of routine clinical practice (Table 9.2). Where practicing clinicians work to reduce variation, innovators actively seek deviation. Although the former view standardization as a loss of potential options, the latter view it as an essential learning tactic. For clinicians, daily work is the implementation of established science into practice; for innovators, it is the practice of science in routine care. And although clinicians avoid risk, innovators deliberately perturb systems and conduct experiments. Hence leaders of clinical change need to help a team of practicing clinicians learn the skills of innovation and improvement.

Those leading learning can equally find it personally challenging. Many of the leadership behaviors described previously run counter to the norm. It is hard for clinicians to publicly acknowledge uncertainty when they have, after all, been trained to know the right answer. Undergraduate and ongoing training, licensure examinations, professional discipline, reaccreditation, and professional practice all test their personal mastery of a body of science. And in care delivery, they usually "lead" by either doing it themselves or instructing subordinates,[21] especially when change is framed as the execution of a known best practice and the reduction of variation.

Clinicians can be uncomfortable with the methods of organizational experiments run in real time in the context of routine care (in manufacturing terms, on the "shop floor"): they fear uncontrolled trials on unconsenting patients. But in a learning system every patient is a test of the current system's operating capability. The successful adopters of a new minimally invasive surgical procedure were those units that treated every early case as an "experiment": the team met beforehand to plan the procedure and afterward to review what went well and what went badly, implementing operating system changes in the very next case.[22] They asked, "What went well or badly today and what will we do differently tomorrow?"

Those leading learning cannot shy away from the hard choices discussed previously. But it can be a difficult balance for practicing clinicians because these decisions often affect the leader's colleagues. Collegiality and the professional respect of one's peers are central values among clinicians. Physicians' income and the quality of their work environment depend on it. We want to be liked by our medical and nursing colleagues. The chance that relationships will be preserved are greater if the process is fair and transparent, even if the choice goes against someone's preferred idea.

Finally, there is the problem of the time that organizational learning takes. Leaders of units reeling from volume and revenue pressure can be forgiven for keeping their staff focused on the task at hand. However, taking time out to huddle to review and plan is not a waste of staff time if it results in new learning. It is the only way to address what may seem at times an irreducible tension: effective learning and more informed planning would reduce the need for firefighting, but firefighting reduces the time available for planning.

AN OLD NORMAL

It has become common to credit the 2020 Covid-19 pandemic as heralding a new normal.[23,24] But the uncertainty introduced by Covid-19 is not a new normal, it is the old normal. It has ever been thus: the pandemic only made obvious what has always been the case. Better understanding of individuals and populations has improved the probability estimates, but medical care still requires judgment under uncertainty. The need to constantly push back the frontier of our ignorance and learn about what care to deliver and how to deliver it will always remain. All delivery organizations need to become learning systems, not only to cope with whatever their current crisis is, but also to perform better under more normal conditions and to be already armed with the structures and routines they will need to manage whatever the next crisis is, when it comes.

But transforming a delivery organization into a learning system requires managing it differently than usual. First, because both clinical and operational knowledge and perspective are essential for organizational learning, an effective learning system integrates clinical and administrative structures and activities. Learning systems do not treat them as separate universes, as is more commonly the case. So much of what we need to learn, and redesign, is at the intersection of clinical care and operations.

Second, in effective learning systems learning is indistinguishable from normal work. The mechanisms that support systematic learning are part of the organization's normal structure and routines: the learning system is not separated from the usual management and governance processes. Those things being learned, and what they imply for future clinical practice and operations redesign, are the focus of the delivery organization's normal decision-making bodies and executive functions. A learning system is an organizational architecture that links all the activities of learning into a closed loop of observation, analysis, and action that is integrated into the institution's usual routines so that ultimately it becomes the way the institution is managed.

IMPLICATIONS FOR ACTION: LEARNING SYSTEMS AND LEADING LEARNING

Leading organizations have two notable characteristics: they learn faster than everyone else, and they put that learning into action faster and more reliably than everyone else. Creating a learning organization requires building new structures and processes and introducing new behaviors.

To create these structures and processes consider the following questions:

1. How will your system collect a rich data set that includes both qualitative and quantitative data drawn from electronic sources and the personal experiences of patients and staff?
2. By what mechanism will these data be collated and analyzed? How will you integrate externally and inter-

nally sourced data? How will you detect patterns and meaningful signals within and among data sets?

3. Who or which internal groups will be responsible for acting immediately on issues that can be immediately fixed or evaluating issues that need further investigation and solution design?

4. How will significant changes be authorized?

5. What are the mechanisms for implementing change?

6. What is the mechanism for auditing the accuracy with which a new design is implemented?

7. How is the impact of change evaluated?

In addition, consider your role in leading learning. Leading learning can be hard work, potentially demanding behaving in a new way. Are you comfortable with the new behaviors that might be required? Table 9.3 summarizes some of them.

Table 9.3. Leadership actions for learning

Task	Goal	Challenges to address	Learning leader actions
Frame the problem	Clarity about the nature of the undertaking: learning not execution	• Presumption of certainty: healthcare delivery viewed as a production industry • Tendency to jump to a solution before fully characterizing the problem	• Describe the problem as one of learning rather than implementation of a known model. • Publicly acknowledge your own uncertainty. • Articulate a simple goal.
Establish structures	A team well matched to the nature of the problem to be solved	• Clinical and operational problems often treated separately, staff often working in uni-professional teams • Authority often based on seniority, status, and hierarchy, not suitability to problem	• Convene a multidisciplinary team of content experts with diverse skills: clinical, operational, and patient representation. • Choose team members based on capability not seniority. • Delegate authority and clearly articulate your expectations. • Focus the search on areas of known high uncertainty.

Establish routines	Learning routines and data flows seamlessly embedded in day-to-day activity	• Fragmented data streams and limited feedback loops • Reluctance to experiment in real time and in routine care setting	• Encourage teams to "try it and see." • Insist measurement and reporting are integrated into every experiment and change. • Shorten the feedback loop: create regular meetings to share data and insights, plan next steps, and report on progress.
Support the learning process	Culture and individual behaviors supporting team-level learning	• Senior leaders are often distant, and approval processes Byzantine • Staff can be reluctant to express counter-normative views • Experimentation is reserved for clinical research	• Be available: spend time with the team in their environment, go looking for trouble. • Make decisions quickly (including saying "no"), explaining your rationale. • Ask, don't tell: invite input from even the most reticent team members and treat even the most outlandish ideas as worthy of evaluation. • Invite team to create small-scale local working examples to practice the method.

CHAPTER 10

Transformation at Scale

Although an individual can undoubtedly have a powerful impact on an entire organization, transformation usually needs the commitment and orchestrated action of many. Local leaders addressing the unique aspects of a population, disease, or technology by changing their local systems to improve their ability to deliver what their patients value are really only addressing one problem, or the needs of one subpopulation, at one point in time. Although individuals can lead change in their own services and practices, doing so at organizational scale requires something else. For an organization or a system as a whole to transform, it needs to leverage the benefits of many leaders, each exercising greater control locally. As one academic observed in the midst of the 2020 Covid-19 pandemic, "In a small crisis power moves to the center...in a big one it moves to the periphery."[1]

An organization aiming to transform, therefore, needs to find and nurture a group of smart, motivated people who want to make a difference. The work of operational redesign must be done at scale: multiple, simultaneous leaders, teams, and redesigns, all acting in concert in pursuit of a common global aim. This is no small task.

Historically, scaling promising ideas across entire systems has proven difficult, and it has been hard to engage large numbers of clinicians in organizational change. This inability can limit an organization's capacity to take advantage of promising innovations such as new therapies and enhanced analytics. Having better data or technology is no advantage if the organization cannot make the operational changes needed to put them to best use. The healthcare industry's structure, which separates the professionals from the organizations in which they practice, promotes a strong professional identification among clinicians. This structure can create goal conflict between physicians and their organizational leaders and reduce clinicians' commitment to the broader organizational goals for transformation.[2] In spite of research linking organizational performance to the delivery of safe and effective care, clinicians do not necessarily see organizational reform as their business. Their professional commitment to first do no harm reduces their willingness to engage in the experimentation that is central to innovation and innovation adoption.[3]

OPTIONS FOR WIDESPREAD CHANGE

So how do delivery organizations scale change? By far the most popular approach is to drive change from the top. This approach uses senior leadership–sponsored interventions to specify changes centrally and force their implementation at the front line. Such interventions usually involve either investing in the organization-wide infrastructure needed to create the conditions for high-quality clinical and managerial practice or launching large-scale, cross-departmental, programmatic initiatives that focus on specific issues of quality and efficiency. Examples of the former include defining a culture and a set of corporate values and behavioral expectations consistent with clinical and managerial excellence, implementing an EHR and computerized drug and radiology order entry system, and establishing performance metrics and targets along with associated physician incentives and the analytic resources needed to run them. The latter include service reconfigurations and projects focused on process standardization, length of stay reduction, operating room turn-over and productivity, or ambulatory clinic utilization.

Top-down action tends to appeal to boards and senior executives because it affords a high level of control over central resources and the change process itself, and allows senior leaders to drive the pace at which change can be achieved. For this reason, large-scale interventions originating from the upper echelons and aimed at changing individual clinician behavior can be found in delivery organizations all over the world.

Although popular, this approach risks underestimating the influence local operating systems exert on individual clinician performance and patient outcome. Worse, it can also promote an "us-and-them" relationship between management and clinical staff. And externally imposed change that reduces staff sense of control and self-determination can contribute to burnout. Experience has shown that despite well-intentioned efforts, top-down implementation of the rules and protocols of "evidence-based medicine" is not enough on its own to transform a system of care or individual practice at the unit level. Recall Schein: "You can't impose anything on anyone and expect them to be committed to it." Finally, not only does this approach risk disenfranchising frontline clinicians but it also excuses them from responsibility for their local system's performance and for making changes to improve it. It makes clinical change a manager's job.

Staff resistance to top-down change derives in part from the fact that it can be insensitive to legitimate local variation. Not only do community preferences, patterns of disease, capital and real estate resources, staff numbers and skill sets, and institutional history all vary from one care delivery site to the next, but also a dermatology outpatient clinic may function very differently from a surgical one. For this reason, both local clinicians and patients necessarily have a central role in the transformation of a care system. They have the necessary technical knowledge and the understanding of the local resources and politics needed to design effective organizational arrangements for care delivery and to see them implemented.

The unfortunate reality is that to transform an entire organization in a way that recognizes the legitimate variance in patient values, technological capability, subspecialty skill sets, staffing needs, and workforce models is painstaking and time-consuming work. Each local operating system redesign creates one of the many changes that collectively scale to a larger institutional impact: transformation is the aggregation of marginal gains from multiple small-scale local changes. The hard work of healthcare transformation is achieved by the following:[4]

- Multiple, small-scale, local clinical and administrative operating system redesigns
- Undertaken by clinically led, multiprofessional teams
- In partnership with patients and referrers
- Over long periods of time
- Applying a structured and repeatable redesign method
- Using whatever imperfect data are available
- Managed as a series of experiments

Recognizing this, a few organizations have opted for more of a bottom-up approach to managing a transformation that places the skills, tools, responsibility, and authority for operational redesign in the hands of frontline staff. Returning control to frontline staff, who have felt increasingly disempowered over recent years, engages them in the wider organizational enterprise and enables them to account for warranted variance in their redesigns of their local operating systems.

However, this approach too has its risks. Clinicians are often unprepared to lead change at the local level, and many are too disengaged to be interested. Unless carefully orchestrated from above, frontline change can be ill disciplined, fragmented, and unconnected to the broader organizational strategy or the realities of the organization's current financial constraints. Senior leaders often worry that engaging clinicians in operational design and management is tantamount to handing the keys of the henhouse to the fox. They fear that too much local design authority and discretion will simply lead to unfiltered demands for more resources, rather than a careful rethinking of the way in which current resources are deployed.

An alternative, therefore, that allows organizational transformation to be achieved through coordinated and disciplined frontline change is to structure, guide, and orchestrate it centrally: a "top-guided bottom-up" approach, analogous to Gulati's notion of "freedom within a framework."[5] This approach combines the deployment of multiple frontline teams, each assigned responsibility for managing some aspect of the organization's clinical and operational performance, with clear oversight and output expectations.

A top-guided, bottom-up approach has the benefit of engaging staff in the development of clinically sensitive designs that blend clinical requirements with organizational imperatives and constraints, but its downside is the additional investment required in data analytics, staff training, and governance. Organizations that have chosen this route to transformation have had to resource a number of institutional supports including identifying and training a cadre of frontline change leaders interested and able to lead local redesign teams and then exercise ongoing managerial control; articulating a model of clinical change leadership and defining its roles and responsibilities; equipping leaders in the middle of the organization with a rigorous operating system redesign methodology; exercising appropriate oversight of their actions; and embedding the system for frontline change in a wider organizational culture that facilitates and guides local action.

Organizations that have successfully brought about a transformation this way have combined a capability for the redesign of clinical operating systems by frontline teams with a model of central coordination and governance: together creating a capability for constant change. However, especially in those institutions caught between increasing patient demand and worsening resource shortages, boards of trustees are reluctant to invest staff time and institutional capital in anything other than the maintenance of current care delivery or programs that promise a very rapid return. For example, by the end of nine years of austerity budgets, cash-strapped English hospitals had to divert funds that might have been used for maintenance and long-term capability development to such an extent that they faced a deferred maintenance bill estimated to be £6 billion.

STRUCTURES TO SUPPORT WIDESPREAD LOCAL CHANGE

The infrastructure to support a top-guided, bottom-up approach is made up of frontline tools and central resources (Table 10.1). The most obvious frontline component is a large set of teams, each focusing on the operating system design and management for a subpopulation, pathway, or location of care. Organizations such as Virginia Mason Medical Center and Intermountain Healthcare deploy many multidisciplinary redesign teams concurrently. They target both administrative issues (e.g., the supply chain, patient flow, and recordkeeping and financial administrative processes) and clinical processes and care models supporting individual patient populations. They redesign single processes and whole operating systems. Unsurprisingly, because

Table 10.1. Requirements for clinician-led frontline change

Supporting frontline change	Exercising central control
• Unit or pathway level multiprofessional teams	• Institution or division level oversight body
• Structured and repeatable redesign method	• Tracking metrics and reporting systems
• Widely available team-based operational redesign and change leadership training program	• Project management support
• Defined role for clinical change leaders	• Data and analytics support
• Ongoing mentorship post-training	• Access to advice from corporate services

the teams' purpose is to improve care quality and efficiency simultaneously, they are genuinely multidisciplinary: managers covering finance, operations, IT, and human resources are well represented. Teams often cycle back repeatedly to refine the same process or operating system. Some teams are permanent, others temporary: Virginia Mason brings hundreds of small teams together transiently to redesign key processes, whereas Intermountain Healthcare has a permanent team structure responsible for both redesign and long-term oversight. In both organizations convening and managing multidisciplinary teams has become an important local skill.

The second frontline component is, of course, is a group of local leaders. If leaders are practicing clinicians, they need protected time for their leadership activities. This is a bona fide managerial role as clinical leaders are accountable for their teams' performance and for delivering improved results for their patients. All too often organizations fail to provide time for change leaders. However, the unfortunate reality is that transformation is hard to achieve while relying solely on the professionalism of volunteer enthusiasts working nights and weekends.

The leader's primary job is to connect clinical practice and local system performance to the organizational and departmental goals. The resources they need to discharge this responsibility include time, mentorship and development, administrative and analytic support, and such capital investment as an operational redesign may need. Hence, transformation does not come for free, which is often a sticking point for boards.

Third, redesign teams need a repeatable redesign methodology which specifies a standard approach to analysis, redesign, improvement, and management. The approach chosen varies from organization to organization and is often a popular source of controversy as aficionados of different methodologies—such as lean manufacturing, CQI, Six-Sigma—jockey with one another. Many organizations apply some version of the TPS. Others create their own method that draws from a wide range of tool sets. Intermountain Healthcare has famously developed its own approach based on the tools of continuous process improvement. Although devotees promote their chosen system over all others, what appears most important is that whatever the chosen approach to redesign it is internalized, repetitive, and consistent so that the same language is used throughout the organization, and independent teams can undertake redesign without needing outside consultant support.

Several centralized resources are also necessary. The first is training in leadership and redesign to address the unfamiliarity or discomfort many practicing clinicians feel with the tasks of leading change among their colleagues and exercising stewardship over institutional resources. Transforming organizations invest, often heavily, in leadership development. They usually develop their own leadership training programs[6] that are closely tied to the organization's strategy, culture, and values, rather than solely relying on external providers such as the professional societies or local business schools. Leadership development is *in situ* and for a purpose and training is available to as many of their staff as possible.

Other important resources are provided centrally. These include data relevant to a team's issue of focus and analytic support to help the team acquire and then make meaning of these data. Redesign teams also need access to specialized information on a range of topics such as labor law, financial analysis, process design, system engineering, organizational development, and IT, which can be provided by the appropriate corporate groups. They need project management support to help them stay on track and keep up the pace of work. And finally, they need a point of access to senior decision makers for those occasions when they encounter any institutional barriers to change that they need help removing. One of the defining characteristics of successful early responses to the Covid-19 pandemic was easy access to senior decision makers.

Although the temptation, especially for smaller organizations or systems, is to rely on management consultants to provide much of this support, most transforming organizations have developed these capabilities internally. In practice, this means a separate unit, even if only a few full-time employees (FTEs), that serves as an internal consultancy to the frontline. For example, at Virginia Mason the Kaizen Promotion Office serves this role, and at Intermountain it is the Healthcare Delivery Institute, and at the Massachusetts General Hospital the Center for Quality and Safety. Project managers, health economists and financial analysts, process engineers, and statisticians staff units such as these.

INTEGRATED APPROACH TO TRANSFORMATION

Multiple frontline teams, even when applying a consistent operating system redesign process, need to be guided, coordinated, and overseen. A body charged with this role has several tasks, the first of which is to identify and select targets for redesign that correspond to wider institutional priorities: most frequently the reform of processes, operating systems at a location of care, or pathways that map patient journeys across multiple locations. Redesign and change use expensive staff time which should be focused on the issues of highest organizational value: aimed at the right targets. Because not all targets will need the same magnitude of intervention, teams and targets must be matched to an appropriate approach: the *fix-improve-change* model discussed in Chapter 9. Teams focused on process improvement or a whole system reconfiguration and redesign each need a different composition, approach to data collection, and of course different amounts of time to complete their work. Finally, teams' progress must be monitored and the impact of their implemented redesigns assessed. At Intermountain Healthcare monitoring, and responding to, variance in the performance of their clinical designs (i.e., the clinical process models) is one of the roles of the institution's nine "Clinical Program Guidance Councils." This oversight task could be summarized as targeting, triage, and tracking.

One other essential resource is, of course, leadership talent. Redesign targets must be matched not only to teams but also to change leaders. The oversight body has an important role in identifying and recruiting staff interested in these roles and willing to be trained.

A second body of work relates to integration of operating system redesign with the rest of the organization's managerial work. In many instances, redesign of the process, staffing model, technology use, and control systems will have resource implications for the wider organization: recruitment, buildings, and information systems, for example. In effect, local operating system redesigns create need specifications for the organization's finance, operations, materials management, nursing, diagnostic services, information system, and real estate departments. Any healthcare delivery organization can be thought of as having a demand side, related to the substance of the clinicians' work with their patients, and a supply side, made up of those institutional resources that are used to meet these needs, such as (in case of a hospital) nursed beds, operating room slots, radiology appointments, radiotherapy sessions, clinical supplies, data, or outpatient clinic appointments. Redesigning local approaches to care delivery has the potential to create new internal demands for these supply side departments so these redesign activities cannot be undertaken in isolation from the rest of the organization's managerial structures. Sequence is important also. Many organizations redesign their facilities first and then plan their care models subsequently, when in reality it is better the other way around. It usually falls to an oversight group to manage this interface.

A third task for the oversight group relates to integration of another kind: the management of multiple, concurrent, and potentially interacting operating system redesign activities. Multiple redesign teams can make conflicting demands on shared organizational resources, such as IT, radiology, laboratory, emergency department, or nursing services. For instance, teams responsible for the design and management of the stroke network and multiple cancer pathways are all likely to have ideas of how to use CT scanning capacity. Their combined demands may not match the capability or current work pattern of radiology services, so these teams' competing demands must be adjudicated centrally. The same can be true of their use of the emergency department and the wards.

Yet another integration challenge is to ensure that the institution's various initiatives support and enhance each other. Large healthcare institutions frequently have multiple initiatives going on simultaneously at one or more of five levels: large-scale infrastructure investments, one-time programmatic initiatives, local operating system redesigns, unit-specific process improvement projects, and the daily management of patient flow routines. The first two tend to be less frequent, episodic, and managed by relatively few staff, whereas the latter three are more frequent or even continual, and usually involve training more staff.

Ensuring that all these activities are aligned—vertical coordination—is important and constantly challenging. Large-scale information system overhaul, for instance, is usually easier where institutions already have a well-practiced routine for frontline operating system redesign and a large group of experienced local change leaders.[7] All too often organizations mount multiple organizational change projects that are independent and oblivious to the others, at best inconsistent and at worst in direct conflict with each other. High-level interventions can dominate senior leaders' attention and can leave myriad lower-level activities unmanaged so that the potential institutional benefits of local redesign may be lost. Conversely, an exclusive focus on individual physician behavior, often the result of payer-driven performance measurement and reward systems, risks underinvestment in the local environment that shapes professional behavior and patient outcome.

It is commonly held that strategy execution is driven from the top by aligning it with the objectives, actions, and rewards of mid- and lower-level managers all the way down the hierarchy. However, in practice, aligning interventions at the five levels has proven more difficult than it sounds. Staff may not appreciate the overall strategy or the way its components fit together: research by Sull and colleagues found that only 55 percent of managers could name even one of the company's five top priorities.[8] And their thinking and action all too often remain fixed in their silos: in their survey Sull and colleagues also found that although 84 percent of managers said they could rely on their boss and direct reports to get things done, only 9 percent said they could rely on other units.

Integration among departments and between senior leaders and frontline caregivers is aided not only by a clear narrative of purpose (see Chapter 2) but also by uniform language, a single methodology, discipline in the targeting and sequencing of change activities, the creation of structured opportunities for staff across silos to work together, and above all, clear communication from the top to prevent departmental power struggles and set the stage for collaboration between operational and clinical leaders. It also requires that performance improvement priorities and redesign team focus be rapidly adjusted in response to evolving medical insights, changes in technological capability or regulations, or progress made in other parts of the organization or system. In Sull's study 80 percent of managers said that unsuccessful initiatives were not killed quickly enough. Research such as this highlights just how strong the central coordinating function must be.

MANAGING SUPPLY AND DEMAND CONCURRENTLY

These issues of horizontal and vertical integration raise a fundamental question. What will be the organization's model of leadership and control? Any approach to transformation based on scaling local operational change forces a senior leadership team to consider how the clinical enterprise of the future should be managed.

Unsurprisingly, the management approach taken by most healthcare delivery organizations is rooted in control over their physical assets such as the beds, clinics, operating rooms, staff, and investigative and therapeutic technologies. This, after all, is where the money is. This approach is reflected in the typical organization's structure with operating managers, in the case of a hospital, in charge of the emergency department, operating theaters, nursing and allied health services, diagnostic services, and outpatients, and so on reporting to the classic departments such as operations, finance, and human resources. Non–hospital delivery organizations have similar silos. Most organizational charts look the same. Each manager is predominantly responsible for maximizing the capacity utilization* of the resources and reducing their unit cost, and performance is usually assessed with such transactional performance measures as length of stay, waiting times, visit numbers, and cancellation rates.

This management approach implicitly treats demand for the physical services as exogenous. Consistent with a job shop model, patients move from one generic service to the next as their individual needs dictate. Medical, nursing, and allied health professional leaders, whose position in the organizational structure is usually separate from the operational managers, develop condition-specific protocols and pathways that give some structure to the paths patients take through the delivery system. But the clinicians still largely practice independently (although with lots of external influence on their behavior through incentives or information system–mediated clinical rules) and the management of demand and supply is not synchronized.

Some organizations do it differently. The integrated practice unit (IPU) model, for example, allows demand management and supply delivery to be managed concurrently. Dartmouth-Hitchcock's Spine Center, for instance, uses shared decision-making tools to effectively shape the demand that other resources

---

* Usually defined as a resource's actual output as a proportion of its potential output: for example, the ratio of the amount of time procedures are occurring in an operating room to the amount of time that operating room is available for use.

in the center, such as surgical and physical therapy teams, exist to meet.

Other organizations taking the approach of scaling local change and control have also tightened the link between clinical practice and operations management. For example, Intermountain Healthcare has nine clinical programs each headed by a guidance council made up of clinicians and their administrative counterparts.* The council's role is to "review current clinical results, track progress on goals, and assign resources to overcome implementation barriers at the local level."[9] These organizational structures help ensure integration of clinical practice, defined by the clinical process models, and operational management of the resources needed to support the delivery of that care. Supply and demand are not treated as unrelated activities to be managed independently but are managed in concert. The care process and patient pathway, the design of work and the deployment of the workforce, the selection and use of technology, the configuration of the physical space, and the selection of such managerial control policies as metrics and targets, job designs, accountability frameworks, and assessment processes are treated as a single set of management activities.

Intermountain's guidance councils are also a structured setting in which staff of all professions collaborate in pursuit of a common goal, thus beginning to address the poor relationship between clinicians and managers that characterizes so many delivery organizations. Organizations that are learning systems integrate the activities of operational redesign and ongoing over-

---

* A clinical dyad—physician leader and nurse/support staff leader—from each of the system's three regions sits on this council along with regional hospital administrators, finance, and information system representatives, etc.

sight so that "transformation" becomes a capability for local change and control that is built into daily routines, rather than an event or a program.

Many practicing clinicians eschew managerial work and the change leadership role, however. The leadership skills to help a team learn and implement a new way of working together and then manage that system's performance over the long term are often unfamiliar. Language and approaches common to management models drawn from other industries can clash with core values and behaviors of clinical practice. What appears obvious to management consultants and academics is foreign to clinicians. Hence, organizations actively engaging clinicians in managerial activities have had to develop a clinically coherent management model and language and invest in training. Intermountain's management model focuses on shared baselines (the care process models), clinical workflow, and clinical programs, for instance. And at Milan's Istituto Clinico Humanitas, which has similarly engaged clinicians in management, senior clinicians are taught financial literacy.

MEASUREMENT AND MANAGEMENT

In any organization, what is measured and how these measures are used are central to its management model. It is often taken as axiomatic that "you manage what you measure." The measures to which senior managers and clinical leaders attend signify what is considered important, so the measurement system can be both an expression of the delivery organization's culture and a message to the organization intended to shape the behavior of the entire staff. Measures are a strong signal of an organization's values, and the design of metrics and the measurement system is a powerful tool for making change. In healthcare measurement has particular significance because data and evidence

are at the very core of the enterprise. After all, the rigorous acquisition and analysis of data are what separates modern medicine from the quackery of old, and clinicians are trained scientists
with high expectations for what constitutes adequate evidence.

Unfortunately, measures used for management purposes often do not meet the standards expected of measurement for clinical purposes. On the contrary, measurement for management
is fraught with challenge in healthcare. High-quality data are often lacking, and sample sizes can be too small for the kind of
rigorous analysis that would satisfy clinicians. Clinicians and
managers in delivery organizations face a proliferation of externally mandated performance measures, some appearing inconsistent with their own personal mission or their understanding
of how care should be delivered. Metrics seem to be chosen
based as much on what is possible to measure as what is meaningful to patients and clinicians. Much of the drive for measurement comes from regulators and payers which are nonclinical
bodies that operate at some distance from care delivery.

In recent years, delivery organizations have faced an increasing
reporting burden as the number of required metrics has bur-
geoned. Professional societies, independent bodies such as the
National Quality Forum, and government agencies such as the
U.S. Centers for Medicare and Medicaid Services (CMS) all develop, validate, and promulgate performance measures, what one
leader, only partly in jest, termed the "measurement-industrial
complex."[10] There can be little overlap between the reporting requirements of different agencies and insurers, and for many
specialties some standard measures have little relevance. As
Mountford and Shojania noted, "Mortality rates thankfully have
little relevance to most pediatric or obstetric care, never mind
fields such as ophthalmology, rehabilitation medicine or palliative
care."[11] This can impose a significant reporting burden on delivery

organizations.[12] One U.S. hospital reported that its infrastructure to support external quality metric reporting consumed about 1 percent of net patient revenue, money that might be better used to support internal quality improvement activities.[13]

In addition to placing a burden on delivery organizations, the heavy reporting requirements have had one other important consequence. It has caused them to focus their measurement apparatus externally such that reporting has become an administrative burden to serve external masters that takes resources and focus away from the internal use of measurement. Yet, most of measurement's utility comes from its internal use in allowing board oversight of progress toward implementation of strategic goals and supporting the work of clinical leaders and local managers responsible for managing the performance of their units in pursuit of those goals. Meyer and colleagues suggest that the balance should be tipped heavily in favor of internal uses and that 70 percent of quality measurement dollars should be invested in local improvement needs as assessed by the individual provider.[14]

MEASUREMENT SYSTEMS

However, to serve internally as an effective lever of control, metrics must be part of a wider system of measurement and reporting. All too often delivery organizations collect reams of data but do not react effectively to them, not adequately defining how data will be collected in the context of routine care, how they will be analyzed and reported (to whom, how, and in what setting), what the consequences will be, and what actions will be taken. It is not sufficient to simply create a set of metrics without also determining how the measurements will be used.

A measurement system has five essential elements (Figure 10.1). Whether these interact effectively will ultimately be judged by the

Figure 10.1. Elements of a measurement system

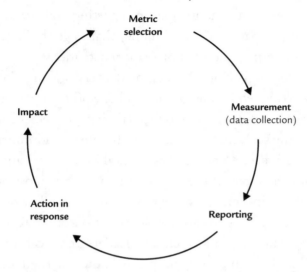

impact the measurement system has on the organization's ability to deliver patient value.

Maximizing the usefulness of data relies on making these five elements work as integral components in the measurement system:

- **Metric selection:** Agreeing on a set of metrics, either imported from external sources or developed internally, requires ongoing clinician input, statistical and epidemiological advice, and IT support. Metric definition is not a one-time activity as metrics change constantly as medical science evolves and organizational experience with the metrics accrues. Thus, organizations need a permanent process for metric identification, validation, and selection and for retiring metrics deemed no longer useful and replacing them with higher-utility alternatives.

- **Measurement (data collection):** Separate processes collect the raw data, manipulate it to create the measurements, and analyze their meaning. Much of the needed raw data will already be collected—health systems are usually awash in data—but some may need to be collected de novo. Clinicians tend to default to IT-based data collection and analysis tools and often forget the power of small amounts of hand-collected data manipulated in a simple spreadsheet.

- **Reporting:** This includes defining not only the report format—whether data are presented as time series, ratios, or "red, amber, green" (RAG) ratings, how variance is identified, and the selection of the service, institution, or national database to serve the reference for comparison (i.e., benchmarking)—but also the audience for the reports and the venue in which they are reviewed.

- **Actions:** All performance measures should be associated with a visible action, either at the level of an individual clinician or at the organizational level: training or reaccreditation in the case of the former and adjustment or outright changes to one or more of the levers of operational control in the latter. The expected actions should be considered at the same time as a given metric is defined or selected, helping identify to whom, and on what basis, it will be reported.

- **Impact/feedback loop:** Measurement is effective when it results in actions that have impact, either by improving the fidelity with which a process is executed or by improving the process and operating system's ability to create patient value. Did the action taken in response to any meaningful variance observed lead to a better patient outcome? Was the preferred process conformed to, and if so, did this process create its intended result? If not, why not?

Feedback of longer-term results is essential for improving care but also allows the measurement system itself to improve. Metric selection, data collection, analysis and reporting, actions taken, and assessment of impact evolve with experience. Over time, better metrics replace underperforming ones. In this way, a measurement system is dynamic.

DESIGN ISSUES FOR MEASUREMENT SYSTEMS

In developing an effective measurement system, leaders face two sets of design choices: one relating to developing or selecting a group of metrics to create a balanced portfolio and the other to building a reporting system.

Although all delivery organizations have a substantial external reporting obligation, some make the needs of the internal audience, from board members to frontline workers, a deciding factor in their choice of metrics. They report hundreds of measures, many more than are required by regulators and payers,[15] although an individual clinician or clinical group within the organization may only track a small number of metrics at any one time.

To inform operating system design and act as a lever of control, clinicians and managers need a set of metrics that provide information about the functioning of the care unit for which they are responsible. They need to answer two key questions about their operating system: "How do we know that our system is performing the way we want it to?" and "How can we know that this performance is achieving the outcomes for our patients that we desire?" To answer these questions they need metrics that not only allow local control but also allow them to be aware of what is happening in the wider care system and longer patient pathway of which their operating system is a part. In essence, they need to know their patients' upstream and downstream health, health care, and experience. Situating the operating system in the context of the wider enterprise of which it is a part informs its local design.

Control measures give an understanding of whether the operating system is functioning in the way it was intended. Metrics include process compliance, resource utilization, flow measures, and intermediate outcome measures—including patient and staff experience—that provide information about the performance of processes and individuals, and the utilization of key resources in the unit.

Awareness metrics allow a system focus, first by providing some insight into issues of access and the precipitants of entry into a healthcare system. They help answer the questions, "What puts the patient at risk for needing our service in the first place?" and "How do patients come to us?" Understanding how patients get into the operating system helps staff exercise even a small amount of input control and shape their internal processes. Second, these metrics inform questions such as, "Where do patients go after they leave our unit and what further care do they subsequently receive?" and "What are the longer-term outcomes of our care?" Knowledge of subsequent care and experience allows clinical tasks to be allocated along the longer patient journey. Outcome measures are essential as they allow evaluation of whether the care the unit delivers is making a positive difference. As Foucault pointed out, "People know what they do; frequently they know why they do what they do; but what they don't know is what they do does."[16]

Understanding how the patient arrives and where the patient goes next is of more than theoretical interest. Many clinicians have simply no insight into their patients' lives, and care, outside their consulting rooms. If the patient does not return, they could be cured, dead, or have sought care elsewhere either by choice or because they were obliged to by their payer. In all cases, an important opportunity for performance improvement is lost. The counterexample is a group of New York cardiac surgeons that made a practice of seeing their valve replacement patients, or their echocardiograms, at five years postoperatively. The insights gained enabled them to make improvements in virtually every aspect of their practice. Of course, like all data, these also have the potential for bias. Of those patients readmitted within 30 days of cardiac surgery at one Massachusetts hospital, not only were about half not readmitted to the original hospital but also those readmitted to other hospitals in the state were significantly different. Patients with wound infections tended to be readmitted to the initial hospital, whereas those with rhythm disturbances were more likely to be admitted to hospitals that did not perform the original surgery.[17]

Taken together, a portfolio of control and awareness measures describes cause and effect in an operating system: the causes of the need for a unit's services and the effect of those services on the patient's long-term well-being. Hence, the specific metrics chosen for control and awareness in any given unit will reflect clinicians' and managers' current hypotheses of cause and effect in the care of their patients.

Between disease-specific outcome measures published by such organizations as ICHOM[18] and pathway-specific process measures developed by professional societies, regulators, and individual delivery organizations, clinicians and managers have thousands of potential metrics from which to choose. The temptation is usually to measure more than less. However, experience suggests benefit in applying some broad principles to metric selection including the following. Aim for metrics that meet the following criteria:

- **Care centered:** Although some metrics must necessarily focus on higher-level corporate goals or the requirements of regulators and payers, ultimately it is the frontline teams that make changes to improve outcome, experience, and financial performance. Their data needs are paramount, so as many metrics as possible should focus on the needs of frontline clinicians and clinical service managers. To the greatest extent possible, measures should be defined, tested, and evaluated in consultation with clinical staff.

- **Research based:** Clinician engagement on metric selection implies a need for metrics to be derived from a robust research base. Of course, this is not always possible. The research base supporting many business processes is often not as robust as that supporting such clinical practices as the choice of a therapy. In spite of this limitation, a clinical organization must be able to justify why it is asking a clinician to pay attention to a particular metric.

- **Varied:**[19] Because patients' needs and delivery systems designed to meet them are complex and vary from one population to another, metrics must also vary. Some will focus on resource utilization and will necessarily be condition-nonspecific tracking processes or outcomes for heterogeneous groups of patients (e.g., operating room turnaround time or on-time starts or hospital-acquired infection rates). Others will be condition-specific and focus on more homogeneous subpopulations (e.g., diabetes HBA_1C measures). Definitions of the numerator and denominator may change with experience.

- **Parsimonious:**[20] Practicing clinicians can only focus on a limited number of metrics at any one time.

Although there should be a broad range of metrics in use across the whole organization, any individual should only be required to pay attention to a few. Moreover, selecting a metric is much like ordering a diagnostic test. Before ordering a test, thoughtful physicians will ask themselves, "Will the result change my decision?" If not, they do not order the test. Parsimony is achieved by asking of each metric, "Will seeing these data change what we do?"

Different outcome measures serve different functions, even within the same condition. Each potential metric thus must be tested by asking, "What is the purpose of measuring this factor?" The case of deep brain stimulation for movement disorders, discussed in Chapter 2, provides an example of the problem.

The severity of the movement disorder condition and the impact of interventions are both assessed using the three domains of the International Classification of Functioning (ICF): impairment of body structure and function, limitation of activity, and restriction on social participation. A significant disparity exists between what patients' families report to be important to them and what is measured in scientific reports and drug and device trials. In one study parental/carer concerns at the initial assessment were compared to the metrics used in 70 interventional studies.[21] Top patient/carer concerns were pain, difficulty in delivering the activities of daily living, difficulties with hand use, and seating: outcomes predominantly captured by the activity and participation scales of the ICF. However, most of the 46 neurosurgical and 24 pharmacological studies reviewed in this paper reported only changes in the impairment scale (i.e., a reduction in muscle tone or abnormal movements), and only one study used pain as its primary end point. Improvements in impairment are easier to measure than activity or participation and thus serve as useful trial end points when evaluating potential interventions. However, these do not necessarily correlate with improvements in function or quality of life and do not capture what parents care about: the impact of the impairment on the patient's family's or carer's daily lives. Outcome measures serving the investigator's needs may not help the practitioner concerned about the delivery of patient value.

Finally, when selecting metrics, be alert to a measurement's potential for unintended consequences and adverse effects, especially when a metric implies a target. Distortions can occur when metrics initially designed for internal control are used for external judgment. For instance, when CMS introduced a measure assessing whether the first dose of antibiotic for community-acquired pneumonia was delivered within six hours of the patient's presentation, it led to inappropriate antibiotic prescribing to patients with asthma and heart failure, who also presented with the same symptoms of shortness of breath and coughing that are characteristic in community-acquired pneumonia.[22,23] There are similar concerns about readmission rate measurement driving the overuse of observation beds or the four-hour emergency room waiting time target driving unnecessary admissions.

A second set of key measurement system design choices relates to reporting. The way an organization's leaders and managers choose to report measures internally will be a reflection of the way they have chosen to manage. The first choice relates to the level at which measurements are analyzed and reported. Data can be reported at the individual or group level. Reasons to report at the group level include mitigating small sample sizes and accurately reflecting the team nature of care, as well as encouraging teamwork. Many individuals typically contribute to the work reflected in measurements of resource utilization, process compliance, and patient outcomes.

When measures relate to the performance of individuals, leaders have a second choice relating to whether data are reported anonymously. Options for reporting individual clinicians' compliance with protocols, productivity targets, or resource utilization include to report to the individual only, to the department head only, to the individual and department head, or to the entire department in a group meeting. Because peer review of individualized performance data is such an effective way of influencing clinician behavior, some institutions choose to report measures either semi-anonymously (reports that compare the performance of multiple clinicians in which the index clinician is identified but the other clinicians are not), or completely unblinded (a comparative performance report in which all the clinicians are named).

Although "high-stakes" reporting, in which an individual's behavior is tracked, reported, and tied to an organizational consequence such as a bonus or sanction, exploits the powerful incentive of social acceptance among peers, it is fraught with difficulty. Aside from small sample sizes and multicausality, most administrative databases are prone to errors, and many measures used for this purpose are not well validated. For these reasons, some organizations have chosen to dispense with individual performance measurement altogether and rely on group or department-level measurement and reporting.

Ultimately, measurement is only helpful when measurements are made, analyzed, reported, and acted upon in a systematic way. An effective measurement system begins with a clear understanding of the organization's purpose in measurement and the actions to be undertaken in response to any meaningful patterns detected. The difficulty collecting data need not affect whether a metric is chosen: first identify a useful metric and then figure out how to collect the necessary data. In pursuit of parsimony, metrics that do not provide decision makers with meaningful information should be discarded. This way, the measurement system will evolve into an effective tool for day-to-day operational control and long-term improvement.

Developing a measurement system takes time, especially if one of the goals is to promote system thinking, clinician self-reflection, and frontline involvement in operating system design and control. Institutions such as the Cleveland Clinic and the Massachusetts General Hospital have taken a gradual approach in developing their measurement systems. Metrics each clinical division initially proposed to track its own performance were usually drawn from existing measurement activities (promoted by the professional society or disease registry to which the division was already contributing) and were more often than not process rather than outcome measures. With each passing year, divisional metric sets broadened to include more outcome and patient experience metrics. Initially data were collected and reported back to the division without a benchmark, target, or consequence: these elements were added subsequently. Intermountain Healthcare has a long history of involving clinicians in performance management and improvement. Metrics developed and deployed by its divisions make up a significant portion of routine performance reporting to the board so that clinicians are being held accountable for measures they deem appropriate.

TRANSLATING OPERATIONAL CONTROL INTO IMPROVED FINANCIAL PERFORMANCE

The infrastructure described comes at a cost. Institutions have taken years to develop their supporting systems and grow their pool of clinical change leaders. Boards and senior executives, especially if under revenue and regulatory pressure, naturally want a return on any investment they make in the staff and

Table 10.2. Classes of cost in healthcare delivery

Cost	Effect of reduction in use	Example
Variable	The item is not consumed, does not need to be replaced, and is available for later use.	Supplies, medications
Semi-variable	The item is not consumed, but the ability to repurpose the item is limited by time. Costs of providing the service may be reduced with sufficient reduction in volume.	Direct hourly nursing, respiratory therapists, physical therapists
Semi-fixed	The item is not consumed, but the obligation to continue to pay for the item does not change.	Equipment, operating-room time, physician salaries, ancillary services
Fixed	Resource consumption is not altered in the short run but may be altered in the next operating cycle.	Billing, organizational overhead, finances

technology needed to support widespread unit-level redesign. Unfortunately, the reality is that improved operational design and control do not automatically translate into financial gain.

Although reducing a delay or the use of an ineffective test or therapy has immediate quality benefits for the next patient, stopping an ineffective activity or reducing the amount of something consumed often does not save the organization any money because healthcare costs are largely fixed (Table 10.2).[24] Staff, buildings, and expensive technology must still be paid for even if their utilization is reduced. In reality the only way to reduce outgoings is to close or repurpose buildings, reduce staff numbers or pay rate, or reduce the services offered. Reducing length of stay tends to save little because the service nonetheless remains open, staff are still paid, and the costs of the building and technologies must still be borne. Variable costs are the only class of costs in which reducing an activity or use of a consumable directly and immediately translates into cash savings. In all other classes of cost (semi-variable, semi-fixed, and fixed), some other, often administratively difficult or politically unpopular, contraction is needed to release cash from waste reduction and performance improvement efforts. Boards expecting large savings are often disappointed.

Experience at the Mayo Clinic suggests what savings can be expected. The Mayo Clinic has reported significant operational improvements, reflected in improvements in parameters such as total cost of care, length of stay, blood product utilization, cancellation rates, appointment wait time, readmission rates, and complication and error rates.[25] However, when valuing the impact of its quality and performance improvement programs, it makes a clear distinction between "hard" and "soft" savings. The former are those that have a definite and measurable effect on cash flow over a reasonably short time (less than one to two years). Examples include equipment no longer needed that can be sold, contracted services no longer needed, or a decrease in the FTE count. Soft savings are changes with a definite impact on operations but that are only indirectly connected to cash flow, such as length of stay decrease with no impact on net income, avoided malpractice costs, or FTE reduction with redeployment to other activities.[26] Of a reported U.S. $46 million average annual savings, approximately $15 to $20 million were in "hard savings" and $25 to $30 million were in "soft." The reported program support costs were U.S. $3.5 million, giving a return on investment (to generate "hard" savings) of 5:1.

The majority of returns on investment in better operations design and control are realized through capacity enhancement. This increases the volume of services provided with the same resources: more patients or more care per patient, but no more staff. In effect this is doing more for the same, rather than the same for less. In an era of aging populations and increasing demand, freeing capacity is no small thing, but it does not necessarily generate an improvement in the short-term cash position. Capacity enhancement also prepares an institution to handle sudden, unexpected influxes of patients such as those experienced during the first and second waves of Covid-19 cases.

The unhappy reality that improved operational performance may not help the financial position can actually be worse than described previously. In what is the Achilles heel of any fee-for-service reimbursement model, institutional finances can actually worsen because smoother and more effective operations are often rewarded with lower per-patient revenues. For example, although Intermountain's success in managing elective Caesarean section rates reduced revenue by $50 million (a savings to its payers), its costs only went down by $41 million, a net loss from improved performance of $9 million.[27] The fact that this loss was a gain to Intermountain's insurers is behind current interest in gainsharing contracts between insurers and the professionals and organizations delivering care. Otherwise, the reward for excellence is a reduced budget. One theoretical advantage of national healthcare systems that both insure the population and own the delivery organizations is that they can avoid this perverse incentive, although this does not necessarily occur in practice. Budgets may still be cut when performance improves. Finally, better quality care is only cheaper if reduced waste and improved outcomes do not demand more expensive technologies. Contrary to one popular narrative, better-quality care can, and sometimes should, be more expensive.

Intermountain's experience points to another important consideration for senior teams intent on supporting local operational design and control. Institutional performance gains are usually the aggregation of many marginal gains from multiple local operational redesigns. Studies of the nature and extent of waste in healthcare suggest that, although its total value is eye watering, the sources of waste are widely and thinly distributed. Berwick and Hackbarth, for example, estimated that an impressive 33 percent of all U.S. healthcare expenditure was wasted. They categorized waste as overtreatment, failure to coordinate care, failure in care delivery, administrative complexity, excessive prices, and fraud and abuse. They found that only administrative complexity contributed more than 10 percent of the overall 33 percent estimate and that all the other categories each contributed less.[28] The IOM reports similar findings.[29] Each target for waste reduction efforts has the potential for only a few percent gain.

In practice there are, unfortunately, only a limited number of mechanisms of improving performance, measured as either the quality or efficiency of care. Some act by affecting the demand for services, for example, by intervening earlier in the course of disease through improved primary or secondary prevention (thereby preventing the need for more complex care later), increasing the appropriateness of care by undertaking only those interventions that are safe and effective, or reducing error and therefore the need for later "rework" to address iatrogenic injury or hospital-acquired infection.

Other interventions influence the costs of supply. We can optimize the number of activities existing resources may safely produce through technological support or improved scheduling and patient flow, or reduce the cost of providing a service by deploying less expensive staff or negotiating reduced prices for nonstaff inputs such as equipment and real estate. Taken together these are all ways of delivering the right care to the right person at the right time in the right place, done right.

In practice therefore, although there are many potential targets for performance improvement, there are relatively few fundamental mechanisms of achieving an improvement and often only modest gains to be had from any individual operating system redesign. One reason Intermountain and Virginia Mason have made such progress has been that they have deployed so many teams and leaders to focus on such a wide range of operating systems throughout their organizations. But gains are more likely to be realized in the form of released capacity than freed cash. Senior leaders therefore need to be realistic about how much financial gain they can achieve in the short term and be prepared for the politically difficult additional work required if real cost reduction is their end goal. Growing revenue using released capacity has been a much easier route for many organizations.

Regardless of whether a board and senior leadership team are motivated by cost reduction, revenue growth, or preparation for coming technological change, the clear implication is that any organization serious about transformation has to plan to support multiple local, small-scale activities over long periods of time, be prepared to invest in the infrastructure described here, and devote energy to its design. All else is simply tilting at windmills.

Conclusion

The environmental conditions driving the need to transform healthcare are likely to be with us for the foreseeable future. Demand continues to rise as populations age and a constant stream of new and expensive technologies enables more to be done for each individual. This potent cocktail of more patients and more cost per patient comes exactly at the time when nations' healthcare budgets are becoming increasingly strained.

Delivery organizations and caregiving professionals are inevitably caught in the middle, squeezed between increasing patient demand and constrained national resources. Although increased delivery system efficiency is only part of the solution, organizations and clinicians will continue to be subject to relentless pressure to improve productivity.

Yet not only is increasing transaction velocity and volume in our current institutions a recipe for further staff burnout but it is also unlikely to be enough. Technological and service developments are changing the very nature of care: who can deliver what care, where, and how. The inability of delivery systems to adopt and make the most of them can retard the very innovation we need. Local operating system redesign executed by engaged, enabled, and supported mid-level leaders is needed throughout the wider delivery system. At the organizational level, the ability to orchestrate multiple local operating system redesigns and change efforts is essential for both the widespread adoption of innovations in analytics and diagnostic and therapeutic technology, as well as the implementation of its strategy into practice.

In orchestrating widespread reform of their organizations' operating systems, senior leaders will need to address three fundamental tensions raised in the preceding chapters. First, organizations need to find a balance between central and local control. The role of clinicians, who were in prior eras exclusively trained and hired as individuals, is changing. Although doctors are being increasingly treated as workers, they and other clinicians have a key role in designing and managing the operating systems in which they practice. However, making clinicians part of the solution means more than teaching them new skills. They also need support as they apply these in their organizational settings. This, in turn, means that senior leaders' roles also need to change: they must adopt more of a mentoring style than the pacesetting one they are used to, a shift many find challenging in the current environment.

Second, organizations need to develop a sophisticated approach to variation. A common narrative in healthcare frames variation as bad, yet advancing science is enabling us to untangle the complexity in populations once thought of as homogeneous, thereby increasing warranted variation. Better understanding of the particular needs of different patient subgroups has allowed us to deliver greater patient value. Greater operational diversity seems inevitable, increasing the importance of accurately matching the operating system design to the type of care to be provided.

Improved operational performance is achieved both by reducing unwarranted practice variation and by exploiting the learning potential of appropriate variation. For example, Intermountain Healthcare has been successful exactly because it simultaneously works to reduce unwarranted variation—through specification and standardization—and encourage warranted variation through clinician autonomy and the ease of overriding the standard when necessary. It is able to deliver better value to its patients by supporting both a culture of conformance and a culture of dissent.

The third tension relates to uncertainty. Healthcare delivery organizations are often exhorted to implement best practice, roll out proven models, and rely on tools honed in production industries to do so. Yet regional variations in disease, personal preferences, community values, technology availability, and staff skills make it difficult to uniformly apply a single model. Healthcare delivery reform is anything but a linear journey to a known destination. On the contrary, uncertainty both underpins much of clinical practice and bedevils operating system redesign and management reform. Hence each delivery system must experiment to learn which model works best for it. No clinician or CEO wants to be seen not to know the right answer, yet this is exactly what it takes to establish an effective experimental and learning system. Furthermore, boards are often under pressure to think quarter by quarter, yet developing new delivery models and establishing the internal capabilities needed to do so over and over again are long-term projects that require continuing support. This is not something board members like to hear.

Finally, leaders must navigate these tensions against a background of healthcare delivery's special challenges. Its foundational biological science is incomplete and rapidly evolving. Patient relationships are long-term and constantly changing. When other industries interact with repeat customers, they usually provide the same product or service they did the last time. In healthcare, the product evolves as diseases progress and patients' preferences change, often influenced by previous interactions. Diversity and complexity are parts of the landscape, yet care is often still being delivered in the context of a model largely created in the nineteenth century.

So the hard work of transforming care—design, implement, learn from implementation, redesign—is ongoing. Not only does it demand new perspectives and skills but also a new group of leaders who are motivated and able to take on responsibility for shepherding local redesign. We need a generation of leaders in the middle of delivery organizations skilled in helping their colleagues through change. Clinicians, initially trained for one thing, are now needed to do another. Because operating systems exert such a powerful influence over the care a patient ultimately receives, all clinicians arguably need some basic redesign and management skills.

It is usually in the interests of management consultants, academics, and regulators to propose universally applicable single solutions to complex problems. This book intentionally takes the opposite perspective: that there are multiple legitimate approaches and tools available. Hence, at its heart it is about matching: matching the operating system to the nature of the care and the value to be delivered, matching the behavior change technique to the behavior and its barriers, and matching the leadership style to the nature of the change. And it is about selecting the approach and tool that best suit the circumstances you are facing. It is a reaction against the one-size-fits-all mindset of so much management advice and policy regulation.

This book is also about the locus of control: the idea that those with the best understanding of the nature of patients' needs, values, and disease are those best positioned to design and control the local systems that are the primary mechanism by which care is delivered. And last, it is about service: the argument that not only do professionals serve their patients, but so do the systems in which they practice. But systems do not naturally serve their clients: they must be built to do so. This is detailed and slow work, not something that happens overnight but something that can be achieved deliberately and purposefully.

The conditions may never be right for transforming care and redesigning operating systems. Boards' perspectives are likely to remain short term. Complete data and perfect data quality may be an illusion. Reimbursement systems may not protect against the losses that better care can incur and incentives may never completely align. Nonetheless, the institutions described here, and many others, have shown that substantial progress can be made in spite of local conditions, not because of them. Given the pace of technological change, we do not have the luxury of waiting for ideal circumstances. The time for redesign is now.

Notes

Chapter 1

1. Pallok K, De Maio F, Ansell DA. Structural racism—a 60-year-old black woman with breast cancer. *N Engl J Med.* 2019;380(16):1489-1493.

2. Shanafelt TD, Dyrbye LN, West CP. Addressing physician burnout: the way forward. *JAMA.* 2017;317(9):901-902.

3. Nembhard IM, Alexander JA, Hoff TI, Ramanujam R. Why does the quality of health care continue to lag? Insights from management research. *Acad Manag Perspect.* 2009;24-42.

4. Laloux F. *Reinventing Organizations.* Brussels: Nelson Parker; 2014.

5. Eisenstein L. To fight burnout, organize. *N Engl J Med.* 2018;379(6):509-510.

Chapter 2

1. Gulati R. Structure that's not stifling. *Harv Bus Rev.* 2018;96(3):68-79.

2. Porter ME. What is strategy? *Harv Bus Rev.* 1996;74(6):61-78.

3. Waitemata District Health Board, unpublished study (J Christensen, 2014).

4. Fowler FJ, Collins MM, Albertsen PC. Comparison of recommendations by urologists and radiation oncologists for treatment of clinically localized prostate cancer. *JAMA.* 2000;283(24):3217-3222.

5. Davies HTO, Hodges C-L, Rundall TG. Views of doctors and managers on the doctor-manager relationship in the NHS. *BMJ Br Med J.* 2003;326(7390):626-628.

6. Rundall TG, Davies HTO, Hodges C, Diamond M. Doctor-manager relationships in the United States and the United Kingdom. *J Healthc Manag.* 2004;49(4):251-268.

7. Powell A, Davies H. Managing doctors, doctors managing. Research Report, Nuffield Trust. Published 2016. https://www.nuffieldtrust.org.uk/files/2017-01/doctors-managers-web-final.pdf.

8. Degeling P, Maxwell S, Kennedy J, Coyle B. Medicine, management, and modernisation: a "danse macabre"? *BMJ Br Med J.* 2003;326(7390):649–652.

9. Beckman HB. Lost in translation: physicians' struggle with cost-reduction programs. *Ann Intern Med.* 2011;154(6):430–433.

10. For a detailed description of the sources of uncertainty in clinical practice see chapter 2 in Bohmer RMJ. *Designing Care: Aligning the Nature and Management of Health Care.* HBS Press; 2009.

11. Berwick DM, Nolan TW, Whittington J. The triple aim: care, health, and cost. *Health Aff.* 2008;27(3):759–769.

12. Bodenheimer T, Sinsky C. From triple to quadruple aim: care of the patient requires care of the provider. *Ann Fam Med.* 2014;12:573–576.

13. Porter ME. What is value in health care? *N Engl J Med.* 2010;363(26):2477–2481.

14. Lee TH. Putting the value framework to work. *N Engl J Med.* 2010; 363(26):2481–2483.

15. Porter ME, 2010.

16. Blumenthal D, Stremikis K. Getting real about health care value (September 17, 2013). *Harv Bus Rev Blog Network.* Accessed Nov 15, 2020. https://hbr.org/2013/09/getting-real-about-health-care-value.

17. Porter ME, 2010.

18. International Consortium for Health Outcomes Measurement (ICHOM). Standard sets. Accessed Nov 15, 2020. https://www.ichom.org/standard-sets.

19. Sinsky C, Colligan L, Li L, et al. Allocation of physician time in ambulatory practice: a time and motion study in 4 specialties. *Ann Intern Med.* 2016;165:753–760.

20. Gawande A. Why doctors hate their computers. *New Yorker.* November 12, 2018.

21. Detsky AS. What do patients really want from health care? *JAMA.* 2011:306(22); 2500–2501.

22. Dan Lumsden, Consultant Paediatric Neurologist, Guy's and St. Thomas' NHS Foundation Trust, personal communication, 2020.

23. Joffe S, Manocchia M, Weeks JC, Cleary PD. What do patients value in their hospital care? An empirical perspective on autonomy centred bioethics. *J Med Ethics.* 2003;29:103–108.

24. Klaber RE, Bailey S. Kindness: an underrated currency. *BMJ Br Med J.* 2019;367:l60–199.

25. Berry LL, Danaher TS, Chapman RA, et al. Role of kindness in cancer care. *J Oncol Pract.* 2017;13(11):744–750.

26. UK Department of Health. Healthy Foundations life stage segmentation toolkit. Published 2010. Accessed Nov 15, 2020. https://www .cancerresearchuk.org/prod_consump/groups/cr_common/@nre/@hea /documents/generalcontent/cr_045215.pdf.

27. The Waitemata District Health Board's purpose can be accessed at https://www.waitematadhb.govt.nz/about-us/board-priorities/.

28. Gulati R. Structure that's not stifling. *Harv Bus Rev.* 2018;96(3): 68–79.

29. Waitemata District Health Board Annual Plan 2015/16. Accessed Nov 15, 2020. https://www.waitematadhb.govt.nz/assets/Documents /annual-plan/WDHB-AnnualPlan2015-16.pdf.

Chapter 3

1. Bloom N, Genakos C, Sadun R, Van Reenen J. Management practices across firms and countries. *Acad Manag Perspect.* 2012;26(1):12–33.

2. Dorgan S, Layton D, Bloom N, et al. *Management in Healthcare: Why Good Practice Really Matters.* McKinsey and Company/London School of Economics; 2010.

3. Nelson EC, Batalden PB, Huber TP, et al. Microsystems in health care: Part 1. Learning from high-performing front-line clinical units. *Jt Comm J Qual Improv.* 2002;28(9):472–493.

4. Jaikumar provides a wonderful history of manufacturing systems through the lens of the history of Beretta, one of the world's oldest companies and still owned by the family that founded it. (Jaikumar R. From filing and fitting to flexible manufacturing: a study in the evolution of process control. *Found Trends Technol Inf Oper Manag.* 2005;1[1]:1–120.)

5. Press MJ. Instant replay: a quarterback's view of care coordination. *N Engl J Med.* 2014;371(6):489–491.

6. Swensen SJ, Meyer GS, Nelson EC, et al. Cottage industry to postindustrial care—the revolution in health care delivery. *N Engl J Med.* 2010;362:e12. Published online February 4, 2010. doi: 10.1056/NEJMp0911199.

7. Schmemann S. Moscow eye doctor hails assembly-line surgery at clinic. *New York Times.* July 2, 1985.

8. Hayes RH, Wheelwright SC. Link manufacturing process and product life cycles. *Harv Bus Rev.* Jan–Feb 1979.

9. Hayes RH, Wheelwright SC, 1979.

10. Bohn RE. Measuring and managing technological knowledge. *Sloan Manag Rev.* 1994;36(1):61–72.

11. For a detailed discussion of the stage of knowledge in health care see Bohmer RMJ. *Designing Care.* HBS Press, 2009:80–85.

12. Skinner W. The focused factory. *Harv Bus Rev.* May–June, 1974;113–121.

13. Skinner W, 1974.

14. Herzlinger RE. *Market Driven Health Care.* Addison-Wesley; 1996.

15. Porter ME. What is value in health care? *N Engl J Med.* 2010;363(26):2477–2481.

16. Glouberman S, Mintzberg H. Managing the care of health and the cure of disease: Part I—differentiation. *Health Care Manag Rev.* 2001;26(1):56–69.

17. Bohmer RMJ. *Designing Care.* HBS Press; 2009.

18. Edmondson AC. Strategies for learning from failure. *Harv Bus Rev.* 2011;89(4):48–55.

19. Christensen CM, Grossman JH, Hwang J. *The Innovator's Prescription: A Disruptive Solution for Health Care.* McGraw-Hill; 2009.

20. Sepucha KR, Fowler FJ, Mulley AG. Policy support for patient-centered care: the need for measurable improvements in decision quality. *Health Aff.* 2004.

21. Wennberg JE. Unwarranted variations in healthcare delivery: implications for academic medical centers. *BMJ Br Med J.* 2002;325:961–964.

22. Mulley A, Trimble C, Elwyn G. Patient preferences matter. Kings Fund. Published 2012. Accessed Nov 15, 2020. https://www.kingsfund .org.uk/sites/default/files/field/field_publication_file/patients -preferences-matter-may-2012.pdf.

23. Hayes RH, Wheelwright SC, 1979.

24. A good discussion of variability and its impact on healthcare services can be found in Hopp WJ, Lovejoy WS. *Hospital Operations: Principles of High Efficiency Health Care.* FT Free Press; 2013:507–513.

Chapter 4

1. Brent James, quoted in Bohmer RMJ, Edmondson AC, Feldman LR. 2002. Intermountain health care. Harvard Business School Case, No. 603066.

2. James BC, Savitz LA. How Intermountain trimmed health care costs through robust quality improvement efforts. *Health Aff.* 2011;30(6):1185–1191.

3. Evans MK, Rosenbaum L, Malina D, et al. Diagnosing and treating systemic racism. *N Engl J Med.* 2020;383:274–276.

4. Professor Terrance Chua, National Heart Centre, Singapore, personal communication, 2013.

5. Vaughn L, Edwards N, Imison C, Collins B. Rethinking acute medical care in smaller hospitals. Nuffield Trust. Published 2018. https://www.nuffieldtrust.org.uk/files/2018-10/nuffield-trust-rethinking -acute-medical-care-in-smaller-hospitals-web-new.pdf.

6. Bohmer RMJ, Imison C. Lessons from England's health care workforce redesign: no quick fixes. *Health Aff.* 2013;32(11):2025–2031.

7. OECD. *Health Workforce Policies in OECD Countries: Right Jobs, Right Skills, Right Places.* OECD Health Policy Studies, OECD Publishing; 2016.

8. Drucker PF. Managing for business effectiveness. *Harv Bus Rev.* Published May 1963. https://hbr.org/1963/05/managing-for-business -effectiveness.

9. Bohmer RMJ, Imison C, 2013.

10. Mundinger MO, Kane RL, Lenz ER, et al. Primary care outcomes in patients treated by nurse practitioners or physicians: a randomized trial. *JAMA.* 2000;283(1):59–68.

11. Imison C, Castle-Clarke S, Watson R. Reshaping the workforce to deliver the care patients need. Nuffield Trust. Published 2016. Accessed Nov 16, 2020. https://www.nuffieldtrust.org.uk/files/2017-01/reshaping -the-workforce-web-final.pdf.

12. Bohmer RMJ, Imison C, 2013.

13. Gawande A. Why doctors hate their computers. *New Yorker.* November 12, 2018. https://www.newyorker.com/magazine/2018/11/12 /why-doctors-hate-their-computers.

14. Bohmer RMJ, Imison C, 2013.

15. Arno PS, Levine C, Memmott MM. The economic value of informal caregiving: President Clinton's proposal to provide relief to family caregivers opens a long-overdue discussion of this "invisible" health care sector. *Health Aff.* 1999;18(2):182–188.

16. Massachusetts General Hospital. MGH mission. Accessed Nov 15, 2020. https://www.massgeneral.org/assets/MGH/pdf/equity-and -inclusion/credo-and-boundaries.pdf.

Chapter 5

1. Dafny LS, Lee TH. The good merger. *N Engl J Med.* 2017;372(22): 2077–2079.

2. Dafny LS, Lee TH, 2017.

3. Ross JS, Normand ST, Wang Y, et al. Hospital volume and 30-day mortality for three common medical conditions. *N Engl J Med.* 2010;362(12):1110–1118.

4. Epstein AM. Volume and outcome—it is time to move ahead. *N Engl Med J.* 2002;346(15):1161–1164.

5. NHS England. Next steps on the NHS Five Year Forward view. https://www.england.nhs.uk/five-year-forward-view/next-steps-on-the -nhs-five-year-forward-view/primary-care/.

6. Robertson R, Sonola L, Honeyman M, et al. Specialists in out of hospital settings. King's Fund, 2014. Accessed Nov 16, 2020. https:// www.kingsfund.org.uk/sites/default/files/field/field_publication_file /specialists-in-out-of-hospital-settings-kingsfund-oct14.pdf.

7. Bohmer RMJ. *Designing Care.* HBS Press; 2009:137.

8. Huckman RS, Porter ME, Gordon R, et al. Dartmouth-Hitchcock Medical Center: Spine Care. Harvard Business School Case No. 609-016, 2009.

9. Huckman RS. Are you having trouble keeping your operations focused? *Harv Bus Rev.* 2009;87(9):90–95.

10. Huckman RS. *Harv Bus Rev.* 2009.

11. James BC, Savitz LA. How Intermountain trimmed health care costs through robust quality improvement efforts. *Health Aff.* 2011;30(6):1185–1191.

Chapter 6

1. Klaber RE, Blair M, Lemer C, Watson M. Whole population integrated child health: moving beyond pathways. *Arch Dis Child.* Published online May 23, 2016. doi: 10.1136/archdischild-2016-310485.

2. Heifetz R, Grashow A, Lansky M. *The Practice of Adaptive Leadership.* *Harv Bus Rev.*; 2009:19–23.

3. Adapted from Edmondson AC. The competitive imperative of learning. *Harv Bus Rev.* July–August 2008.

4. Edmondson AC, Bohmer RMJ, Pisano G. Speeding up team learning. *Harv Bus Rev.* 2001;79(9):125–132.

5. Barley SR. Technology as an occasion for structuring: observations on CT scanners and the social order of radiology departments. *Admin Sci Q.* 1986;31:78–108.

6. Lewin K. Frontiers in group dynamics: concept, method and reality in social science; social equilibria and social change. *Hum Relat.* 1947;1:5–41.

7. Phillips JR. Enhancing the effectiveness of organizational change management. *Hum Resour Manag.* 1983;22(1–2):183–199.

8. Kotter JP. Leading change: why transformation efforts fail. *Harv Bus Rev.* March 1995:59–67.

9. Edmondson AC. *Teaming: How Organizations Learn, Innovate, and Compete in the Knowledge Economy.* Jossey-Bass; 2012.

10. King's Fund. Leadership and engagement for improvement in the NHS. 2012.

11. King's Fund. The future of leadership and management in the NHS: no more heroes: a report for the King's Fund Commission on Leadership and Management in the NHS. 2011.

12. Edmondson AC, 2012.

13. Heifetz R. *Leadership Without Easy Answers*. Harvard University Press; 1994.

14. Mintzberg H. Structure in 5's: a synthesis of the research on organization design. *Manage Sci.* 1980;26(3):322–341.

15. Welch HG, Mogielnicki J. Presumed benefit: lessons from the American experience with marrow transplantation for breast cancer. *BMJ Br Med J.* 2002;324:1088–1092.

16. Lee TH. Turning doctors into leaders. *Harv Bus Rev.* 2010;88 (4):50–58.

17. Lee TH, 2010.

18. Neily J, Mills PD, Young-Xu Y, et al. Association between implementation of a medical team training program and surgical mortality. *JAMA.* 2010;304(15):1693–1700.

19. Haynes AB, Weiser TG, Berry WR, et al. A surgical safety checklist to reduce morbidity and mortality in a global population. *N Engl J Med.* 2009;360:491–499.

20. Chen J, Radford M, Wang Y, et al. Do America's best hospitals perform better for myocardial infarction? *N Engl J Med.* 1999;340:286–292.

21. Dean N, Bateman K, Donnelly S, et al. Improved clinical outcomes with utilization of a community-acquired pneumonia guideline. *Chest.* 2006;130:794–799.

22. Edmondson AC. Learning from mistakes is easier said than done: group and organization influences on the detection and correction of human error. *J Appl Behav Sci.* 1996;32(1):5–28.

23. Curry L, Spatz E, Cherlin E, et al. What distinguishes top-performing hospitals in acute myocardial infarction mortality rates? *Ann Intern Med.* 2011;154:384–390.

24. Interview at the King's Fund available at https://www.kingsfund .org.uk/audio-video/don-berwick-importance-and-challenge-clinical -leadership.

25. Goodall A. Physician-leaders and hospital performance: Is there an association? *Soc Sci Med.* 2011;73(4):535–539.

26. Bloom N, Sadun R, Van Reenan J. Does management matter in healthcare? Center for Economic Performance, London School of Economics Working Paper. Accessed Nov 16, 2020. https://cep.lse.ac.uk /textonly/_new/staff/vanreenen/pdf/HospitalPaper_ver11.pdf.

27. Lee TH, 2010.

28. Berwick DM. Eleven worthy aims for clinical leadership of health system reform. *JAMA.* 1994;272(10):797–802.

29. Adapted from Bohmer RMJ. *The Instrumental Value of Medical Leadership.* King's Fund; 2012.

30. Beckman HB. Lost in translation: physicians' struggle with cost-reduction programs. *Ann Intern Med.* 2011;154(6):430–433.

31. Feynman RP. Personal observations on reliability of shuttle. Report of the Presidential Commission on the Space Shuttle Challenger Accident. Vol 2, App F. https://history.nasa.gov/rogersrep /v2appf.htm.

32. Rashid F, Edmondson AC, Leonard HB. Leadership lessons from the Chilean Mine Rescue. *Harv Bus Rev.* 2013;91(7–8):113–119.

33. Stockdale J. Cited by Collins JC. *Good to Great: Why Some Companies Make the Leap . . . and Others Don't.* Harper Business; 2001.

34. Gulati R. Structure that's not stifling. *Harv Bus Rev.* 2018;96(3):68–79.

35. Gulati R, 2018.

36. President Nixon's 1972 announcement on the space shuttle. Accessed Nov 16, 2020. https://history.nasa.gov/stsnixon.htm.

37. Roberto MA, Bohmer RMJ, Edmondson AC. Facing ambiguous threats. *Harv Bus Rev.* 2006;84(11):16–113.

38. Report of the Mid-Staffordshire NHS Foundation Trust Public Inquiry. Accessed Nov 16, 2020. https://assets.publishing.service.gov.uk /government/uploads/system/uploads/attachment_data/file/279124 /0947.pdf.

39. Bohmer RMJ, Bloom JD, Mort EA, et al. Restructuring within an academic health center to support quality and safety: the development of the Center for Quality and Safety at the Massachusetts General Hospital. *Acad Med.* 2009;84:1663–1671.

40. Data from Edmonson AC, Roberto MA. Children's Hospital and Clinics (A). HBS Case No. 203-050. HBS Press; 2007.

41. Porter ME, Nohria N. What is leadership? The CEO's role in large complex organizations. In Nohria N, Khurana R, eds. *Handbook of Leadership Theory and Practice.* HBS Press; 2010.

42. Porter ME, Nohria N, 2010.

43. Wennberg J, 2011. Accessed Nov 17, 2020. https://www.slideshare .net/grouphealth/wennberg-at-group-health-32511.

44. Edmondson AC, Bohmer RMJ, Pisano GP. Speeding up team learning. *Harv Bus Rev.* 2001;79(9):125–132.

45. Langewiesche W. Columbia's last flight. *Atlantic Monthly.* Nov 2003:82.

46. Schein EH. *Humble Inquiry: The Gentle Art of Asking Instead of Telling.* Berrett-Koehler Publishers; 2013.

47. Porter ME, Nohria N, 2010.

48. Hickson GB, Pichert JW, Webb LE, Gabbe SG. A complementary approach to promoting professionalism: identifying, measuring, and addressing unprofessional behaviors. *Acad Med.* 2007;82(11):1040–1048.

49. Hickson GB, Pichert JW. One step in promoting patient safety: addressing disruptive behavior. *Physician Insurer.* 2010:40–43.

50. Leape LL, Shore MF, Dienstag JL, et al. A culture of respect, part 1: the nature and causes of disrespectful behavior by physicians. *Acad Med.* 2012;87(7):1–8.

51. Leape LL, Shore MF, Dienstag JL, et al., 2012.

52. Hickson GB, Pichert JW, Webb LE, Gabbe SG, 2007.

53. Johnson & Johnson credo. Accessed Nov 17, 2020. https://www.jnj .com/about-jnj/jnj-credo.

54. Simons R. *Levers of Control: How Managers Use Innovative Control Systems to Drive Strategic Renewal.* HBS Press; 1994:39.

55. Massachusetts General Hospital. Mission statement. Accessed Nov 16, 2020. https://www.massgeneral.org/assets/MGH/pdf/equity-and -inclusion/credo-and-boundaries.pdf.

56. Waitemata District Health Board.

57. Kornacki MJ, Silversin MJ. *Leading Physicians Through Change: How to Achieve and Sustain Results.* American College of Physician Executives; 2000.

58. Bohmer RMJ, Ferlins EM. 2005. Virginia Mason Medical Center, HBS Case 606-044.

59. Hickson GB, Pichert JW, Webb LE, Gabbe SG. A complementary approach to promoting professionalism: identifying, measuring, and addressing unprofessional behaviors. *Acad Med.* 2007;82(11): 1040–1048.

60. Hickson GB, Pichert JW, Webb LE, Gabbe SG, 2007.

61. Pichert JW, Hickson GB, Moore I. Using patient complaints to promote patient safety. In: Henriksen K, Battles JB, Keyes MA, et al, eds. *Advances in Patient Safety: New Directions and Alternative Approaches.* Vol 2. Agency for Healthcare Research and Quality (US); 2008.

62. David Lawrence, chairman emeritus of the Kaiser Foundation Health Plan and Hospitals, personal communication, July 11, 2020.

63. Lawrence DM. *Best Care Best Future: A Guide for Health Care Leaders.* Second River Healthcare Press; 2014.

64. Cochran J. *Healer, Leader, Partner: Optimizing Physician Leadership to Transform Healthcare.* Lioncrest Publishing; 2018.

Chapter 7

1. Relman AS. Medicine as a Business and a Profession. The Tanner Lectures on Human Values; 1986.

2. Relman AS, 1986.

3. Davis DA, Thomson MA, Oxman AD, et al. Evidence for the effectiveness of CME; A review of 50 randomized controlled trials. *JAMA.* 1992;268(9):1111–1117.

4. Greco PJ, Eisenberg JM. Changing physicians' practices. *N Engl J Med.* 1993;329(17):1271–1274.

5. Oxman AD, Thomson MA, Davis DA, et al. No magic bullets: a systematic review of 102 trials of interventions to improve professional practice. *Can Med Assoc J.* 1995;153(10):1423–1431.

6. Balas EA, Boren SA. *Managing Clinical Knowledge for Health Care Improvement.* Yearbook of Medical Informatics; 2000.

7. McGlynn EA, Asch SM, Adams J, et al. The quality of health care delivered to adults in the United States. *N Engl J Med.* 2003;348(26): 2635–2645.

8. McGlynn EA. Improving the quality of U.S. health care—what will it take? *N Engl J Med.* 2020;383:801–803.

9. Cabana MD, Rand CS, Powe NR, et al. Why don't physicians follow clinical practice guidelines. *JAMA.* 1999;282:1458–1465.

10. Michie S, Van Stralen MM, West R. The behaviour change wheel: a new method for characterising and designing behaviour change interventions. *Implementation Sci.* 2011:6(1):42–52.

11. Lorencatto F, Charani E, Sevdalis N, et al. Driving sustainable change in antimicrobial prescribing practice: how can social and behavioural sciences help? *J Antimicrob Chemother.* 2018;73(10): 2613–2624.

12. Data from Atkins L, Francis J, Islam R, et al. A guide to using the Theoretical Domains Framework of behaviour change to investigate implementation problems. *Implementation Sci.* 2017;12(1):77–94; Lorencatto F, Charani E, Sevdalis N, et al. *J Antimicrob Chemother,* 2018; Michie S, Van Stralen MM, West R. *Implementation Sci,* 2011; West R, Michie S, Atkins L, Chadwick P, Lorencatto F. Achieving behaviour change: A guide for local government and partners. Accessed Nov 23, 2020. https://assets.publishing.service.gov.uk/government/uploads/system /uploads/attachment_data/file/875385/PHEBI_Achieving_Behaviour _Change_Local_Government.pdf.

13. Lorencatto F, Charani E, Sevdalis N, et al. *Journal of Antimicrobial Chemotherapy,* 2018.

14. Hunter DJ. Uncertainty in era of precision medicine. *N Engl J Med.* 2016;375(8):711–713.

15. Tinetti ME, Bogardus ST, Agostini JV. Potential pitfalls of disease-specific guidelines for patients with multiple conditions. *N Engl J Med.* 2004;351(27):2870–2874.

16. Rosenthal E. Patients' costs skyrocket; specialists' incomes soar. *The New York Times.* January 18, 2014. Accessed Nov 17, 2020. https:// www.nytimes.com/2014/01/19/health/patients-costs-skyrocket -specialists-incomes-soar.html?_r=0.

17. Kassirer JP. *On the Take: How Medicine's Complicity with Big Business Can Endanger Your Health.* Oxford University Press; 2005.

18. Wynia MK, Latham SR, Kao AC, et al. Medical professionalism. *N Engl J Med.* 1999;341:1612–1616.

19. Herzberg, F. The motivation-hygiene concept and problems of manpower. *Personnel Administration.* Jan–Feb 1964 (27):3–7.

20. Hackman JR, Oldham GR. *Work Redesign.* Pearson Education; 1980:78–80.

21. Landro L. A new way to get doctors to take better care of patients: bribe them. *Wall Street Journal.* April 10, 2003.

22. Rosenthal MB. Beyond pay for performance—emerging models of provider-payment reform. *N Engl J Med.* 2008;359(12):1197–1200.

23. Van Herck P, De Smedt D, Annemans L, et al. Systematic review: effects, design choices, and context of pay-for-performance in health care. *BMC Health Serv Res.* 2010;10(1):247.

24. Robinson JC. Theory and practice in the design of physician payment incentives. *Milbank Q.* 2001;79(2):149–177.

25. Song Z, Ji Y, Safran DG, Chernew ME. Health care spending, utilization, and quality 8 years into global payment. *N Engl J Med.* 2019;381(3):252–263.

26. Rosenthal MB, Frank RG, Li Z, Epstein AM. Early experience with pay for performance: from concept to reality. *JAMA.* 2005;294(14):1788–1793.

27. Karlsberg SS, Sussex J, Feng Y. Incentives to follow best practice in health care. Office of Health Economics Briefing 55, February 2015. https://www.ohe.org/publications/incentives-follow-best-practice-health -care.

28. Berwick DM. Payment by capitation and the quality of care. *N Engl J Med.* 1996;335(16):1227–1230.

29. Van Herck P, De Smedt D, Annemans L, et al., 2010.

30. Epstein AM, Lee TH, Hamel MB. Paying physicians for high-quality care. *N Engl J Med.* 2004;350(4):406–410.

31. Van Herck P, De Smedt D, Annemans L, et al., 2010.

32. Data from Van Herck et al., 2010; Karlsberg Schaffer et al., 2015.

33. Emanuel EJ, Ubel PA, Kessler JB, et al. Using behavioral economics to design physician incentives that deliver high-value care. *Ann Intern Med.* 2016;164(2):114–119.

34. Emanuel EJ, Ubel PA, Kessler JB, et al., 2016.

35. Mehrotra A, Sorbero MES, Damberg CL. Using the lessons of behavioral economics to design more effective pay-for-performance programs. *Am J Manag Care.* 2010;16(7):497–503.

36. Rosenthal MB, Frank RG, Li Z, Epstein AM. Early experience with pay for performance: from concept to reality. *JAMA.* 2005;294(14): 1788–1793.

37. Kahneman D, Tversky A. Prospect theory: an analysis of decision under risk. *Econometrica.* 1979;47(2):263.

38. Mehrotra A, Sorbero MES, Damberg CL, 2010.

39. England's plastic bag usage drops 85 percent since 5p charge introduced. *The Guardian.* July 30, 2016. https://www.theguardian.com /environment/2016/jul/30/england-plastic-bag-usage-drops-85-per-cent -since-5p-charged-introduced.

40. Fung CH, Lim Y-W, Mattke S, et al. Systematic review: the evidence that publishing patient care performance data improves quality of care. *Ann Intern Med.* 2008;148:111–123.

41. Fung CH, Lim Y-W, Mattke S, et al., 2008.

42. Geng EH. Implementation science for the bedside. *N Engl J Med.* 2019;381(4):304–305.

43. Hibbard JH, Greene J, Sofaer S, et al. An experiment shows that a well-designed report on costs and quality can help consumers choose high-value health care. *Health Aff.* 2012;31(3):560–568.

44. Fung CH, Lim Y-W, Mattke S, et al., 2008.

45. Karlsberg Schaffer S, Sussex J, Feng Y, 2015.

46. Scott I. What are the most effective strategies for improving quality and safety of health care? *Int Med J.* 2009;39(6):389–400.

47. Hall KW. Using peer pressure to improve performance. *Harv Bus Rev.* 2010;88(4):54–55.

48. Westert GP, Groenewoud S, Wennberg J, et al. Medical practice variation: public reporting a first necessary step to spark change. *Int J Qual Health Care.* 2018;30(9):731–735.

49. Bohmer RMJ, Ferlins EM. Clinical change at Intermountain Healthcare. Harvard Business School teaching case 606-149, 2006.

50. Emanuel EJ, Ubel PA, Kessler JB, et al., 2016.

51. Brent James, personal communication.

52. Ham C. Reforming the NHS from within: Beyond hierarchy, inspection and markets. King's Fund, 2014. Accessed Nov 16, 2020. https://www.kingsfund.org.uk/sites/default/files/field/field_publication _file/reforming-the-nhs-from-within-kingsfund-jun14.pdf.

53. Sir Chris Ham, ex-chief executive of the King's Fund, personal communication.

54. Torchiana DF, Colton DG, Rao SK, et al. Massachusetts General Physicians Organization's quality incentive program produces encouraging results. *Health Aff.* 2013;32(10):1748–1756.

55. A full list of the measures used by the MGPO Quality Incentive Program can be found at the site https://www.healthaffairs.org/doi /suppl/10.1377/hlthaff.2013.0377/suppl_file/2013-0377_torchiana _appendix.pdf.

56. Torchiana DF, Colton DG, Rao SK, et al., 2013.

57. Meyer GS, Torchiana DF, Colton D, et al. The use of modest incentives to boost adoption of safety practices and systems. In: Henriksen K, Battles JB, Keyes MA, Grady ML, eds. *Advances in Patient Safety: New Directions and Alternative Approaches.* Vol 3. Agency for Healthcare Research and Quality; 2008. Accessed Nov 18, 2020. https:// www.ahrq.gov/downloads/pub/advances2/vol3/Advances-Meyer_41.pdf.

58. Meyer GS, Torchiana DF, Colton D, et al., 2008.

59. Torchiana DF, Colton DG, Rao SK, et al., 2013.

60. Rogers EM. *The Diffusion of Innovations.* Free Press; 1962.

61. Data from Rogers EM, 1962.

62. Gregg Meyer MD, personal communication.

Chapter 8

1. Berwick DM. Continuous improvement as an ideal in health care. *N Engl J Med.* 1989;320(1):53–56.

2. Laffel G, Blumenthal D. The case for using industrial quality management science in health care organizations. *JAMA.* 1989;262(20):2869–2873.

3. W. Edwards Deming. Quality, Productivity and Competitive Position, 1982.

4. Hartzband P, Groopman J. Medical Taylorism. *N Engl J Med.* 2016;374(2):106–108.

5. Swensen SJ, Meyer GS, Nelson EC, et al. Cottage industry to postindustrial care—the revolution in health care delivery. *N Engl J Med.* 2010;362(5):e12.

6. Swensen SJ, Meyer GS, Nelson EC, et al., 2010.

7. Spear D, Bowen HK. Decoding the DNA of the Toyota Production System. *Harv Bus Rev.* 1999;77(5):96–106.

8. Tucker AL, Edmondson AC, Spear S. When problem solving prevents organizational learning. *J Organ Change Manag.* 2002;15(2):122–137.

9. Deng X. A political wizard who put China on the capitalist road. *New York Times*, February 20, 1997.

10. Spear D, Bowen HK, 1999.

11. Argyris C. Teaching smart people how to learn. *Harv Bus Rev.* 1999;69(3):99–109.

12. Intermountain's protocols are publicly available at https://intermountainphysician.org/clinical/Pages/Care-Process-Models-%28CPMs%29.aspx.

13. Henderson RM, Clark KB. Architectural innovation: the reconfiguration of existing product technologies and the failure of established firms. *Adm Sci Q.* 1990;35(1):9–30.

14. Dewey J. *Logic: The Theory of Inquiry.* Holt, Rinehart and Winston; 1938.

15. Asch DA, Terwiesch C, Mahoney KB, Rosin R. Insourcing health innovation. *N Engl J Med.* 2014;370(19):1775–1777.

16. Christensen CM, Hall T, Dillon K, Duncan DS. Know your customers' "jobs to be done." *Harv Bus Rev.* 2016;94(9):14.

17. Austin RD, personal communication.

18. Leonard DL, Rayport JF. Spark innovation through empathic design. *Harv Bus Rev.* 1997;75:102–115.

19. Zenios S, Makower J, Yock P, eds. *Biodesign: The Process of Innovating Medical Technologies.* Cambridge University Press; 2010.

20. Zenios S, Makower J, Yock P, et al., 2010.

21. Jeremy Myerson, director of the Helen Hamlyn Centre for Design. Presentation to the King's Fund, 2012. Accessed Nov 19, 2020. https://www.kingsfund.org.uk/sites/default/files/media/jeremy-myerson-design-thinking-in-health-care-kingsfund-jun13.pdf.

22. Asch DA, Terwiesch C, Mahoney KB, et al., 2014.

23. Peter Skilman, 1999. ABC Nightline documentary. Accessed Nov 19, 2020. https://www.youtube.com/watch?v=M66ZU2PCIcM.

24. Pisano GP. *The Development Factory: Unlocking the Potential of Process Innovation.* HBS Press; 1997.

25. Bosk CL, Dixon-Woods M, Goeschel CA, Pronovost PJ. Reality check for checklist. *Lancet.* 2009;374(9688):444–445.

26. Edmondson AC. Strategies for learning from failure. *Harv Bus Rev.* 2011;89(4):48–55.

27. Roth AM, Lee TH. Health care needs less innovation and more imitation. *Harv Bus Rev.* Published online November 19, 2014. https:// hbr.org/2014/11/health-care-needs-less-innovation-and-more -imitation.

28. Rogers EM. *The Diffusion of Innovations.* Free Press; 1962.

29. Narayan VA, Mohwinckel M, Pisano G, Yang M, Manji HK. Beyond magic bullets: true innovation in health care. *Nat Rev Drug Discov.* 2013;12(2):85–86.

30. Edmondson AC, Bohmer RMJ, Pisano GP. Speeding up team learning. *Harv Bus Rev.* 2001;79(9):125–132.

31. Edmondson AC. Framing for learning: lessons in successful technology implementation. *California Manage Rev.* 2003;45(2):34–54.

32. Nembhard IM, Tucker AL. Deliberate learning to improve performance in dynamic service settings: evidence from hospital intensive care units. *Organ Sci.* 2011;22(4):907–922.

Chapter 9

1. Gregg Meyer MD, former colonel USAF MC, personal communication.

2. Bohmer RMJ. *Designing Care: Aligning the Nature and Management of Health Care.* HBS Press; 2009:chap 6.

3. Bohmer R, Shand J, Allwood D, et al. Learning systems: managing uncertainty in the new normal of COVID-19. *NEJM Catal Innov Care Deliv.* 2020;1(4).

4. Nwaru BI, Friedman C, Halamka J, Sheikh A. Can learning health systems help organisations deliver personalised care? *BMC Med.* 2017;15(1):177. doi: 10.1186/s12916-017-0935-0.

5. Senge PM. *The Fifth Discipline: The Art and Practice of the Learning Organization.* ed 2. Broadway Business; 2006.

6. Bohmer RMJ, Shand J, Allwood D, et al. *NEJM Catal Innov Care Deliv.* 2020.

7. Bohmer RMJ. *Designing Care.* HBS Press; 2009.

8. Adapted from Bohmer RMJ. *Designing Care.* HBS Press; 2009.

9. Hickson GB, Federspiel CF, Pichert JW, et al. Patient complaints and malpractice risk. *JAMA.* 2002;287(22):2951–2957.

10. Cooper WO, Guillamondegui O, Hines OJ, et al. Use of unsolicited patient observations to identify surgeons with increased risk for postoperative complications. *JAMA Surg.* 2017;152(6):522–529.

11. Connolly HM, Crary JL, McGoon MD, et al. Valvular heart disease associated with fenfluramine–phentermine. *N Engl J Med.* 1997;337(9):581–588.

12. Bohmer RMJ, Shand J, Allwood D, et al. *NEJM Catal Innov Care Deliv.* 2020.

13. Bohmer RMJ, Shand J, Allwood D, et al, 2020.

14. Bohmer RMJ, et al. *NEJM Catalyst,* 2020.

15. Garvin DA, Edmondson AC, Gino F. Is yours a learning organization? *Harv Bus Rev.* 2008;86(3):109–116.

16. Data from Garvin DA, Edmondson AC, Gino F. Is yours a learning organization? *Harv Bus Rev.* 2008;86(3):109–116.

17. Edmondson AC, Bohmer RMJ, Pisano GP, 2001.

18. Bohmer RMJ, Ives Erickson JR, Meyer GS, et al. 10 Leadership lessons from COVID field hospitals. *Harv Bus Rev.* 2020. Accessed Nov 18, 2020. https://hbr.org/2020/11/10-leadership-lessons-from-covid-field-hospitals?ab=hero-main-text.

19. Rashid F, Edmondson AC, Leonard HB, 2013.

20. Pisano GP. The hard truth about innovative cultures. *Harv Bus Rev.* Jan–Feb 2019:62–71.

21. Lee TH. Turning doctors into leaders. *Harv Bus Rev.* 2010;88(4):50–58.

22. Edmondson AC, Bohmer RMJ, Pisano G. Speeding up team learning. *Harv Bus Rev.* 2001;79(9):125–132.

23. Berwick DM. Choices for the "new normal." *JAMA.* 2020;323(21):2125–2126.

24. Cutler DM, Nikpay S, Huckman RS. The business of medicine in the era of COVID-19. *JAMA.* 2020;323(20):2003–2004.

Chapter 10

1. Hammel G. Quoted in *The Economist,* 25 April 2020, 58.

2. Nembhard IM, Alexander JA, Hoff TI, Ramanujam R. Why does the quality of health care continue to lag? Insights from management research. *Acad Manag Perspect.* 2009;24–42.

3. Nembhard, Alexander JA, Hoff TI, et al., 2009.

4. Bohmer RMJ. The hard work of healthcare transformation. *N Engl J Med.* 2016;375(8):709–711.

5. Gulati R. Structure that's not stifling. *Harv Bus Rev.* 2018;96(3): 68–79.

6. Blumenthal DM, Bernard K, Bohnen J, Bohmer RMJ. Addressing the leadership gap in medicine: residents' need for systematic leadership development training. *Acad Med.* 2012;87(4):513–522.

7. Meyer GS, O'Neil B, Gross D. Seven challenges and seven solutions for large-scale EHR implementations. *NEJM Catalyst,* 2018. Accessed Nov 22, 2020. https://catalyst.nejm.org/doi/full/10.1056/CAT .18.0073.

8. Sull D, Homkes R, Sull C. Why strategy execution unravels–and what to do about it. *Harv Bus Rev.* 2015;93(3):57–66.

9. James BC, Lazar JS. Sustaining and extending clinical improvements: a health system's use of clinical programs to build quality infrastructure. In Nelson EC, Batalden PB, Lazar JS, eds. *Practice-Based Learning and Improvement: A Clinical Improvement Action Guide.* ed 2. Joint Commission on Accreditation; 2007.

10. Gregg Meyer MD, personal communication.

11. Mountford J, Shojania KG. Refocusing quality measurement to best support quality improvement: local ownership of quality measurement by clinicians. *BMJ Qual Saf.* 2012;21(6):519–523.

12. Cassell CK, Conway P, Delbanco S, et al. Getting more performance from performance measurement. *N Engl J Med.* 2014;371(23):2145–2147.

13. Meyer GS, Nelson EG, Pryor DB, et al. More quality measures versus measuring what matters: a call for balance and parsimony. *BMJ Qual Saf.* 2012;21(11):964–968.

14. Meyer GS, Nelson EG, Pryor DB, et al., 2012.

15. Bohmer RMJ. The four habits of high-value healthcare organizations. *N Engl J Med.* 2011;365(22):2045–2047.

16. Foucault M. *Madness and Civilization: A History of Insanity in the Age of Reason.* Howard R, trans-ed. Vintage; 1988.

17. Bohmer RMJ, Newell J, Torchiana DF. The effect of decreasing length of stay on discharge destination and readmission after coronary bypass operation. *Surgery.* 2002;132(1):10–15.

18. International Consortium for Health Outcomes Measurement. https://www.ichom.org.

19. McGlynn EA, Schneider EC, Kerr EA. Reimagining quality measurement. *N Engl J Med.* 2014;371(23):2150–2153.

20. Meyer GS, Nelson EG, Pryor DB, et al., 2012.

21. Lumsden DE, Gimeno H, Tustin K, et al. Interventional studies in childhood dystonia do not address the concerns of children and their carers. *Eur J Paediatr Neurol.* 2015;19(3):327–336.

22. Cassell CK, Conway P, Delbanco S, et al., 2014.

23. The six-hour first antibiotic dose for community-acquired pneumonia metric was retired in 2012.

24. Rauh SS, Wadsworth EB, Weeks WW, et al. The savings illusion—why clinical quality improvement fails to deliver bottom-line results. *N Engl J Med.* 2011;365:e48.

25. Swensen SJ, Dilling JA, McCarty PM, et al. The business case for health-care quality improvement. *J Patient Saf.* 2013;9:44–52.

26. Swensen SJ, Dilling JA, McCarty PM, et al., 2013.

27. James BC, Savitz LA. How Intermountain trimmed health care costs through robust quality improvement efforts. *Health Aff.* 2011;30(6):1185–1191.

28. Berwick D, Hackbarth A. Eliminating waste in US health care. *JAMA.* 2012;307(14):1513–1516.

29. *Best Care at Lower Cost.* Institute of Medicine; 2012.

Acknowledgments

This book would not exist without my family, especially my wife, Lynette, who supported and encouraged me the whole way. She debated the ideas with me, read and critiqued chapters, and was a constant voice of reason. My children, Asher and Isobel, both gave much of their time to discussing the subject. In my son, I am lucky to have both a wonderful editor and a talented designer. Once again, the cover is his.

I have been very fortunate to have a group of readers whose comments have made this a better book. These include Amy Edmondson, Jeannette Ives Erikson, David Lawrence, Jean Larson, Ned Lebow, Lesley Lura, and Gregg Meyer.

Finally, I have had the benefit of an extended group of friends and colleagues, both academics and practitioners, who have helped me hone the theory of the argument and test it in practice. These include Dominique Allwood, Penny Andrew, Rachel Bell, Steve Bradley, Dale Bramley, Ronny Cheung, Nigel Edwards, Arie Franx, Rob Huckman, Candace Imison, Bruce King, Lester Levy, James Mountford, Ivy Ng, Steve Phoenix, Gary Pisano, Quay Keng Wah, Jaume Ribera, John Scoble, Celia Skinner, Jenny Shand, Simon Steddon, Peter Tufano, Jo Turville, Dave Upton, Michele van der Kemp, and Robyn Whittaker.

As ever, despite these peoples' best efforts, the failures are all mine.

Index

Page numbers followed by "f," refer to figures. Page numbers followed by "t," refer to tables. Page numbers followed by "b," refer to boxes.

About the Author

Richard Bohmer is a New Zealand–educated doctor and a management academic. He has practiced as a hospital and primary physician. He was the Clinical Director for Quality Improvement at Massachusetts General Hospital and then spent 18 years on the faculty of Harvard Business School. He has published in the medical and management literature and is the author of *Designing Care: Aligning the Nature and Management of Health Care* (HBS Press, 2009). Dr. Bohmer currently works independently with numerous hospitals and health authorities around the world to help them establish clinical leadership and management models and to improve their performance.

⊛ Berrett–Koehler
B̄K̄ Publishers

Berrett-Koehler is an independent publisher dedicated to an ambitious mission: *Connecting people and ideas to create a world that works for all.*

Our publications span many formats, including print, digital, audio, and video. We also offer online resources, training, and gatherings. And we will continue expanding our products and services to advance our mission.

We believe that the solutions to the world's problems will come from all of us, working at all levels: in our society, in our organizations, and in our own lives. Our publications and resources offer pathways to creating a more just, equitable, and sustainable society. They help people make their organizations more humane, democratic, diverse, and effective (and we don't think there's any contradiction there). And they guide people in creating positive change in their own lives and aligning their personal practices with their aspirations for a better world.

And we strive to practice what we preach through what we call "The BK Way." At the core of this approach is *stewardship,* a deep sense of responsibility to administer the company for the benefit of all of our stakeholder groups, including authors, customers, employees, investors, service providers, sales partners, and the communities and environment around us. Everything we do is built around stewardship and our other core values of *quality, partnership, inclusion,* and *sustainability.*

This is why Berrett-Koehler is the first book publishing company to be both a B Corporation (a rigorous certification) and a benefit corporation (a for-profit legal status), which together require us to adhere to the highest standards for corporate, social, and environmental performance. And it is why we have instituted many pioneering practices (which you can learn about at www.bkconnection.com), including the Berrett-Koehler Constitution, the Bill of Rights and Responsibilities for BK Authors, and our unique Author Days.

We are grateful to our readers, authors, and other friends who are supporting our mission. We ask you to share with us examples of how BK publications and resources are making a difference in your lives, organizations, and communities at www.bkconnection.com/impact.

Dear reader,

Thank you for picking up this book and welcome to the worldwide BK community! You're joining a special group of people who have come together to create positive change in their lives, organizations, and communities.

What's BK all about?

Our mission is to connect people and ideas to create a world that works for all.

Why? Our communities, organizations, and lives get bogged down by old paradigms of self-interest, exclusion, hierarchy, and privilege. But we believe that can change. That's why we seek the leading experts on these challenges—and share their actionable ideas with you.

A welcome gift

To help you get started, we'd like to offer you a **free copy** of one of our bestselling ebooks:

www.bkconnection.com/welcome

When you claim your **free ebook**, you'll also be subscribed to our blog.

Our freshest insights

Access the best new tools and ideas for leaders at all levels on our blog at ideas.bkconnection.com.

Sincerely,

Your friends at Berrett-Koehler